MacBook Pro

For Seniors

Unleashing the Power of the Ultimate MacBook Pro for Beginners & Senior Technophobes

Robinson Cortez

Copyright © 2023 *Robinson Cortez*

All Rights Reserved

This book or parts thereof may not be reproduced in any form, stored in any retrieval system, or transmitted in any form by any means—electronic, mechanical, photocopy, recording, or otherwise—without prior written permission of the publisher, except as provided by United States of America copyright law and fair use.

Disclaimer and Terms of Use

The author and publisher of this book and the accompanying materials have used their best efforts in preparing this book. The author and publisher make no representation or warranties with respect to the accuracy, applicability, fitness, or completeness of the contents of this book. The information contained in this book is strictly for informational purposes. Therefore, if you wish to apply ideas contained in this book, you are taking full responsibility for your actions.

Printed in the United States of America

TABLE OF CONTENTS

TABLE OF CONTENTS III
INTRODUCTION 1
    DISPLAY 2
    PORTS 2
    DISPLAY AND AUDIO 3
    PERFORMANCE 3
    GRAPHICS AND GAMING 3
    WEBCAM 4
    MACOS VENTURA 4
    NEW ADDITIONS 5
        Performance with Unmatched Power Efficiency with M2 Pro and M2 Max 5
        Enhanced Connectivity 6
    MACOS VENTURA 7
    MACBOOK PRO AND THE ENVIRONMENT 7
CHAPTER ONE 8
GETTING STARTED 8
    OVERVIEW 8
    SPECIFICATIONS 8
    APPLE M2 PRO CHIP 9
        Apple M2 Max chip 9
        Operating System 9
        Keyboard and Trackpad 9
    STORAGE 9
        Apple M2 Pro chip 9
        Apple M2 Max chip 10
    NEW FEATURES ON YOUR NEW MACBOOK PRO 10
    HOW TO SET UP YOUR NEW MACBOOK PRO 12
    HOW TO CREATE A COMPUTER ACCOUNT 15
    HOW TO MOVE DATA TO YOUR NEW MACBOOK PRO 17
    HOW TO SET UP TOUCH ID 18
    HOW TO USE THE MAGIC MACBOOK PRO KEYBOARD 21
    HOW TO CHARGE THE BATTERY AND ADJUST BATTERY VOLTAGE 22
        Charging the battery 22
        Adjusting Battery Voltage 23
        Battery Health & Management 23
    HOW TO BACK UP AND RESTORE DATA 24
        Backing up Data (using Time Machine): 24
        Restoring Data (With Migration Assistant) 26
    HOW TO SHUT DOWN OR SLEEP YOUR NEW MACBOOK PRO 27

Put your MacBook Pro to sleep	*27*
How to turn off/shut down your MacBook	*28*
FREQUENTLY ASKED QUESTIONS	28

CHAPTER TWO 29

APPLE PAY AND AIRPRINT 29

OVERVIEW	29
HOW TO SET UP APPLE PAY	29
HOW TO MAKE PURCHASES USING APPLE PAY	31
HOW TO ENABLE APPLE PAY IN SAFARI	33
HOW TO CHANGE OR REMOVE PAYMENT CARDS WITH APPLE PAY	34
How to Add a Credit Card to Apple Pay	*34*
Removing Payment Card from Apple Pay	*35*
ABOUT AIRPRINT	36
How to use AirPrint	*36*
How to print wirelessly from your MacBook Pro to an AirPrint printer	*37*
FREQUENTLY ASKED QUESTIONS	39

CHAPTER THREE 40

DOCK AND MENU BAR 40

OVERVIEW	40
HOW TO USE AND CUSTOMIZE THE DOCK	40
Using the Dock	*40*
Customizing the Dock	*41*
HOW TO CHANGE THE DOCK'S SIZE	41
Method 1: Using System Settings	*41*
Method 2: Using the Dock	*42*
HOW TO CHANGE THE DOCK'S ORIENTATION	42
HOW TO HIDE/SHOW DOCK ON MACBOOK PRO	43
Hiding the Dock	*43*
Showing the Dock	*43*
HOW TO CHANGE THE MENU BAR SIZE ON YOUR MACBOOK PRO	43
Displays	*44*
Accessibility	*44*
HOW TO ADJUST THE MENU BAR SIZE	45
HOW TO HIDE THE MENU BAR	46
HOW TO REDUCE YOUR MAC'S WINDOW	46
FREQUENTLY ASKED QUESTIONS	47

CHAPTER FOUR 48

ICLOUD 48

OVERVIEW	48

How to Set up & Edit iCloud 48
    Setting Up iCloud.. 48
    Changing iCloud settings 49
    Access your iCloud Account Information 49
    Access Payment & Shipping Information 50
How to manage iCloud Sync Permissions 51
How to Sign Out of iCloud 52
    How to use iCloud Private Relay 54
Activate and Deactivate iCloud Private Relay 57
    How to turn off iCloud Private Relay 57
Frequently Asked Questions 57

CHAPTER FIVE 58

SCREEN TIME AND FAMILY SHARING 58

Overview 58
Set Up & Use Screen Time 58
    Using Screen Time.. 59
    How to Enable Screen Time... 61
How to Monitor App Usage 61
    Impose App Limits 63
How to Set Downtime 64
    Customize App Limits (Optional) 65
    Customize Communication Limits (Optional) 65
    Always Allow Apps 66
    Set Communication Limits... 67
Manage Content and Privacy 68
How to Setup Family Sharing 70
Invite Family Members in Family Sharing 72
Invite People to Family Sharing 73
Join Family Sharing Group 74
Set up App Store Purchase Sharing 75
Set up iCloud Storage Sharing 76
Setting up Screen Time for Kids in Family Sharing Group 77
Set up Apple Music in the Family Sharing Group 78
Set up Apple Arcade in the Family Sharing Group 79
Frequently Asked Questions 80

CHAPTER SIX 81

FOCUS MODE AND QUICK NOTES 81

Overview 81
How to Enable Focus Mode 81
Activate Focus from the Control Center and System Settings 82
Create a New Focus Filter 83

Edit an Existing Focus Filter	84
Allow Notifications from Specific Persons & Apps	85
Allow Time-Sensitive Notifications	87
Manage Apps to Display your Focus Mode Status	88
How to use Quick Notes	89
How to Access Quick Notes	91
Enable Hot Corners	92
How to Create a Quick Note	93
Add Smart Links to Quick Note	95
Understanding Quick Notes and Smart Links	*95*
Add Smart Links to Quick Notes	*95*
Quick Note Thumbnail	96
Taking Notes Immediately	*97*
Making organization simple	97
Increased productivity and efficiency	97
Insert Text or Photos from Safari to Quick Notes	97
View & Customize Quick Notes in the Notes App	99
Capturing your Thoughts	99
Customizing Quick Notes	99
Saving and Closing Quick Notes	*101*
Frequently Asked Questions	101

CHAPTER SEVEN 102

FOLDERS AND NOTES 102

Overview	102
Arrange Notes with Folders	102
How to Create a Folder	103
How to Rename a Folder	106
How to Rearrange Folders	108
How to Delete a Folder	110
Working with Notes	111
Getting Started with Notes on MacBook Pro	111
Creating and Formatting Notes	*111*
Collaboration in Notes	*112*
Search and Organization	*112*
Privacy and Security	*112*
Syncing and Accessibility	*112*
Markup and Sketching	*113*
How to Create a Note	113
Access the Notes App	*113*
Create a New Note	*113*
Syncing with iCloud	114
Searching for Notes	115

Additional Tips	115
Move a Note	116
Pin a Note	117
Lock a Note	119
Delete a Note	122
Format your Notes	123
Sort your Notes	126
Search Notes	127
Add Media to Notes	129
Add Attachments to Notes	132
Browse Attachments in Notes	134
Add Tables to Notes	136
Add Checklists to Notes	138
Share your Notes	139
Frequently Asked Questions	141

CHAPTER EIGHT 142

FACETIME 142

Overview	142
How to Set Up FaceTime on a MacBook Pro	142
Make a FaceTime Audio Call	146
Make a FaceTime Call via Messages App	148
Additional Tips	*149*
Start a Group FaceTime Call	149
Tips for a Smooth Group FaceTime Experience	*151*
Answer/Decline a FaceTime Call	151
Answering a FaceTime call	*151*
Declining a FaceTime Call	*152*
Additional Tips	*153*
Add another Participant to a Group FaceTime Call	*153*
Share Your Screen on FaceTime	154
Tips for Successful Screen Sharing	156
Activate & Use Screen Sharing	157
Using FaceTime's Screen Sharing feature	*157*
Change Shared Window in FaceTime	*158*
Share Sharing Screen in FaceTime	159
Frequently Asked Questions	161

CHAPTER NINE 162

UNIVERSAL CONTROL AND CONTINUITY CAMERA 162

Overview	162
How to set up & Use Universal Control in MacBook Pro	162
Setting up Universal Control	*162*

- *How to set up Universal Control* 162
- *Using Universal Control* 164
- ADJUST/TURN OFF UNIVERSAL CONTROL 164
  - *Changing the settings on a universal control* 164
  - *Disabling Universal Control* 165
- FIXING UNIVERSAL CONTROL PROBLEMS 165
- HOW TO USE THE CONTINUITY CAMERA 166
  - *What is a Continuity Camera?* 166
  - *Requirements* 166
- USING CONTINUITY CAMERA 167
- TAKE AN IMAGE WITH A CONTINUITY CAMERA 168
- TAKE A PICTURE IN FINDER 170
- SCAN A DOCUMENT USING THE CONTINUITY CAMERA 171
- FREQUENTLY ASKED QUESTIONS 173

CHAPTER TEN 174

SAFARI 174

- OVERVIEW 174
- HOW TO VISIT A WEBSITE 174
- HOW TO BOOKMARK A SITE 176
- HOW TO USE TAB GROUPS IN SAFARI 178
  - *Understanding Tab Groups* 178
  - *Creating a Tab Group* 178
  - *Managing and Customizing Tab Groups* 179
  - *Rename a Tab Group in Safari* 179
  - *Move Safari Tabs from one Group to Another* 181
  - *Rearrange Tab Groups* 182
  - *Access Tabs Group in a Grid* 184
  - *Remove a Tab Group* 185
- FREQUENTLY ASKED QUESTIONS 187

CHAPTER ELEVEN 188

AIRPLAY AND VOICE RECORDINGS 188

- OVERVIEW 188
- HOW TO SET UP AND USE AIRPLAY 188
- USING AIRPLAY FOR SCREEN MIRRORING 189
- HOW TO USE SCREEN MIRRORING 189
- USING AIRPLAY FOR AUDIO STREAMING 190
- USING AIRPLAY FOR VIDEO STREAMING 190
- ENDING THE AIRPLAY CONNECTION 191
- ENABLE MAC TO RECEIVE AIRPLAY CONTENT 191
- ENABLE MAC TO RECEIVE AIRPLAY CONTENT 193
- HOW TO CREATE & CUSTOMIZE VOICE RECORDINGS 194

viii

Create Voice Recordings with Voice Memos	196
Customize Voice Recordings on Voice Memos	198
Replace a Section of the Recording	200
Trim a Section of the Recording	202
Create a Copy of a Recorded Audio	204
Remove Background Noise from the Recorded Audio	206
Frequently Asked Questions	207

CHAPTER TWELVE 208

REMINDER APP 208

Overview	208
How to Use Reminder App	208
Set Up Recurring Reminders	212
Share Reminders	214
Add People to a Shared List	216
Set Up Task Sharing	219
Assign Task to Someone Else	220
Reassign the Task to another Person	222
Set an Alarm via Reminders	224
Frequently Asked Questions	226

CHAPTER THIRTEEN 227

LIVE TEXT 227

Overview	227
How to use Live Text on MacBook Pro	227
Enabling Live Text	*227*
Using Live Text	*227*
Drag & Drop Selected Text	229
Extracting Text	230
Editing Text	*231*
Accessibility Benefits	231
Limitations and Considerations	232
Search the Web for Highlighted Text	232
Translate Text within Pictures	234
Tips for Using Live Text Translation	234
Share the Text in Photos	235
Speak the Highlighted Text	236
Enabling Live Text	*237*
Using Live Text to Speak Highlighted Text	*237*
Customizing the Speech Settings	237
Translate Text on MacBook Pro	238
Frequently Asked Questions	239

CHAPTER FOURTEEN 240

SPOTLIGHT, SPLIT SCREEN, AND SIRI 240

OVERVIEW 240
HOW TO ACCESS AND USE SPOTLIGHT 240
  Enabling Spotlight 240
  Using Spotlight 240
  Customizing Spotlight 242
EDIT SPOTLIGHT SEARCH RESULTS 242
HIDE ITEMS FROM SPOTLIGHT SEARCH 245
HOW TO USE SIRI 247
  Enabling Siri 247
  Siri's Basic Tasks 247
  Advanced Features 248
INTEGRATION WITH APPLE ECOSYSTEM 248
WHAT CAN SIRI DO FOR YOU? 249
  Effortless Productivity 249
  Seamless Multitasking 249
  Voice-Controlled Features 250
  Knowledge at your Fingertips 250
  Personalized Experience 250
  Inclusivity and Accessibility 250
HOW TO USE SPLIT SCREEN 251
USE SPLIT VIEW ON MACBOOK PRO 253
TIPS FOR EFFECTIVE SPLIT VIEW USE 255
ACTIVATE SPLIT VIEW VIA MISSION CONTROL 255
VIEW OTHER APPS IN SPLIT VIEW 257
FIX SPLIT SCREEN NOT WORKING 258
FREQUENTLY ASKED QUESTIONS 260

CHAPTER FIFTEEN 261

MEMOJI AND APP STORE 261

OVERVIEW 261
HOW TO USE MEMOJI 261
  Using your Memoji 262
  Using Memoji in FaceTime 262
CREATE MEMOJI STICKERS 263
EDIT, DUPLICATE, OR REMOVE MEMOJI 265
  Editing your Memoji 265
  Duplicating your Memoji 266
  Removing your Memoji 266
  Use Memoji as Group Picture in iMessage 267
  Use Memoji as Your iMessage Profile Image 268

x

How to Choose a Memoji Profile Picture for iMessage – Tips 269
How to Use the App Store 270
   Accessing the App Store 270
   Browsing and Searching for Apps 270
Installing Apps 271
   Managing Installed Apps 272
   App Store Preferences 272
   How to View Apps that Need Update 272

CHAPTER SIXTEEN 275

BASIC SETTINGS ON YOUR NEW MACBOOK PRO 275

Overview 275
How to Capture Screenshots and Record Your Screen 275
   Capturing Screenshots 275
Recording your Screen 276
Customizing Screenshot and Recording Settings 277
   Change the screenshot and recording settings on your MacBook Pro to suit your requirements. 277
   How to Adjust the Brightness of the Display on your MacBook Pro 277
How to Adjust the Volume 280
How to Perform Gestures Using the Trackpad and the Mouse 282
   The Magic of the Trackpad Gestures 282
   Mastering Mouse Gestures 283
Customizing and Fine-Tuning Gestures 284
How to Use the Stage Manager 284
   Creating and Managing Desktops 285
Using Split View for Enhanced Multitasking 286
Using the App Exposé 286
Customizing the Stage Manager 286
Frequently Asked Questions 287

CHAPTER SEVENTEEN 288

TROUBLESHOOTING ISSUES 288

Overview 288
MacBook Pro Won't Turn On 288
   Check the Battery 288
   Restart the SMC 288
Overheating 288
   Close Resource-Intensive Applications 288
   Learn Debris and Dust 288
Slow Performance 289
   Clear Disk Space 289
   Reset PRAM and NVRAM 289
   Wi-Fi Connectivity Issues 289

TRACKPAD AND KEYBOARD PROBLEMS 289
   Startup Problems 289
   Software Glitches or Crashes 290
   External Devices Not Recognized 290
   Screen Problems (black screen, flickering, etc.): 290
   Data Corruption or Loss 290
TIPS AND TRICKS FOR NAVIGATING THROUGH MACBOOK PRO FUNCTIONS 290
FREQUENTLY ASKED QUESTIONS 309
   CONCLUSION 310

INDEX **311**

INTRODUCTION

Apple unveiled the new 14- and 16-inch MacBook Pro models with M2 Pro and M2 Max, its most advanced professional silicon that offers professional users even more power-efficient performance and battery life. The new MacBook Pro handles demanding activities like effects rendering, which is up to 6x quicker than the fastest Intel-based MacBook Pro, and color grading, which is up to 2x faster, thanks to M2 Pro and M2 Max, the world's most powerful and efficient CPU for a pro laptop.

The battery life of the MacBook Pro is now up to 22 hours, which is the longest battery life ever on a Mac, building on the incredible power efficiency of Apple technology. The new MacBook Pro includes improved HDMI, which for the first time enables 8K screens, as well as Wi-Fi 6E, which is up to twice as fast as the previous version. Creators can work on scenes that are so vast that PC laptops cannot even run them thanks to the M2 Max model's up to 96GB of unified memory. The acclaimed Liquid Retina XDR display, vast range of connections, 1080p FaceTime HD camera, six-speaker sound system, and studio-quality microphones round out the unmatched features of the MacBook Pro. The user experience provided by the MacBook Pro is unparalleled when paired with macOS Ventura. The MacBook Pro 2023 is intended to be the quickest laptop you can carry with you everywhere, and it has the battery life to back it up (prices start at $1,999). In comparison to the M1 Pro, the new M2 Pro is expected to run 20% quicker on the CPU and 30% faster on the GPU. The M2 Max comes with a massive 38-core GPU if you have the money. Even while the design is the same as the previous MacBook Pro 14-inch, there have been some noteworthy improvements made, such as quicker Wi-Fi 6E and a stronger HDMI connector that can handle up to 8K monitors.

Display

It's a good thing that the MacBook Pro 14-inch maintains the same aesthetic as its predecessor. Silver and Space Gray versions of the same very sturdy, squared-off metal chassis are offered. Most people like the little details of this laptop, such as how simple it is to open with one hand (due to the grooved front lip), the simple Touch ID button for quick sign-on, and the beautifully carved **"MacBook Pro"** on the bottom of the device. The MacBook Pro 14-inch is a tad heavy for a 14-inch laptop, measuring 12.31 x 8.71 x 0.61 inches and weighing 3.5 pounds (3.6 pounds for the M2 Max version). The HP Spectre x360 14 is 3 pounds, while the Huawei Matebook X Pro is 2.9 pounds, but none of those devices has as much power.

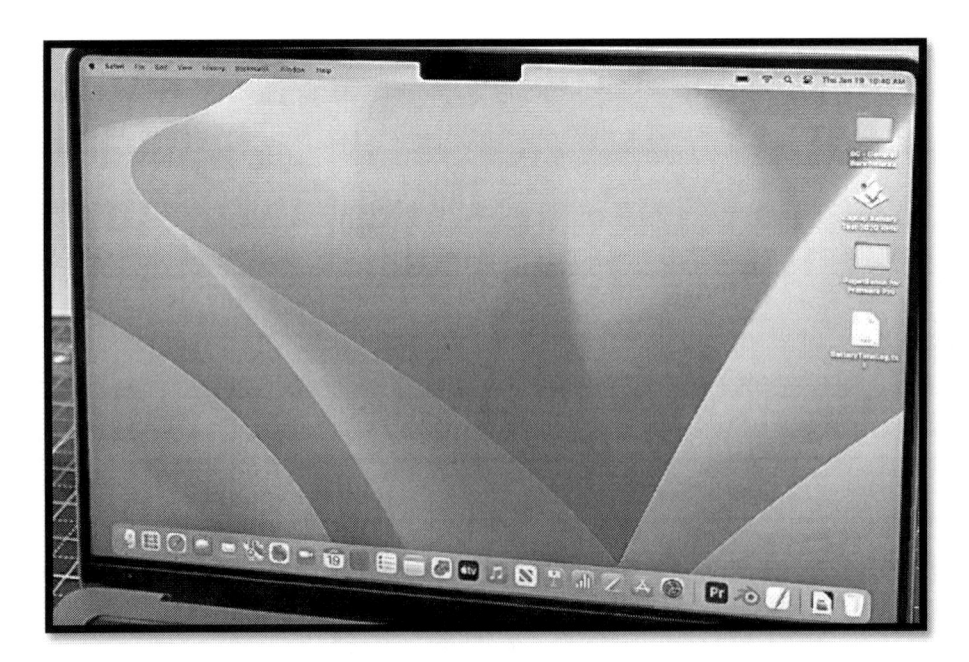

Ports

If you need more than just Thunderbolt/USB-C connectors, the portable MacBook to purchase is still the 14-inch MacBook Pro. Aside from the three Thunderbolt 4 connections, which are a must-have for photographers and filmmakers, you also get an SD card slot and an HDMI connector.

The MacBook Pro supports the HDMI 2.1 standard, which means the HDMI connector can now handle up to 8K resolution on an external monitor at 60Hz. can connect a 4K monitor that runs at up to 240Hz. Keep in mind that the M2 Pro chip can drive a maximum of two external displays, while the M2 Max chip can handle a maximum of four monitors.

Display and Audio

The mini-LED display on the MacBook Pro 14-inch is unquestionably one of the nicest you'll find in any notebook. It has a vibrant color scheme and a fluid 120Hz ProMotion refresh rate. In certain lab testing, the MacBook Pro 14-inch display performed well, beginning with brightness. Using a trusted light meter, we measured HDR content at 1,447 nits for 10% of the display and 1,081 nits for 100% of the screen. The 13-inch MacBook Pro achieves slightly under 500 nits in comparison. The screen of the MacBook Pro 14-inch displayed 117.7% of the sRGB color space and 83.4% of the more difficult DCI-P3 color range. On the two tests, the Dell XPS 15 scored significantly higher 122.7% and 86.9%, respectively. Apple's laptop's display, however, has somewhat more realistic colors since it received a Delta-E score of 0.19 (where 0 is ideal). The MacBook Pro 14-inch's six-speaker audio system, which has four force-canceling woofers and two tweeters, produced a tremendous sound while playing the same clip.

Performance

Whether you choose the M2 Pro model or the M2 Max version, the MacBook Pro can handle everything you throw at it with ease. If you want more visual power or more energy for video applications, choose the M2 Max. A 10-core CPU, 16-core GPU, 16GB of shared memory, and 512GB of storage are the first configurations of the M2 Pro processor. Apple provided us with a $4,099 version to examine, but despite its outrageous price, it has insane power with its 12-core CPU, 38-core GPU, 64GB of RAM, and 2TB of storage.

Graphics and Gaming

Starting with a 16-core GPU, the MacBook Pro 14-inch provides a broad variety of graphics options. There is a noticeable difference in benchmark performance between the 38-core GPU from the M2 Max chip and the 19-core GPU within the M2

Pro chip. Even though Apple still has a long way to go in the gaming department, the new 14-inch MacBook Pro is more than capable of producing reliable frame rates. At 1920 x 1200 resolutions, the M2 Pro MacBook Pro achieved 48.6 frames per second, as opposed to 39.3 for the 2021 model with M1 Pro. However, with the MacBook's native 3024 x 1964 resolution, neither device could achieve a passable 30 frames per second. A substantially higher 73 frames per second at 1920 x 1200 pixels and a playable 34 frames per second were achieved using the M2 Max version's 38-core GPU. With its Nvidia GPU at 1080p, the Dell XPS 15 achieved 38.4 frames per second.

Webcam

Since Apple updated the MacBook Pro in 2021, the FaceTime HD camera hasn't seen much alteration, and that's generally for the better. The 1080p webcam captures excellent detail and has realistic color.

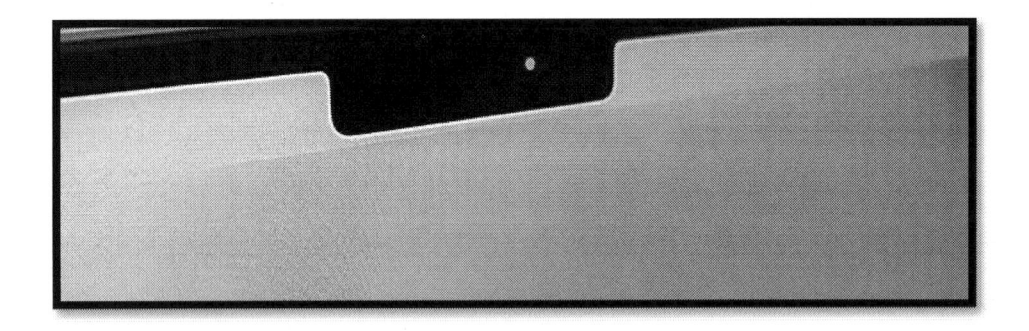

With a feature called Continuity Camera, macOS Ventura also lets you connect your iPhone to your laptop if you want an even better camera. That capability seems more appropriate for older laptops with Intel or Apple M1 processors running Ventura and without 1080p cameras.

macOS Ventura

The new MacBook Pros come pre-installed with macOS Ventura (version 13). Ventura made its debut in the autumn of 2022. Some of the new features include improved picture search in Spotlight; Passkeys that never leave your device for more secure sign-in; editable texts in iMessage; Stage Manager, a method to arrange windows to keep focused; and some long-needed capabilities in mail, such undo and scheduling send Redesigned System Settings, which take some getting used to but more closely mirror what's on iOS, and Continuity Camera, which allows you use your iPhone as a webcam. In contrast to Windows computers, there isn't much fat on macOS. Mail, Messages (excellent for synchronizing with your iPhone or iPad), Notes, Maps, FaceTime, and Safari are all included in the program. Apple Music, Apple TV, Apple News, and Podcasts all have specific applications available for them. Additionally free are productivity programs like Numbers, Pages, and Keynote. Rosetta 2 is still in use to convert applications created for Intel x86 software so that they may operate on Apple Silicon, although an increasing number of applications are now native for M-series CPUs or use universal binaries.

New Additions

Performance with Unmatched Power Efficiency with M2 Pro and M2 Max

With M2 Pro and M2 Max, the MacBook Pro revolutionizes professional processes in a variety of fields, including art, science, and app development. Performance, battery life, connection, and general productivity have all dramatically improved for those upgrading from Mac models based on Intel. Additionally, the MacBook Pro keeps running whether users are plugged in or using battery power. For up to 20% more performance than the M1 Pro, the MacBook Pro with M2 Pro has a 10- or 12-core CPU with up to eight high-performance and four high-efficiency cores. Users can complete massive tasks and operate numerous professional programs at breakneck speed thanks to 200GB/s of unified memory bandwidth and up to 32GB of unified memory, which is twice the amount in M2.

Up to 19 cores on a next-generation GPU increase graphics performance by up to 30%, while a 40% increase in Neural Engine speed makes machine learning activities like image and video processing quicker. Additionally, M2 Pro's powerful media engine rips through the most well-liked video codecs, substantially speeding video playing and encoding while using a small amount of power.

With M2 Pro on MacBook Pro 2023:

- Motion renders titles and animations up to 80% quicker than the fastest MacBook Pro with an Intel processor and up to 20% faster than the previous version.

- Compiling in Xcode is up to 2.5 times quicker than the quickest MacBook Pro with an Intel processor and around 25% faster than the previous generation.
- Adobe Photoshop now processes images up to 40% quicker than it did in the previous version and up to 80% faster than the fastest MacBook Pro with an Intel processor.

With a substantially bigger GPU with up to 38 cores and up to 30% more graphics performance than the M1 Max, the MacBook Pro with M2 Max pushes workflows to the limit. It also has 400GB/s of unified memory bandwidth, which is twice as fast as M2 Pro. With up to 96GB of unified memory, the MacBook Pro pushes the boundaries of laptop graphics memory to support demanding graphics workloads like integrating enormous panoramic panoramas and producing scenes with extraordinary 3D geometry and textures. The performance of M2 Max is up to 20% faster than M1 Max thanks to its next-generation 12-core CPU, which has up to eight high-performance and four high-efficiency cores. It also boasts a more potent media engine than M2 Pro with double the ProRes acceleration, which substantially speeds up video playing and transcoding.

With M2 Max on MacBook Pro 2023:

- Effects rendering in Cinema 4D is up to 30 percent quicker than it was in the previous iteration and up to 6 times faster than the fastest MacBook Pro with an Intel processor.
- DaVinci Resolve's color grading is up to 2x quicker than the fastest MacBook Pro with an Intel processor and up to 30% faster than the prior model.

Enhanced Connectivity

In addition to quicker Wi-Fi 6E and more sophisticated HDMI to handle 8K displays up to 60Hz and 4K displays up to 240Hz, the MacBook Pro now has Wi-Fi 6E for improved wireless communication. The varied connectivity choices currently included in the MacBook Pro, like the three Thunderbolt 4 ports for quick connections to peripherals, the SDXC card slot, and the MagSafe 3 charging, are expanded upon by these additional features.

macOS Ventura

The MacBook Pro offers even more speed and productivity with macOS Ventura. Your MacBook Pro 2023 now uses video conferencing capabilities like Desk View, Center Stage, Studio Light, and more thanks to robust improvements like Continuity Camera. FaceTime's handoff feature enables users to initiate a FaceTime chat on their iPhone or iPad and seamlessly transfer it to their Mac, or the other way around. Additionally, programs like Stage Manager automatically arrange windows and applications so users can focus on their current jobs while still having a clear view of everything. While Safari, the world's fastest Mac browser, ushers in a password-free future with passkeys, Messages, and Mail are better than ever. The new freeform app offers a flexible canvas that helps users be more productive and expressive, whether they are planning or brainstorming on their own or with others. Users can now create and share a separate photo library among up to six family members using iCloud Shared Photo Library. Gaming on Mac has never been better because of Apple silicon's strength and appeal as well as new development tools like Metal 3.

MacBook Pro and the Environment

The enclosure of the MacBook Pro is made entirely of aluminum, rare earth elements are used in all of the magnets, tin is used in the solder of the main logic board, and gold is used in the plating of several printed circuit boards. All of these materials are recycled. It also complies with Apple's strict energy efficiency requirements and includes various components made of at least 35% recycled plastic. Apple is getting closer to its aim of eliminating all plastic from its packaging by 2025 thanks to the fact that the MacBook Pro is devoid of many toxic compounds and that 97 percent of the packaging is made of fiber.

Apple now operates carbon-neutrally on a global scale, and by 2030, the company aims to achieve complete carbon neutrality across the whole manufacturing supply chain and the full product life cycle. This implies that every Apple product sold will have a net-zero climate effect, from component production to assembly to shipping to customer usage to recycling to material recovery.

CHAPTER ONE
GETTING STARTED

Overview

Chapter one introduces us to a whole new level of the MacBook Pro 2023. In this chapter, you will get to see the specifications, new features, how to set up your new MacBook Pro, how to create a computer account, how to back up and resort data, and so much more.

Specifications

Here the various specifications of the new MacBook Pro 2023:

Device name: MacBook Pro 2023 (14- and 16-inch model)
Size and Weight:
- **Height**: 0.66 inch (1.68 cm)
- **Width**: 14.01 inches (35.57 cm)
- **Depth**: 9.77 inches (24.81 cm)
- **Weight (M2 Pro):** 4.7 pounds (2.15 kg)
- **Weight (M2 Max):** 4.8 pounds (2.16 kg

Camera:
- Advanced image signal processor with computational video
- 1080p FaceTime HD camera

Battery and Power:

- Up to 22 hours Apple TV app movie playback
- Up to 15 hours wireless web
- 100-watt-hour lithium-polymer battery
- 140W USB-C Power Adapter
- USB-C to MagSafe 3 Cable
- Fast-charge capable with included 140W USB-C Power Adapter

Memory:

Apple M2 Pro chip

- 16GB unified memory - Configurable to: 32GB (M2 Pro or M2 Max), 64GB (M2 Max), or 96GB (M2 Max with 38-core GPU)

Apple M2 Max chip

- 32GB unified memory - Configurable to: 64GB (M2 Max) or 96GB (M2 Max with 38-core GPU)

Operating System

- macOS Ventura

Keyboard and Trackpad

Backlit Magic Keyboard with:

- Touch ID
- 78 (U.S.) or 79 (ISO) keys including 12 full-height function keys and 4 arrow keys in an inverted-T arrangement.
- Force Touch trackpad meant for precise cursor control and pressure-sensing capabilities; enables Force clicks, accelerators, pressure-sensitive drawing, and multi-Touch gestures.
- Ambient light sensor

Storage

Apple M2 Pro chip

- 512GB SSD - Configurable to: 1TB, 2TB, 4TB, or 8TB

Apple M2 Max chip

- 1TB SSD - Configurable to: 2TB, 4TB, or 8TB

New features on your new MacBook Pro

To help you get the most out of your Mac Pro, macOS Ventura adds new capabilities and enhancements.

Use fresh approaches to accomplish more to boost your creativity and productivity:

- **Email**: Remind yourself to follow up or return to an email later, schedule emails to be delivered whenever you choose, and unsend emails that you have already sent. Recently shared items, such as documents and links, are now suggested when you search in Mail. Additionally, search offers more precise results since it corrects your mistakes and looks for synonyms for the search phrases you provide.
- **Freeform**: A brand-new app that you can use for solo or group brainstorming. Create a board and include text, images, files, and other things. Access your boards from any device and see updates immediately. Beginning with macOS 13.1 and iOS 16.2.
- **Stage Manager**: Keep your desktop clutter-free by automatically organizing your windows and programs. Your other windows are grouped on the side and are easily accessible with a single click, leaving the area you want to concentrate on front and center.
- **Spotlight**: You can carry out Quick Actions using Spotlight, such as establishing a timer. Additionally, Spotlight's improved image search allows you to look for photos in Photos, Messages, and other places. You can now use Live Text to look for actual text in images.
- **Safari**: The fastest browser in the world with a privacy-focused design. Passkeys, an even more secure sign-in method in Safari, will protect you against phishing and data breaches.
- **Focus**: More customization options for a Focus, including the ability to accept alerts from certain persons or applications, incoming calls or forthcoming events, and more. Use Focus filters to block distracting items in applications

like Calendar, Messages, Safari, and Mail by sharing your Focus across devices.

Share experiences and collaborate more easily using your favorite applications:

- **Messages**: You can now invite others to work together on projects in other applications like Keynote, Numbers, Pages, Notes, and more via messages. Other recent additions to Messages include the ability to amend recently sent messages up to five times within 15 minutes of sending them, as well as the option to unsend recently sent messages for up to 2 minutes after sending them.
- **iCloud Shared Photo Library**: Add pictures and videos to an album that you can share with up to five other people using the iCloud Shared Photo Library. Everyone else can see everyone's revisions, comments, and new content, and you can use smart recommendations to have certain images or videos from your library—such as those with a particular subject or date—automatically added.
- **Activity Stream**: When working together on a project in Numbers, Keynote, or Pages, Activity Stream allows you to keep track of every update. All edits, comments, and other file management changes are shown in a thorough list on the sidebar.

Use your MacBook Pro and all of your devices in new ways:

- **Continuity Camera**: You can now wirelessly use your iPhone as your webcam while you're on a video call. Desk View also lets others see your face while sharing the contents of the desk in front of you. Compatible with iPhone 11 or later.
- **FaceTime**: You can now transfer calls between devices using FaceTime. Start a FaceTime call on your iPhone while you're out and about and transfer it to your MacBook Pro when you get home. The FaceTime session may also be started at your workstation and continued when you leave the home.
- **Home**: The Home app now has a completely redesigned interface that makes it simpler to browse, arrange, see, and manage all of your accessories. View every room in your house at once, instantly access all of your useful accessories by room using categories, and use the revised sidebar and new tile style to manage your accessories, categories, and rooms.

Other new features available on macOS Ventura:
- **Notes:** Lock a note using your Mac login password. Additionally, Smart Folders that automatically discover notes by Tags, Mentions, Quick Notes, Date Created, and other criteria might help you organize your notes more effectively.
- **Reminders**: Time- and date-based grouping has enhanced the Today and Scheduled Lists, making it simpler to see and create reminders. Whether it's a project checklist, a packing list for a vacation, or anything else, you may store a list as a template to use later.
- **Clock**: Your Mac now has access to the Clock app found on the iPad and iPhone. You can make personalized Clock shortcuts that you can reach from the menu bar, Finder, or by asking Siri, in addition to setting global clocks, timers, and alarms inside the app.
- **System Settings**: There is now a revamped System Settings interface.
- **Accessibility**: When viewing videos, listening to audio, having chats, or on FaceTime calls, see Live Captions (Beta). To concentrate, listen to background music. To use VoiceOver and spoken notes, choose new languages and voices. To check for common formatting faults, use VoiceOver. Hang up FaceTime conversations with Voice Control, and recite personalized spellings letter by letter. When using a buddy controller, connect two controllers.
- **News**: My Sports allows you to follow your favorite teams, leagues, and players in the News app. You can also tailor your feed to get the newest headlines, view highlights, and receive scores, schedules, and standings for the teams and leagues you like.
- **Weather**: The Weather app is now accessible on your MacBook Pro and has engaging animations, thorough maps, and interactive forecast modules in addition to a design designed for a bigger display.

How to set up your new MacBook Pro

When your MacBook Pro turns on for the first time, Setup Assistant guides you through the straightforward procedures required to begin using your new Mac. You can opt to follow all the instructions or skip some and come back to them later. After initial setup, it could make sense, for instance, to set up Screen Time, which you can establish for various users.

Setup Assistant will guide you through the following:

- **Choose your region or country**: Your Mac's language and time zone are established when you do this.
- **Accessibility options**: Click **Not Now** to skip seeing accessibility options for those with vision, motor, hearing, and cognitive impairments.

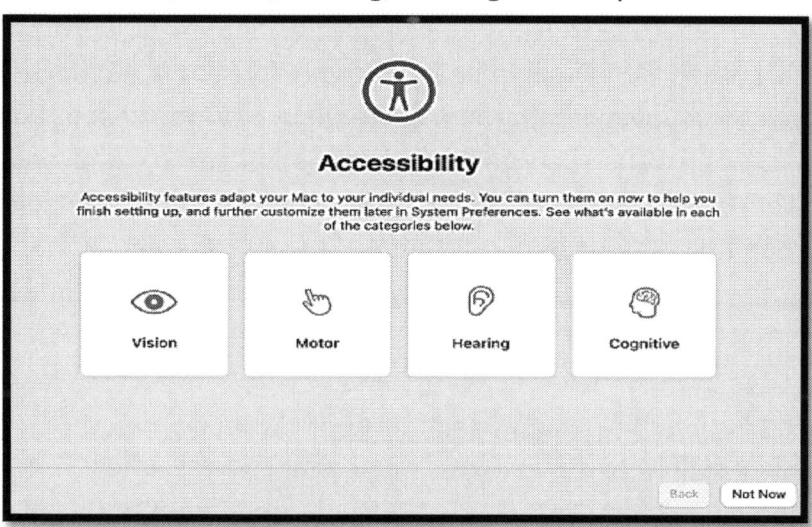

- **Join a Wi-Fi network**: Select the network and, if prompted, enter a password. You can also choose **Other Network Options** if you're using Ethernet. To change the network at a later time, click the Wi-Fi status indicator in the menu bar or click Wi-Fi in the sidebar of **System Settings**, then select a network and input the password. Here, you can also decide whether to switch on or off Wi-Fi.

Note: You can add the Wi-Fi status symbol to the menu bar if you don't see it there after setup. Click **Control Center** in the sidebar of System Settings, chooses "**Show in Menu Bar**" under Wi-Fi, and then clicks **OK**.

- **Transfer Information**: In the Migration Assistant box, select **Not Now** if you're setting up a new computer and haven't previously configured a Mac.
- **Sign in with your Apple ID**: An email address and a password make up your Apple ID. It serves as your primary account for all transactions with Apple, including those involving the App Store, Apple TV app, Apple Books, iCloud, Messages, and other services. It's recommended to keep your Apple ID private and avoid sharing it. During setup, you can create an Apple ID for free if you don't already have one. Whether it's your PC, an iOS device, an iPad device, or an Apple Watch, sign in with the same Apple ID to use any Apple service.
- **Store your files in iCloud**: With iCloud, you can access your content—including documents, images, and more—from anywhere. Make sure you use the same Apple ID to log in across all of your devices. If you haven't already, visit **System Settings** and choose "**Sign in with your Apple ID**" from the sidebar to configure this option later. After logging in, pick the features you want to use by clicking iCloud, then clicking your Apple ID in the sidebar. During setup, you can also decide to use iCloud Keychain to store your credentials.
- **Screen Time**: Keep track of your computer usage and receive reports on it.
- **Enable Siri and "Hey Siri":** During setup, you can activate Siri and "**Hey Siri**" so that you can voice your Siri commands. Speak numerous Siri instructions when asked to activate "**Hey Siri**."
- **Set up Touch ID**: When configuring Touch ID, you have the option of adding a fingerprint. Open **System Settings** and choose **Touch ID & Password** from the sidebar to set up Touch ID later or add more fingerprints. Click and follow the on-screen directions to add a fingerprint.

On your MacBook Pro, you can also choose how Touch ID should be used, including to unlock the computer, use Apple Pay to make purchases from the App Store, Apple TV app, Apple Books, and websites, and auto-fill your password. Each user can add a fingerprint to Touch ID to rapidly unlock, authenticate, and log in to the MacBook

Pro if two or more users are using the device. For a total of five fingerprints across all of your MacBook Pro user accounts, add up to three fingerprints per user account.

- **Set up Apple Pay**: During setup, you can configure Apple Pay for one user account on your MacBook Pro. Other users are still able to use Apple Pay to make purchases, but they must do so with an Apple Watch or iPhone that has Apple Pay enabled. To add and validate your card, adhere to the onscreen instructions. You can be asked to validate a card if you've already used it to buy media.

Open **System Settings** and choose **Wallet & Apple Pay** to set up Apple Pay or subsequently add more cards. To set up Apple Pay, adhere to the onscreen instructions. It should be noted that the card issuer decides whether your card may be used with Apple Pay and may need you to supply further information to finish the verification process.

Apple Pay works with a wide variety of credit and debit cards.

- **Select your look**: To change the appearance of your desktop, click Light, Dark, or Auto. Open **System Settings** > **Appearance**, and then pick a setting if you want to modify the one you selected during setup. Other aesthetic options are also available, including the size and color of sidebar icons and highlights.

How to create a computer account

Follow these steps to create a new user account on your MacBook Pro:

1. Click the Apple logo in the top-left corner of your screen and choose "**System Settings**."
2. Select the "**Users & Groups**" icon in the System Settings pane. To make changes, you may need to enter your admin password.
3. Click on the padlock symbol in the window's lower-left corner and input your admin password to unlock it if it is locked.

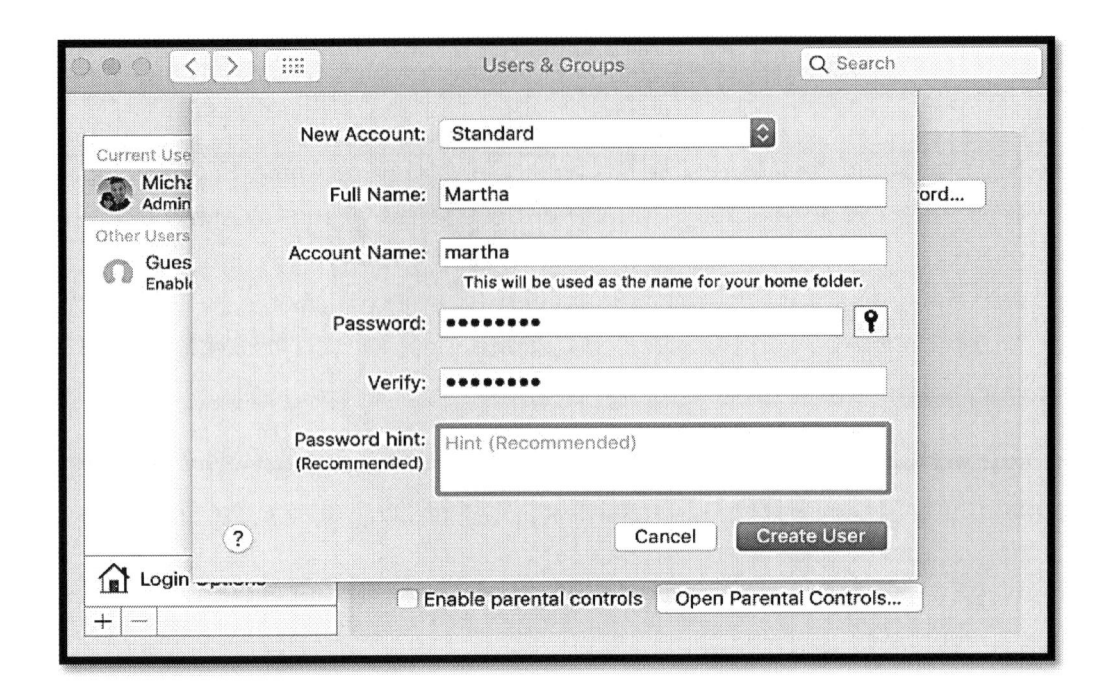

4. To add a new user, use the **"+"** button at the bottom of the left-side user list.
5. Select Account Type to bring up a new window. Select the kind of account you want to create:
- **Administrator**: Complete authority over the whole system and all other users.
- **Standard**: Can install applications and operate the computer, but not modify the operating system.
6. Enter the user's full name, account name (short name), password, and password hint in the appropriate fields. To log in, enter your account name and password. You can also upload a profile photo if you choose.
7. **Select Security Questions (Optional):** If you forget your password, select security questions to aid with account recovery.
8. After entering the necessary information, click the "**Create User**" button.
9. The newly created user account should now be visible in the list on the Users & Groups window's left side.
10. **Configure Account Settings (Optional):** Choose the newly created user account and make any changes you want to it, such as activating parental controls, deciding on login choices, or configuring iCloud settings.

11. **Sign in to the New Account:** First, log out of your existing account by clicking the Apple logo and choosing **"Log Out [Your Username]."** Next, log in to the newly established account to make sure everything is functioning as it should.

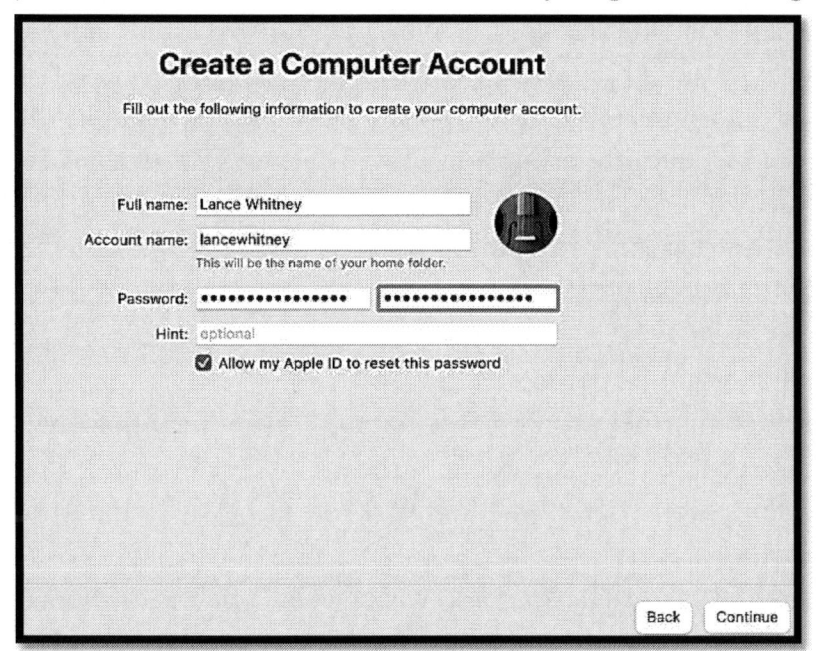

Remember that administrative rights are necessary to create a new user account. You may need to ask the Mac's administrator to create the account for you if you aren't the system administrator.

How to move data to your new MacBook Pro

Transferring your data to your new MacBook Pro allows you to access the information you need whenever you want.

Here are the steps to move data to your new MacBook Pro:

1. **Backup Your Old MacBook**: First of all, to ensure you don't lose any crucial information or settings, you must backup your old MacBook before you begin migrating data. For this, you can use Apple's built-in Time Machine or any alternative backup technique you choose.
2. Install Your New MacBook Pro: Turn it on and go through the installation steps. Choosing your language, region, and keyboard layout as well as

connecting to Wi-Fi and logging in with your Apple ID are required steps in this process.
3. **Migration Assistant:** Data transfer from an old MacBook to a new one may be made easier with the aid of Apple's Migration Assistant app. The "**Utilities**" subfolder of the "**Applications**" folder contains Migration Assistant.
4. Select a Data Transfer Method from those offered by Migration Assistant:
- **From a Mac, backup, or startup disk**: Transfer data straight from your old MacBook, a Time Machine backup, or an external drive using this method.
- **From a Time Machine backup:** Move your data using a recent Time Machine backup of your old MacBook.
- **From a Windows PC**: If you're transferring from a Windows PC to a MacBook, this option might be useful.
5. To connect your old MacBook (or backup) to the new MacBook Pro, follow the on-screen prompts according to the method you choose. This can include connecting over your home network or using a Thunderbolt or USB-C connection.
6. **Choose the Data to Transfer**: You will be given options to choose the Data to Transfer. Applications, documents, user accounts, settings, and more may fall under this category.
7. **Wait for the Transfer to Complete**: Depending on the volume of data being transmitted, the transfer procedure will take some time. Permit the procedure to run uninterrupted.
8. **Set up Certain Apps**: You may need to reinstall certain software when the data transfer is finished. It is necessary to redownload and reinstall certain applications from the Mac App Store or the websites of the creators.
9. Once the transfer is complete, check your new MacBook Pro to make sure all of your data, settings, and apps have been correctly moved.
10. **Organize and Update**: Use this chance to arrange your new MacBook Pro's files and folders. Additionally, be careful to update any programs or software that may need it.

How to Set Up Touch ID

Your new MacBook Pro comes with the option to enable Touch ID and use it for functions such as making transactions with Apple Pay and unlocking your device.

Here are the steps to set up Touch ID:

1. The first step in setting up your MacBook Pro is to turn it on. After that, choose your language, country, and Wi-Fi network.
2. To use Touch ID with different Apple services, you must create or sign in to your Apple ID while configuring a new MacBook Pro.
3. **Create a User Account**: When configuring your MacBook Pro for the first time, you will be requested to create a user account. Touch ID and other system functions will be accessible via this account.
4. **Activate Touch ID**: The steps:
- Select the Apple menu from the screen's top-left corner.
- Then choose "**System Settings**."
- Click on "**Touch ID**."

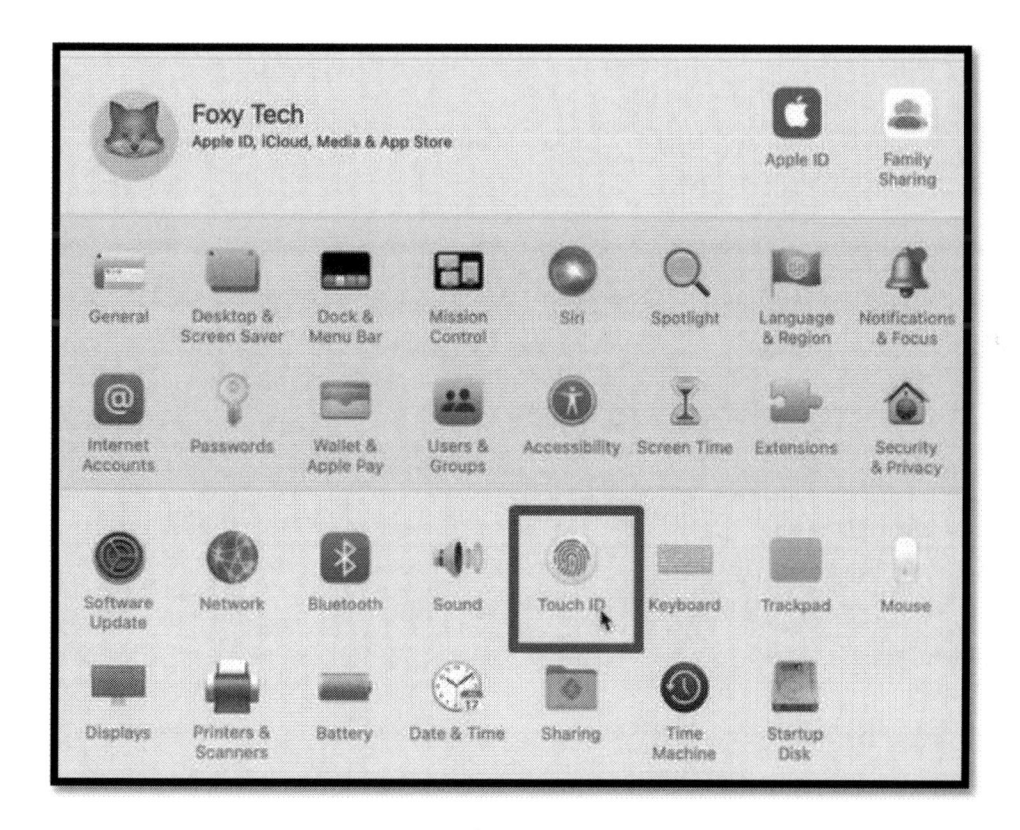

5. **Adding a Fingerprint:**
- If you want to add a new fingerprint, click the "**+**" button.

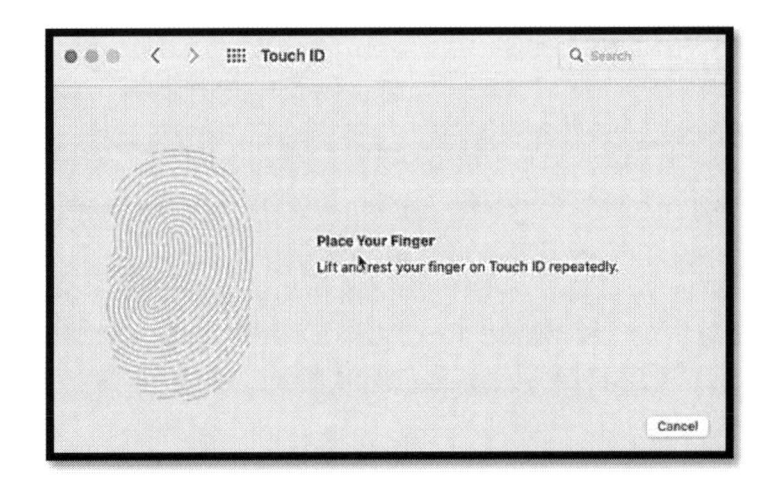

- To put your finger on the Touch ID sensor, adhere to the on-screen instructions.
- Lift and reposition your finger many times to enable the system to record various fingerprint features.
- To achieve a thorough and precise scan, you may need to gently modify the location of your finger.

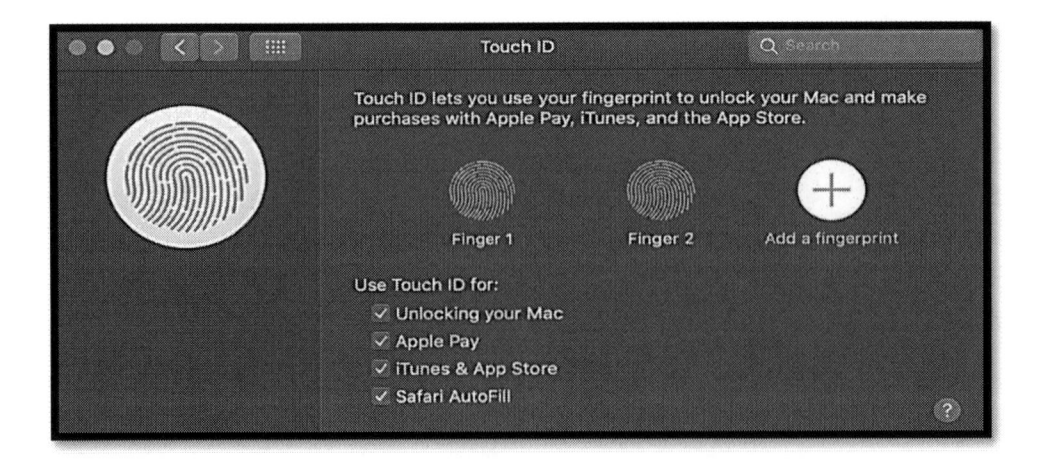

6. **Change Settings:**
- After configuring your fingerprint, Touch ID can be used in a variety of ways. You have the option of using Touch ID to unlock your MacBook Pro, use Apple Pay to make purchases, and more.
7. **Add Additional Fingerprints (optional):**

- If you want to enable several fingers to unlock the laptop or carry out other tasks, you can add more fingerprints.

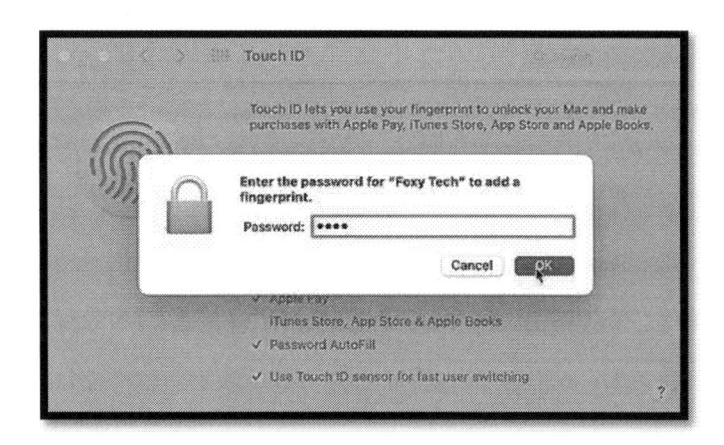

8. **Try Touch ID and Use It:**
- After you've configured Touch ID, you can test it by locking your MacBook Pro and unlocking it with your registered fingerprint.
- Touch ID can also be used to authenticate some tasks, such as installing applications, and making transactions using Apple Pay.

How to use the Magic MacBook Pro Keyboard

With just the press of a key, the Magic Keyboard with Touch ID makes it simple to type emojis, change keyboard languages, lock your MacBook Pro, and access a variety of system services. When Touch ID is on, you can use your fingerprint to instantly lock your screen, unlock your MacBook Pro, and make purchases using Apple Pay from the App Store, Apple TV app, Apple Books, and websites.

- **Set up Touch ID**: You can configure Touch ID during installation or afterward under Touch ID & Password in System Settings.
- **Turn on your MacBook Pro**: Press Touch ID (the power button) or any other key, or raise the lid.
- **Use Touch ID**: When you start up or restart the computer after setting up Touch ID, you will need to enter your password to log in. When prompted for your password after the first login, you can just touch your finger gently on the Touch ID sensor to authenticate. Apple Pay and Touch ID may both be used to safely complete online transactions.
- **Lock your MacBook Pro**: To instantly lock your screen, presses Touch ID.
- **Turn off your MacBook Pro**: Shut down your MacBook Pro by selecting **Apple menu** > **Shut Down**. Select the **Apple menu** > **Sleep** to put your MacBook Pro to sleep.
- **Alternate between keyboard languages or emoji:** To change keyboards, use the **Function (Fn)/Globe key**. If you have Dictation enabled in the Keyboard settings, tap 🌐 twice quickly to start dictation or again to cycle between the emoji choices or other languages you designate there.
- **Set the Keyboard Settings:** Open **System Settings** click **Keyboard** in the sidebar and choose options to change your keyboard or input source, display emoji and symbols, enable dictation, or create functions to set options for your keyboard and the Function (Fn)/Globe key.
- **Discover keyboard shortcuts**: On your MacBook Pro, use key combinations to do actions that you would typically perform with a trackpad, mouse, or other device. For instance, click where you want to paste the text and then press **Command-V** to copy the chosen text.

How to charge the battery and adjust battery voltage

Charging the battery

1. Use the USB-C charging cable and power adapter that comes with your MacBook Pro.
2. The USB-C power adapter should be connected to one end of the USB-C charging cable, and your MacBook Pro should be connected to the other end.

3. Proceed to plug the USB-C power adapter into a power outlet.
4. The charging process for your MacBook Pro will begin instantly. The status of the charge is shown by the battery symbol in the menu bar.
5. Your MacBook Pro won't need to use the battery anymore after the battery is completely charged; instead, it will use the power from the adapter.

Adjusting Battery Voltage

On most MacBook Pro devices, changing the battery voltage is not a commonly available user-configurable option. The internal circuitry of the MacBook controls battery voltage to guarantee a secure and effective operation. Normally, users don't have to manually change battery voltage. It is advised to let the integrated power management system handle these settings.

Battery Health & Management

The built-in Battery Health Management function in Apple products, including the MacBook Pro, helps to extend the battery's overall life. By adjusting charging patterns, this function helps reduce battery deterioration over time.

To use and control this function:

1. In the top-left corner of the screen, choose the **Apple me**nu.
2. Choose "**System Settings**."

3. Click on "**Energy Saver**" or "**Energy.**"
4. Navigate to the "**Battery**" or "**Battery Health**" tab.
5. Look for options concerning battery health management or optimized battery charging. Ensure you adhere to the instructions to manage these features.

How to back up and restore data

When recovering data from another Mac, you can use built-in utilities like Migration Assistant and Time Machine. Here is a detailed instruction:

Backing up Data (using Time Machine):

You can automatically backup your whole system, including files, apps, and system settings, using Time Machine, a built-in backup tool in macOS.

This is how to apply it:

1. **Prepare an External Storage Device**: To store your backups, you'll need an external hard drive, SSD, or network storage device. Ensure that it is formatted to be compatible with macOS.
2. **Connect the Storage Device**: Connect your MacBook Pro to your external storage device using a USB cable.
3. **Set up Time Machine:**
- Select "**System Settings**" from the Apple menu in the top-left corner of your screen.

- Select "**Time Machine**."

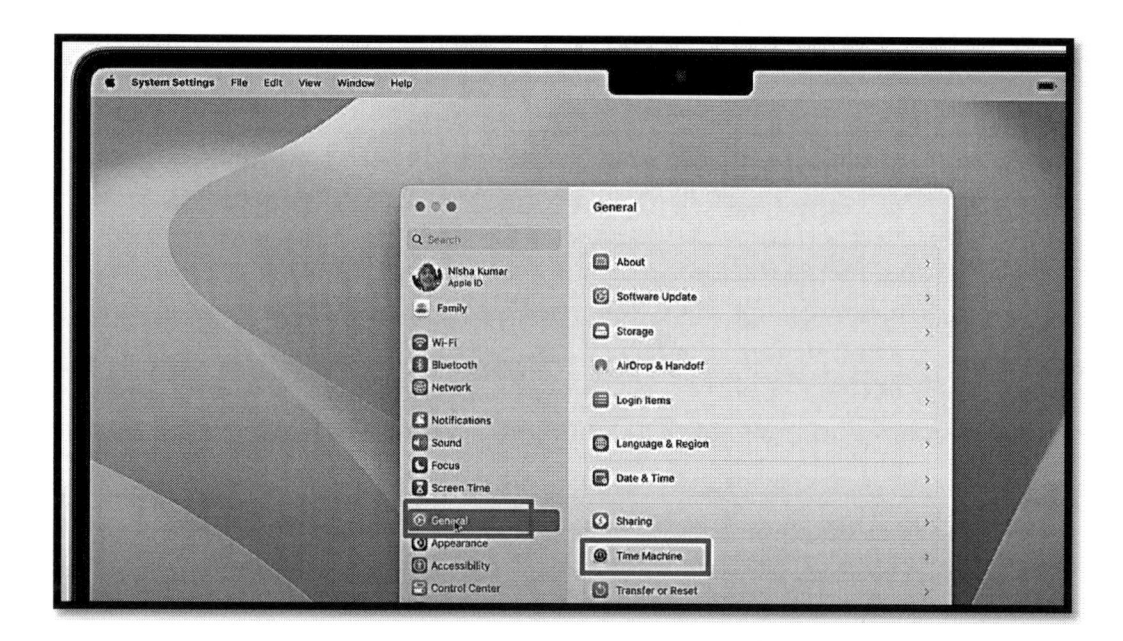

- Select the linked storage device by clicking the "**Select Backup Disk**" button.

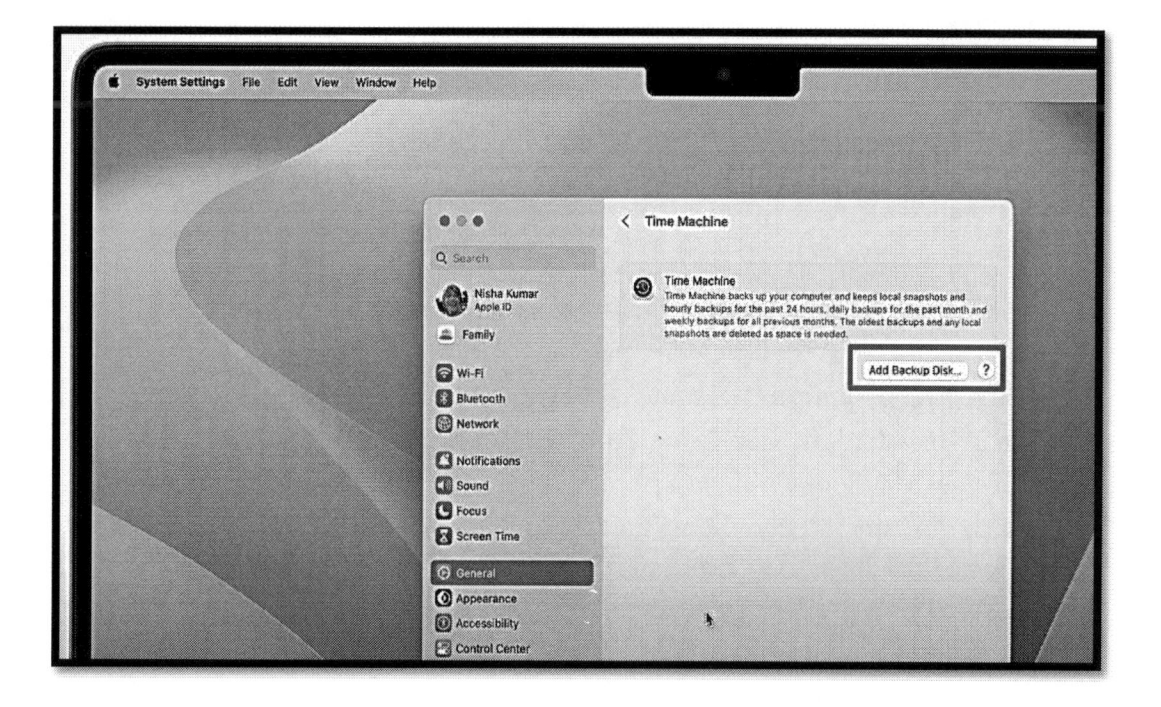

25

- To confirm that you want to use this storage device for Time Machine backups, click "**Use Disk**".
4. **Time Machine Backups**: Once Time Machine is configured, it will routinely back up your data for you. Additionally, you can start a backup manually by selecting "**Back up Now**" in the Time Machine options.

Restoring Data (With Migration Assistant)

Use Migration Assistant to move your files, apps, and preferences from another Mac, a Time Machine backup, or another disk to your new MacBook Pro.

This is how to apply it:
1. **Launch Migration Assistant:**
- Switch on your new MacBook Pro, and then go through the basic setup process until you reach the "**Migration Assistant**" phase.
- Select the starting disk, Time Machine backup, or Mac as the source for your data transfer.

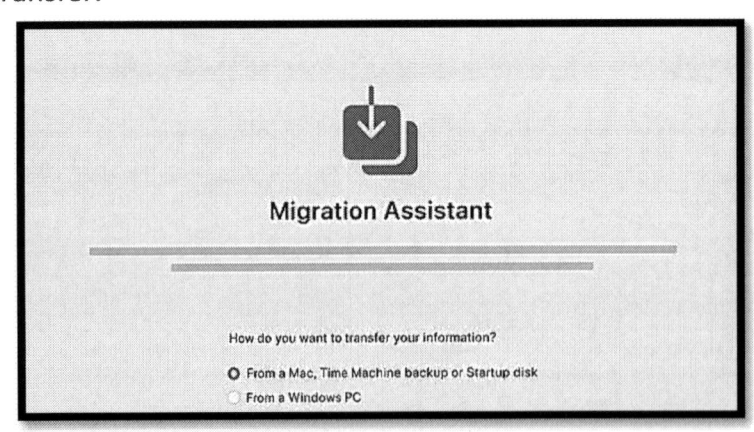

2. **Connecting a Previous Device:**
- Use a Thunderbolt, USB-C, or Ethernet connection to link your old Mac to your new MacBook Pro if you're moving data from one Mac to another.
- Attach the Time Machine backup disk to your MacBook Pro if you're restoring from one.

3. **Choose a Source and Target:**
- Decide whether to use a Time Machine backup or another Mac as the source of your data.

- Make your new MacBook Pro the transfer's target.
4. **Decide which Items to Transfer:**
- You have the option to transfer specific items, including user accounts, apps, documents, settings, and other data.
- Decide what you want, then start the transfer.

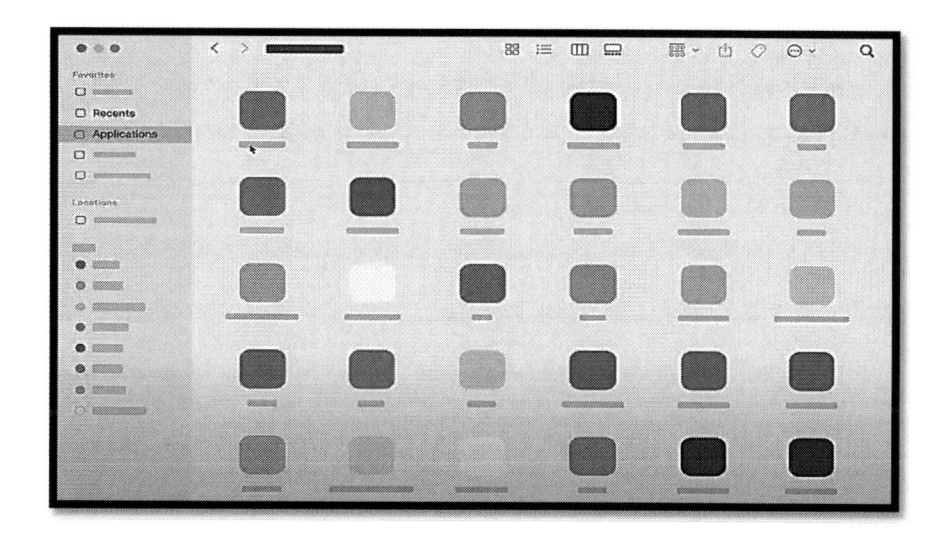

5. **Finish the Transfer:**
- The selected data will start to be transferred to your new MacBook Pro using Migration Assistant.
- You may need to enter your old user account's password when the transfer is finished.

Note: Wait until you are certain that everything has been properly moved to your new MacBook Pro before destroying your old device or Time Machine backup.

How to shut down or sleep your new MacBook Pro

Put your MacBook Pro to sleep

1. **Closing the Lid**: Your MacBook ought to enter sleep mode automatically if you shut the lid. When you open the lid again, this is the default behavior, which enables you to swiftly continue working.
2. Click on the **Apple menu icon** located in the top-left corner of the screen. Go to the dropdown menu and choose "**Sleep**."

3. **Keyboard Shortcut:** Press the "**Control**" key while simultaneously holding down the "**Shift**" and "**Power**" (or "**Eject**") keys. Press the **Control + Shift + Touch ID button** on newer MacBooks without a physical Power key to activate Touch ID.

How to turn off/shut down your MacBook

1. Click on the **Apple menu icon** located in the top-left corner of the screen. Go to the dropdown menu and choose "**Shut Down**."

2. **Keyboard Shortcut**: Press the "**Control**" key, the "**Option**" key, and the "**Power**" (or "**Eject**") key simultaneously. Press the **Control + Option + Touch ID button** on newer MacBooks without a physical Power key to activate Touch ID.

Frequently Asked Questions

1. What are the new features and specifications of the new MacBook Pro?
2. How do you set up your new MacBook Pro?
3. How do you create a computer account?
4. How do you backup and restore your data?
5. How do you use the Magic MacBook Pro keyboard?
6. How do you shut down or sleep your new MacBook Pro?

CHAPTER TWO
APPLE PAY AND AIRPRINT

Overview

Chapter two talks about Apple Pay and Air Print services which allow you to make purchases for items online and print directly from your Apple devices without installing any drivers or software.

How to set up Apple Pay

Apple Inc. created Apple Pay, a mobile payment and digital wallet service. Instead of using real credit or debit cards, it enables consumers to make purchases using their Apple devices, including iPhones, iPads, Apple Watches, and MacBooks. Holding your iPhone close to a suitable payment terminal is all it takes to make a contactless payment using NFC technology, which is how Apple Pay works.

Here's how to set up Apple Pay:

1. **Check Compatibility**: Verify that the MacBook Pro model you are using can accept Apple Pay. The majority of current MacBook Pro models ought to be compatible, but it's wise to double-check on Apple's website or in the system settings.
2. **Add Cards to Wallet**:
- On your MacBook Pro, open the "**Wallet & Apple Pay**" options in the System Settings.

- To add a new card, click on the "+" (plus) button.

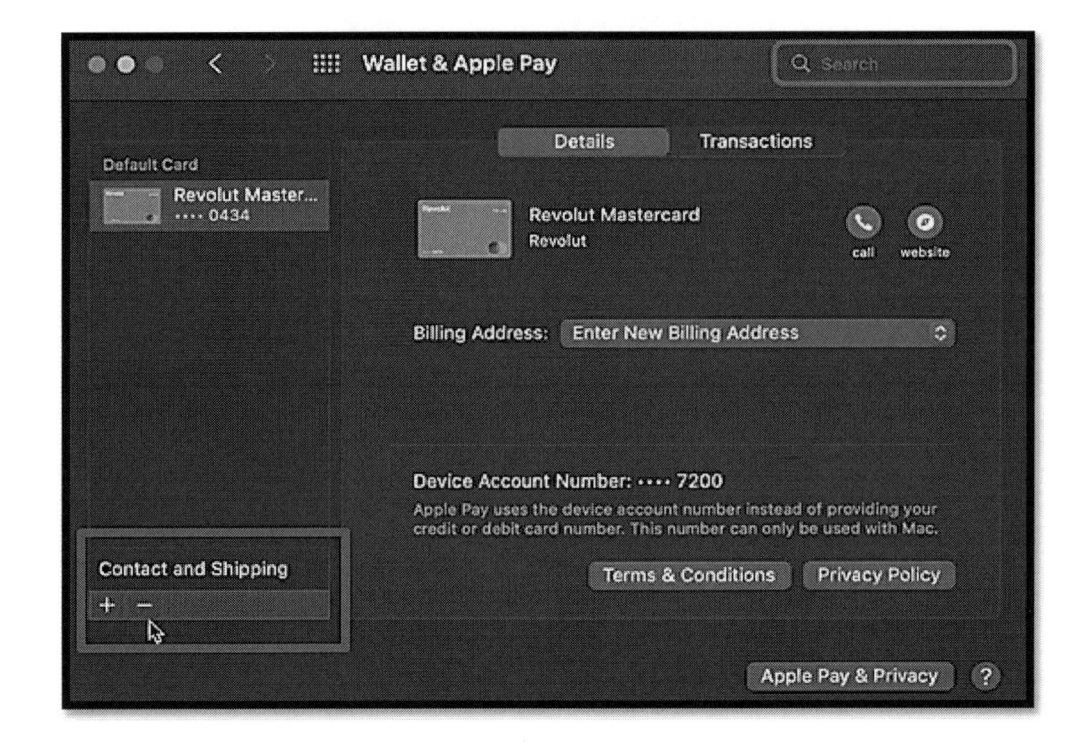

- You can manually input the card information or use the built-in camera to scan your actual card.
- To validate your card, follow the on-screen instructions. You may need to wait for your bank to send you a verification number through text message or email.

3. **Verifying the Card:**
- Your bank will request extra verification once you've inserted your card for security reasons. This can include phoning customer support at your bank or getting a verification number by email or phone.

4. **Set Default Card (Optional):**
- For convenience, you can choose a default card if you have numerous cards in your Apple Pay wallet. *(NB: The default payment method will be made using this card).*

5. **Using Apple Pay:**

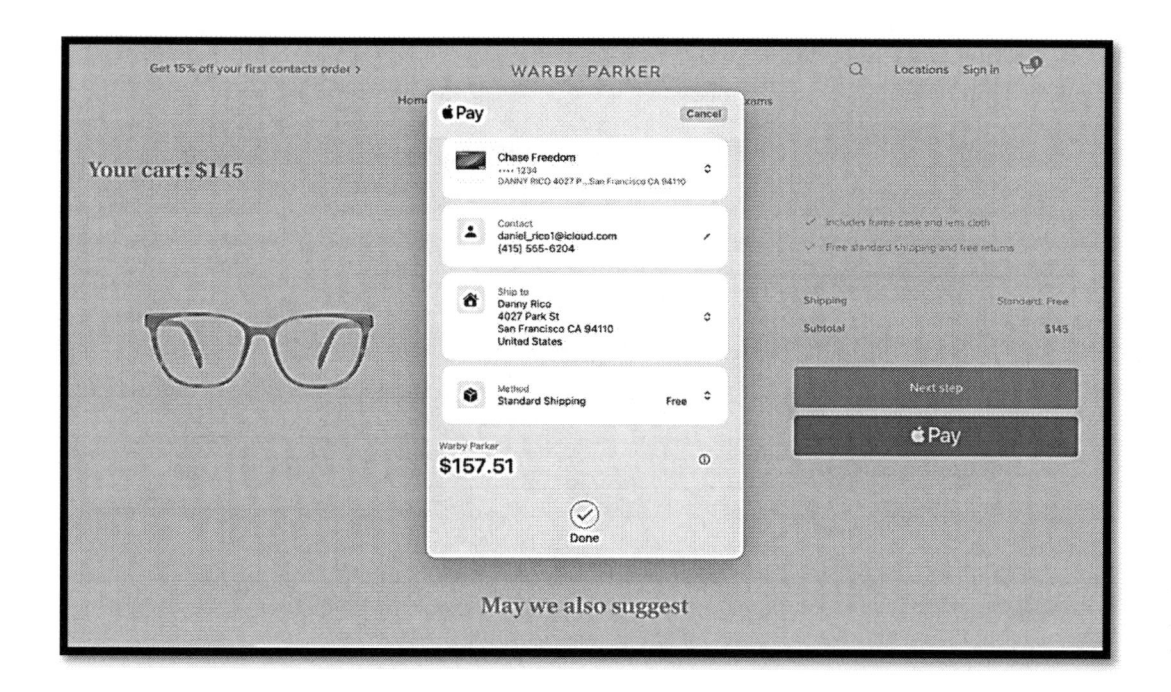

- After configuring Apple Pay, you can use it in Safari or other compatible applications to make online purchases. Look for the Apple Pay option while paying.
- To use Apple Pay for in-store transactions, just place your MacBook Pro next to the payment terminal and approve the transaction using Touch ID or your computer's password.

How to make purchases using Apple Pay

Here are the steps:

1. Make sure your MacBook Pro is compatible with Apple Pay. In general, Apple Pay should work with any Mac that has a Touch ID sensor.
2. **Install Apple Pay**: To install Apple Pay on your MacBook Pro, follow these instructions.
- Select the Apple menu from your screen's top-left corner.
- Then choose "**System Settings.**"
- Choose "**Wallet & Apple Pay**."

- To add a card, click on the **"+"** button.
- Your card details will be requested from you. The card information can be manually entered or taken using your iPhone's camera.
- To finish the setup, adhere to the directions shown on-screen.
3. **Using Apple Pay**: After setting up Apple Pay, you can use it to make purchases online that accept it.
- Head to the checkout page on a website that accepts Apple Pay when you're ready to make a purchase.
- Search for the "**Buy with Apple Pay**" or the "**Apple Pay**" button, which may or may not be labeled as such.
- After you click the button, your MacBook Pro should ask you to authenticate the transaction using Touch ID on the Touch Bar or the MacBook Pro's in-built Touch ID sensor.
- Your payment information will be delivered securely to complete the transaction after authentication.
4. **Using Apple Pay in Apps**: If an app is compatible, you can use Apple Pay to make purchases inside of it.
- Look for the Apple Pay option throughout the checkout process when purchasing a compatible app.

- After choosing Apple Pay, you will be asked to verify your identity using Touch ID.
5. **Managing Cards**: From the "**System Settings**" menu, choose "**Wallet & Apple Pay**." From there, you can change your cards and preferences. You can modify your billing and shipping addresses as well as add or delete cards and change the default card here.
6. **Security**: Apple Pay was created with security in mind. Your credit card information is not kept on the device, and Touch ID is used to verify purchases. Tokenization is another security measure used by Apple Pay to replace your card information with a unique identifier.

How to enable Apple Pay in Safari

Here are the steps:

1. **Check System Requirements**: Before using Apple Pay in Safari, make sure your MacBook Pro and operating system version fulfill the requirements. Typically, you require a MacBook model that is compatible with this functionality and a supported version of macOS (macOS Ventura).
2. **Configure Apple Pay**: If you haven't previously, you should configure Apple Pay on your MacBook Pro. To do this, you must link your credit or debit cards to the Wallet app. Take these actions:
- In the top-left corner of your screen, choose the **Apple menu**.
- Then, choose "**System Settings**."
- Select "**Wallet & Apple Pay**."

- To add a new card, click the "+" button.

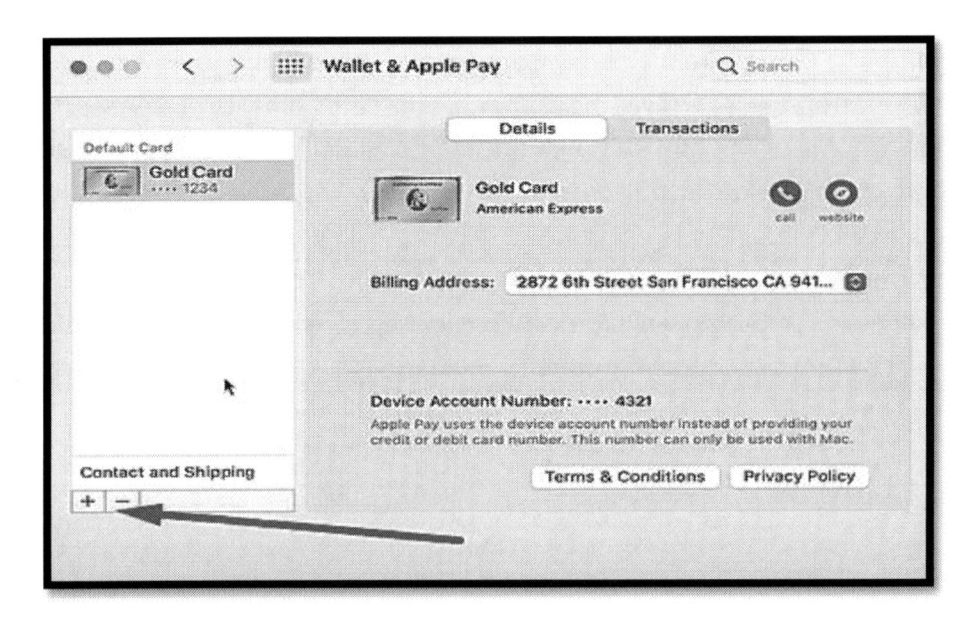

- Add your card information by following the on-screen directions. The card may need to be verified via a method offered by your bank.
3. **Enable Apple Pay in Safari:**
- Start your MacBook Pro's Safari browser.
- Select "**Preferences**" from the Safari menu.
- Select "**Privacy**" from the tabs.
- Verify that "**Prevent cross-site tracking**" is unchecked under "**Website tracking**." Cross-site tracking must be permitted to use Apple Pay.
4. **Test Apple Pay**: Test Apple Pay on approved websites that accept it after configuring it and turning on cross-site tracking in Safari. The Apple Pay button will be there at the checkout when you're ready to make a purchase. When you click the button, a popup to validate the payment with your Touch ID or passcode will appear.

How to change or remove payment cards with Apple Pay

How to Add a Credit Card to Apple Pay

1. **Launch System Settings**: To do this, click the **Apple logo** in the top-left corner of your screen and then choose "**System Settings.**"

2. **Choose Wallet & Apple Pay**: Find and select the "**Wallet & Apple Pay**" icon in the System Settings window.
3. **Add Card:** To begin adding a new credit or debit card, click the "**+**" button (Add Card).

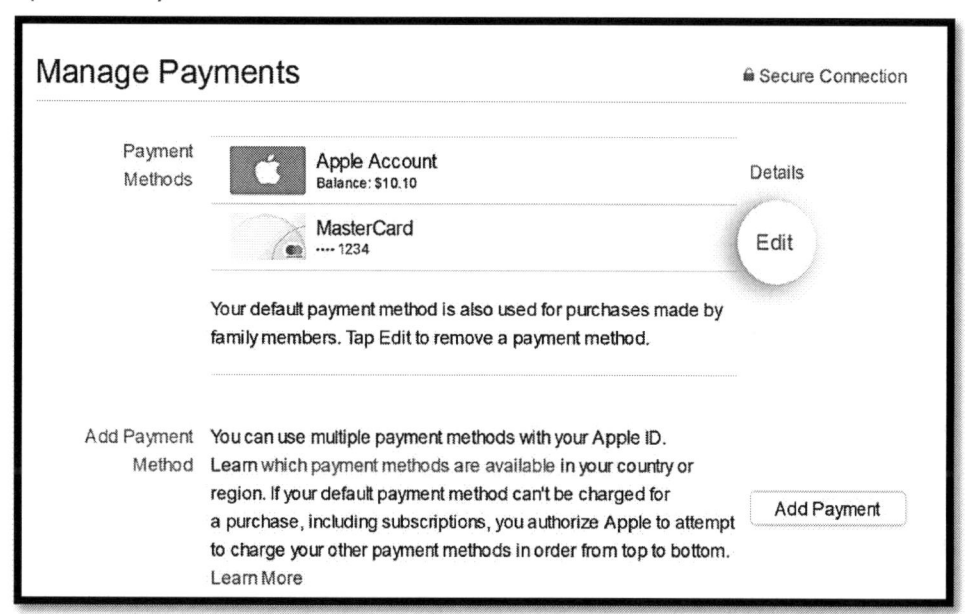

```
Manage Payments                                    🔒 Secure Connection

Payment      Apple Account                              Details
Methods      Balance: $10.10

             MasterCard                                   Edit
             ···· 1234

Your default payment method is also used for purchases made by
family members. Tap Edit to remove a payment method.

Add Payment   You can use multiple payment methods with your Apple ID.
Method        Learn which payment methods are available in your country or
              region. If your default payment method can't be charged for
              a purchase, including subscriptions, you authorize Apple to attempt    Add Payment
              to charge your other payment methods in order from top to bottom.
              Learn More
```

4. You will get instructions on how to add a credit or debit card. Your card information can be manually entered or captured using the camera.
5. **Verification**: Depending on your bank, you may be required to receive a verification number by SMS or email to use the card.
6. **Accept Terms:** Read the terms and conditions that your bank or card issuer has supplied and accept them.

Removing Payment Card from Apple Pay

1. First of all, launch **System Settings**.
2. **Choose Wallet & Apple Pay**: Click the "**Wallet & Apple Pay**" button in the System Settings pane.
3. **Select the Card to Remove**: A list of your added payment cards should appear under the "**Payment Cards**" section. Choose the card you want to discard.
4. **Delete Card**: Select the card you want to delete by clicking the "**Remove**" button (often indicated by a minus sign or trash symbol).

5. **Confirm**: A confirmation popup requesting your confirmation to delete the card will be displayed. Ensure you confirm your decision.
6. **Verification**: Depending on your bank or card provider, you may need to confirm the removal by giving further details or obtaining a verification number.

About AirPrint

Apple created the AirPrint feature, which enables users to print wirelessly from iOS (such as iPhones and iPads) and macOS (such as MacBooks) devices to compatible printers without the need to set up any drivers or software. Users can now easily print documents, photographs, emails, and more without having to fiddle with printer settings, which is handy. Your printer must support AirPrint to use it. This functionality is supported by several contemporary printers from different manufacturers. Your iOS or macOS smartphone should instantly identify the nearby AirPrint printers if you're connected to the same Wi-Fi network as your printer.

How to use AirPrint

You can print wirelessly from your Apple devices using AirPrint, which eliminates the need for extra drivers or software.

Here is how to use AirPrint on a MacBook Pro:

1. **Check Compatibility**: Confirm that your printer is AirPrint-ready. Major manufacturers' contemporary printers often offer AirPrint.
2. **Connect to Wi-Fi**: Ensure that both your MacBook Pro and your AirPrint-capable printer are connected to the same Wi-Fi network.
3. **Open the Document or Image**: Using a suitable app (such as Safari for web pages, Pages for documents, Preview for photos, etc.), open the document, picture, or image that you want to print.
4. **Open Print Dialog**: To open the print settings, choose "**File**" on the menu bar, then "**Print**," or use the shortcut key "**Command + P**."
5. **Choose Printer**: There should be a "**Printer**" dropdown option in the print dialog. To choose your printer from the list of AirPrint-compatible devices, click on it. Your printer should show up in the list if it is correctly connected to the same Wi-Fi network.

6. **Set Printing Settings**: Decide on the print preferences, including the quantity of copies, paper size, orientation, and other factors.
7. **Print**: When you've finished setting everything up, click "**Print**" to send the print job to an AirPrint-enabled printer. The printer should wirelessly take in the work and begin printing.

How to print wirelessly from your MacBook Pro to an AirPrint printer

It's quite easy to print documents wirelessly from a MacBook Pro to an AirPrint printer without the need for any physical connections.

Here are steps:

1. **Check Compatibility**: Confirm that AirPrint is supported by your printer. The majority of contemporary printers do, but it's always a good idea to confirm the manufacturer's recommendations.
2. **Join the same wireless network:**
- Verify that your MacBook Pro is linked to the same Wi-Fi network as the AirPrint printer.
3. **Add the Printer:**
- On your computer screen, click the **Apple menu** in the top-left corner.
- Then choose "**System Settings**."
- To begin, choose "**Printers & Scanners**."

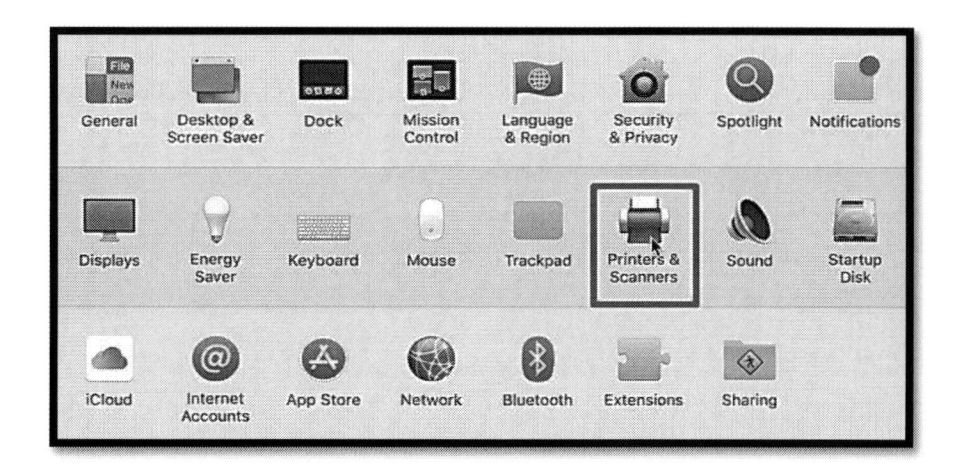

- To add a new printer, click the '**+**' button (Add) on the left.

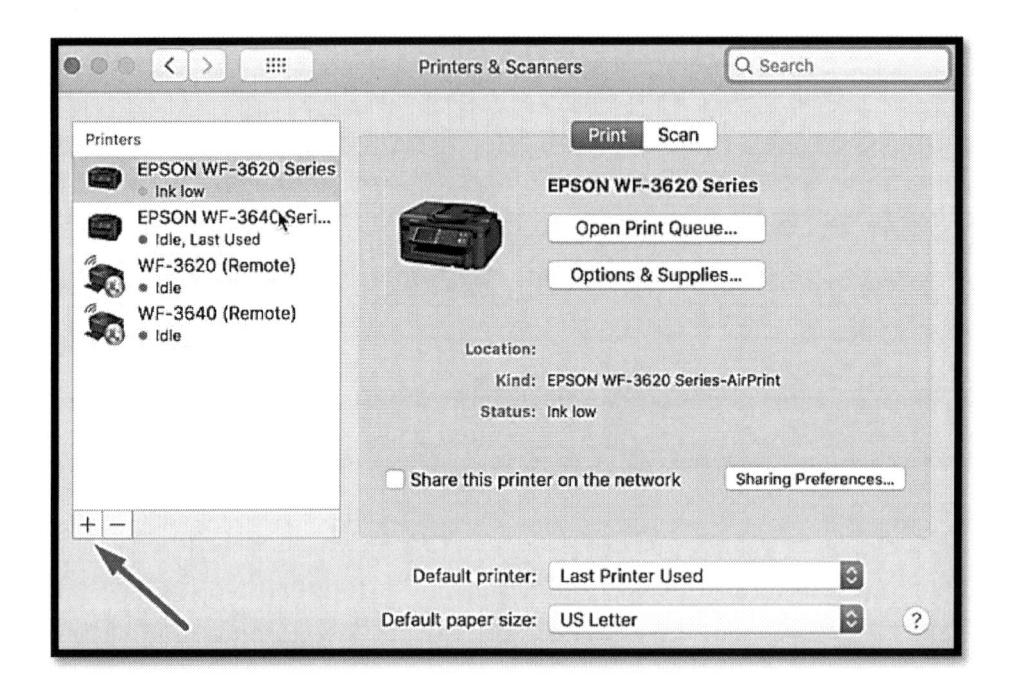

- The AirPrint printer on your network should be immediately detected by your MacBook Pro. Choose it, and then click "**Add**."
4. **Set Printer Options:**
- After adding the printer, you may have to adjust a few things. These could include things like paper quality, size, and orientation. You can change these variables to suit your requirements.

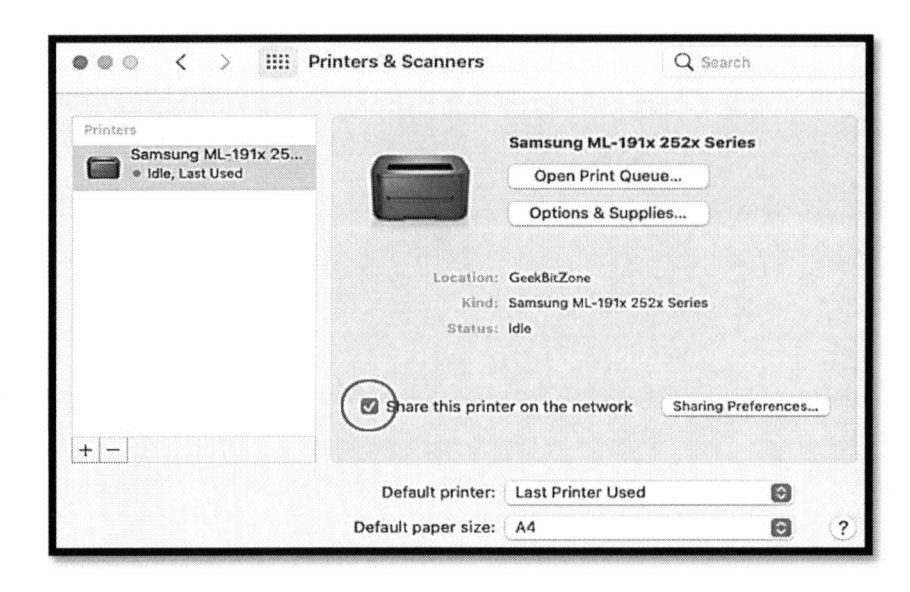

5. **Print a Document:**
   - Open the file or document you want to print.
   - To enter the print dialog, press **"Command + P"** or choose **"File" > "Print"**.
6. **Choose the Printer:**
   - Choose the AirPrint printer you previously installed from the **"Printer"** menu.
7. **Adjust Print Settings:**
   - The print options you have accessible may vary depending on the program you're printing from. If necessary, change these parameters.
8. **Print:**
   - When you're happy with the print settings, click **"Print"** to send the print job to the printer connected to AirPrint.
9. **Track Printing Progress:**
   - The print queue allows you to see the print job's status. To see the print queue, click on the printer icon in the top-right corner of your screen and choose your printer.

The AirPrint printer on your MacBook Pro should now be able to connect wirelessly without any problems. For effective printing, just make sure your MacBook Pro is still plugged into the same Wi-Fi network as the printer.

Frequently Asked Questions

1. How do you set up Apple Pay?
2. How do you enable Apple Pay in Safari?
3. How do you make purchases using Apple Pay?
4. How do you use AirPrint?
5. How do you change or remove payment cards with Apple Pay?
6. How do you print wirelessly from your MacBook Pro to an AirPrint printer?

CHAPTER THREE
DOCK AND MENU BAR

Overview

In this chapter, you will learn all about the dock and menu bar including the process of customizing the dock, changing the dock size, changing the dock's orientation, and so much more.

How to Use and Customize the Dock

The dock, a key component of the macOS interface, gives you easy access to your preferred programs, folders, and documents.

Here is how to use and customize it:

Using the Dock

1. **Accessing Applications**: The Dock is often located at the bottom of your screen. Choose an application icon in the dock to launch the corresponding app. A little dot will appear underneath the symbol of any running applications.
2. **Switching Between Apps**: You can easily move between open programs by using the Dock. An already open app may be brought to the front by clicking its icon.
3. **Adding Apps**: Simply start the app, right-click (or Control-click) its icon in the Dock, and choose "**Keep in Dock**."
4. **Deleting Apps**: To delete an app from the Dock, right-click (or control-click) on the icon of the app and choose "**Remove from Dock**." This will maintain the app itself intact while removing the icon from the Dock.
5. **Files and Folders**: You can now drag files or folders into the Dock to add them there. Fast access to commonly used files and folders is made possible by this.

Customizing the Dock

1. **Position**: Select **"System Settings" > "Dock & Menu Bar"** to change the dock's location. The Dock can now be positioned wherever on your screen—bottom, left, or right.
2. **Size**: Change the size of the Dock icons by dragging the line separating them from the Trash symbol. Your selection will determine whether this enlarges or reduces the size of the Dock icons.
3. **Magnification**: When you enable this feature, the Dock's icons will seem bigger when you hover your mouse over them. The same "**Dock & Menu Bar**" options allow you to change the magnification level.
4. **Minimize Windows**: When you click the yellow minimize button on macOS Ventura, windows are automatically minimized into the Dock. By navigating to **"System Settings" > "Dock & Menu Bar" > "Minimize windows using,"** you can change this behavior to minimize into the application's icon.
5. **Recent Applications**: You can activate the option to display your most recent programs in the Dock under the "**Dock & Menu Bar**" settings.
6. **Adding/Removing Items**: Drag and drop files, directories, and apps into the Dock to put them there. Simply drag an item's icon out of the Dock until it vanishes with a poof animation to delete it.

How to Change the Dock's Size

Here's how to change the MacBook dock's size:

Method 1: Using System Settings

1. Select the **Apple icon** located in the top-left corner of your screen.
2. From the dropdown menu, choose **"System Settings"**.
3. Select "**Dock & Menu Bar**" in the System Settings box.
4. Locate the "**Size**" slider and change it to the dock size you want. To make the dock smaller or bigger, move the slider to the left or right, respectively. The dock's size will change in real-time as you move the slider.
5. After determining the size to your satisfaction, dismiss the System Settings window.

Method 2: Using the Dock

The steps:

1. Scroll to the bottom of your screen and find the Dock. It needs to have a variety of app icons.
2. Place your pointer on the line dividing the screen's app icons from the rest of it.
3. A two-headed arrow will appear as your cursor.
4. To change the dock's size, click and drag the divider line up or down.
5. When the dock reaches the required size, let go of the mouse button.

How to Change the Dock's Orientation

Here's how to change the dock's orientation:

1. First of all, click the Apple logo in the top-left corner of your screen and then choose "**System Settings.**"
2. **Click "Dock & Menu Bar:"** Select "**Dock & Menu Bar**" by clicking the icon in System Settings. Here, you can change several settings for the menu bar and dock.
3. In the "**Dock**" subsection of the settings, there is a dropdown menu titled "**Position on screen**." To see the different options for dock orientation, click this dropdown.
4. **Choose Dock Orientation**: Select one of the various dock locations. The options often consist of:
- **Bottom**: In this setting, the dock always appears at the bottom of the screen.
- **Left**: The dock will be visible on the screen's left side.
- **Right**: The screen's right side will have the dock.
- **Bottom (Prefer left):** If space is at a premium because of other windows, this option allows the dock to be at the bottom but favors the left side.
5. **Adjust Size:** By using the slider next to the "**Size**" label, you can also modify the dock's size. This controls the size at which the dock's icons are shown.
6. **Additional Settings**: There may be extra options affecting the design and operation of the dock, depending on your macOS version.
7. After making your modifications, you can exit the System Settings window.

How to Hide/Show Dock on MacBook Pro

To display or hide the dock on a MacBook Pro:

Hiding the Dock

1. Lower the pointer to the screen's bottom. You should be able to see the Dock.
2. Click with the right mouse button (or the Control key) on the Dock's space.
3. Hover your cursor over the "**Turn hiding on**" option in the context menu that opens.
4. Depending on your desire, choose either the "**Manually**" or "**Automatically**" option.
- **Automatically**: When you choose this option, the Dock will automatically disappear when you aren't using it and return when you move your pointer to the bottom of the screen.
- **Manually**: When you activate this option, the Dock will only be hidden temporarily until you choose to make it visible again.

Showing the Dock

1. If the Dock is configured to automatically hide, move your mouse to the bottom of the screen and it should show up.
2. To make the Dock visible if you manually configured it to be hidden, follow these instructions:
- To display the Dock, move your pointer to the bottom of the screen.
- It's possible that you need to "**unhide**" your Dock if it doesn't show up. Toggle the Dock's visibility by simultaneously pressing the **Command, Option,** and **D keys**.

How to Change the Menu bar Size on Your MacBook Pro

Adjust the menu bar's size as follows:

1. Select the **Apple icon** located in the top-left corner of your screen. In turn, a drop-down menu will appear.
2. In the drop-down menu, choose "**System Settings**."

3. Select "**Displays**" or "**Accessibility**": The menu bar size adjustment option can be found in the "**Displays**" or "**Accessibility**" section, depending on the version of macOS and the particular options accessible. Here's where to look for it in both locations:

Displays

- Select the "**Displays**" icon in **System Settings**.
- Look for a screen zoom, resolution, or display scaling option.
- Change the settings to alter the display scale, which may also have an impact on the menu bar's size.

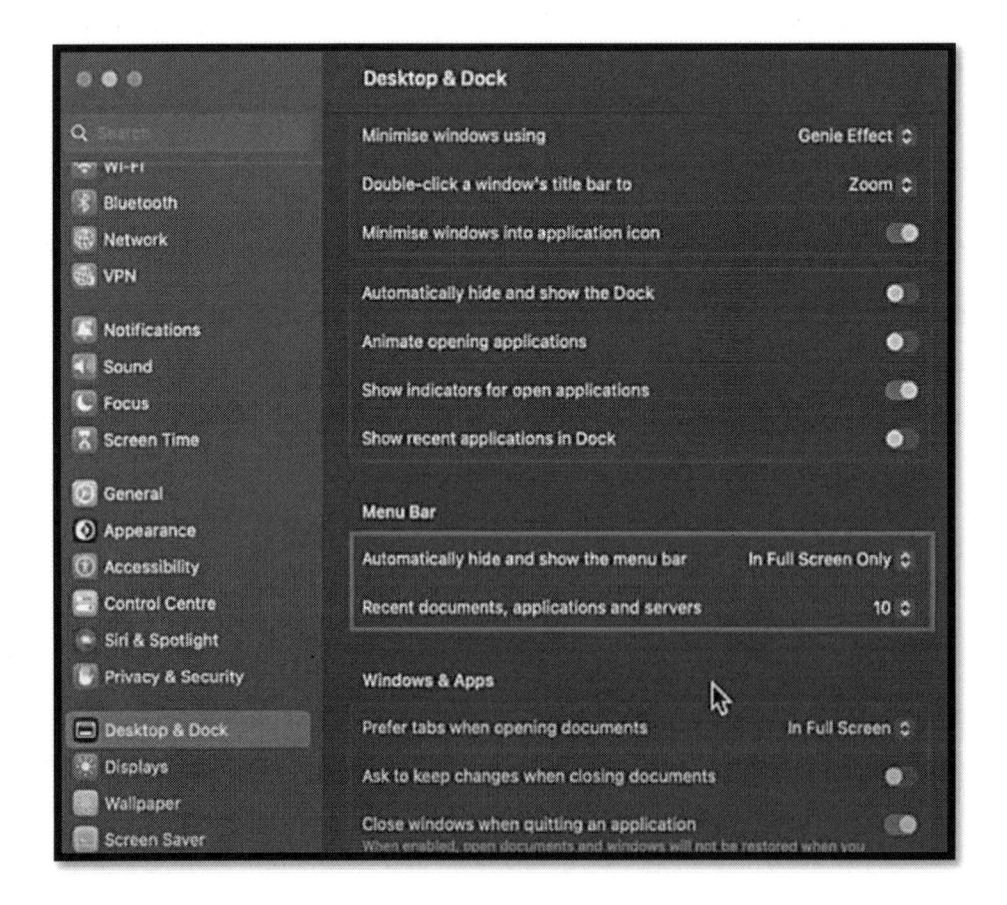

Accessibility

- Select the "**Accessibility**" icon in the System Settings pane.
- Select the "**Display**" category or a related option.
- Check the display zoom or screen magnification settings.

- Change the display's overall size in the settings to see whether the menu bar's size changes as well.
4. **Logout or Restart**: For the changes to take effect, you may need to log out of your Mac or restart your MacBook Pro, depending on the macOS version and your settings.

How to Adjust the Menu bar Size

1. Launch the System Settings menu by clicking the Apple logo in the top-left corner of the screen and choosing **"System Settings."**
2. Find and choose the "**Accessibility**" icon in the System Settings window.
3. **Display**: Click "**Display**" in the accessibility options' left sidebar.

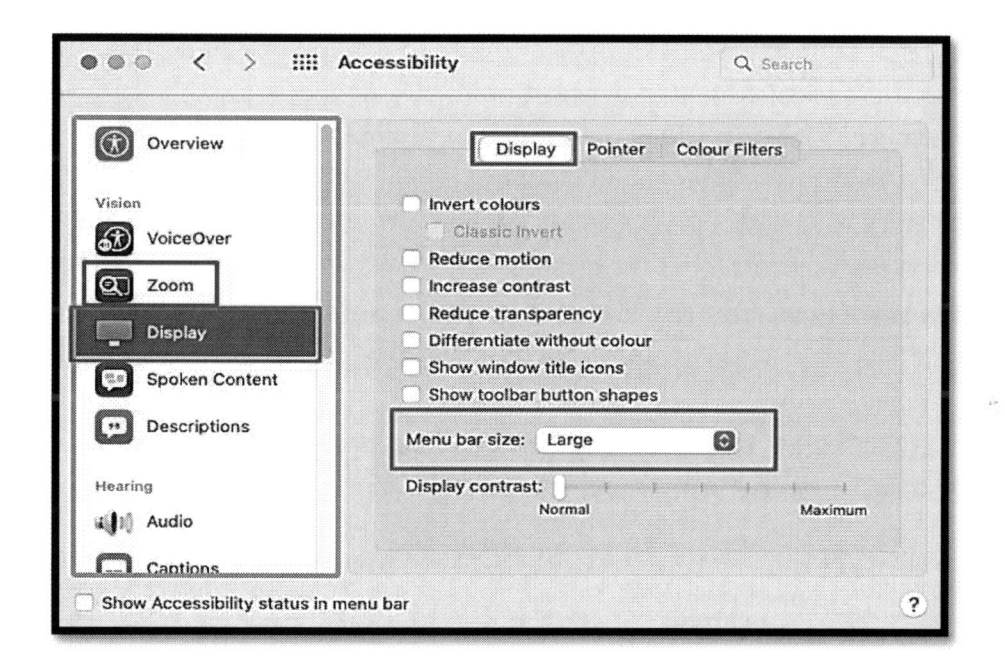

4. When choosing your display options, look for a selection for "**Cursor & Pointer**" or "**Cursor Size**." Depending on the hardware and macOS version, this can change. The menu bar size may be indirectly impacted by the cursor size change offered by certain macOS versions.
5. **Zoom**: As an alternative, check the "**Zoom**" options if the cursor size changes have no impact on the menu bar. The size of the menu bar and the whole screen may grow if Zoom is enabled.

45

6. **Additional Options**: If the aforementioned actions don't provide the expected outcomes, look into additional pertinent Accessibility section options. New settings or features that affect the user interface, notably the menu bar, can be added to macOS.

How to Hide the Menu Bar

The steps:

1. To enter the Apple menu, click on the **Apple logo** in the upper-left corner of the screen.
2. Click the drop-down menu and choose "**System Settings**."
3. **Dock & Menu Bar**: Navigate to and choose the "**Dock & Menu Bar**" option under System Preferences. This preference window ought to let you change how the dock and menu bar operate.
4. **Menu Bar Options**: There needs to be a menu bar option in the "**Dock & Menu Bar**" preference pane. The exact language could change depending on the macOS version in 2023, although it might say something like "**Menu Bar**" or "**Menu Bar Visibility**."
5. **Adjust Settings**: You can find a checkbox or setting in the menu bar choices that enable you to automatically conceal the menu bar. If this checkbox is available, choose it.
6. After changing the menu bar hiding settings, exit the System Settings window.

How to Reduce Your Mac's Window

Here's how to reduce a window on your MacBook Pro:

1. **Reduce Using the Yellow Button**: The yellow button in the window's top left corner is the most popular method to minimize a window on a Mac. The window will be reduced with the help of this button to the Dock. To minimize the window, just click the yellow button. The window may then be restored by clicking the minimized app's icon in the Dock.
2. **Keyboard Shortcut:** To reduce the currently open window, use the keyboard shortcut. Typically, the shortcut is **Command + M**. Press **Command + M** when the window you want to minimize is active, and it will be docked.

3. **Mission Control:** You can use Mission Control to control your windows if you're running a version of macOS that supports it. Use three or four fingers to swipe up on your trackpad, or click the **F3 key** (assuming your keyboard has the corresponding function key). All of your open windows will be shown here as thumbnails. To minimize a window, drag it to the bottom of the screen.
4. **Gesture**: On more recent MacBook models with Force Touch trackpads, you can dismiss a window using a gesture. Put the cursor over the window you wish to reduce, and then use the trackpad's three-finger pinch-out motion to minimize it. The window should now be minimized to the Dock.

Frequently Asked Questions

1. How do you use and customize the dock on your new MacBook Pro?
2. How do you change the dock's size?
3. How do you show or hide the dock?
4. How do you adjust the menu bar size on your MacBook Pro?
5. How do you hide the menu bar?

CHAPTER FOUR
ICLOUD

Overview

There are a whole lot of things you can do by having an iCloud account including storing photos, videos, documents, music, and others. Chapter four teaches you all there is to know about iCloud including setting it up, editing iCloud settings, and others.

How to Set up & Edit iCloud

Apple offers iCloud, a cloud-based storage and syncing service. Users may access numerous sorts of data, including photographs, videos, documents, music, and more, that have been stored on distant servers by using a variety of Apple devices. Automatic device backups, easy app integration, and the capacity to share material with other iCloud users are further capabilities provided by iCloud.

Follow these steps to configure and change iCloud on your new MacBook Pro:

Setting Up iCloud

1. You will be directed through the first setup procedure when you initially set up your new MacBook Pro. You will have the opportunity to sign in with your Apple ID throughout this procedure, which is necessary to use iCloud. Enter your credentials if you have an Apple ID already. In such a case, you can create a new Apple ID.
2. **Enabling iCloud Services**: You will be requested to activate several iCloud services after logging in with your Apple ID. iCloud Drive, Photos, Mail, Contacts, Calendar, Notes, and other services may be among them. Choose the services you want to use, and then sync them across all of your devices. These options are also accessible through the **"System Settings"** menu on your MacBook Pro, where you may make changes afterward.

Changing iCloud settings

The methods below can be used to manage your iCloud storage or update your iCloud settings:

1. Click the Apple logo in the top-left corner of your screen and then choose **"System Settings."**
2. To access iCloud settings, find and click the "**Apple ID**" button in the System Settings window. It has your name written on it and resembles your profile photo.
3. **Manage iCloud Services**: In the Apple ID settings, on the left sidebar, you'll see a list of different iCloud services. To change a service's settings, click on it. For instance, you can modify your Photos settings, pick which folders you want to sync with iCloud Drive, edit your iCloud Mail options, and more.
4. **Manage iCloud Storage**: The Apple ID settings will have an option for "**iCloud Storage**." To adjust your iCloud storage space, click on it. You can see your space use as well as the data that takes up the most room. If you want extra capacity, you may expand your iCloud storage plan.
5. **Sign Out of iCloud:** From the same Apple ID settings, you can sign out of your iCloud account if necessary. Be advised that logging out will prevent your MacBook Pro from synchronizing with iCloud services.

Access your iCloud Account Information

You can retrieve your iCloud account details as follows:

1. **System Settings:**
- In the upper-left corner of your screen, click the **Apple logo**.
- From the drop-down menu, choose "**System Settings**".
- Select "**Apple ID**" in the System Settings box.
2. **Apple ID Settings:**
- An overview of your account details, including your name, email, phone number, and profile image, can be found under the Apple ID settings.
- There are many categories, **including "Overview," "Name, Phone Numbers, and Email," "Password & Security," "Payment & Shipping,"** and others, on the left-hand side. To control certain facets of your iCloud account, click on these pages.

3. **Accessing iCloud Services:**
- Your new MacBook Pro has a lot of integrated iCloud services. For instance, you can view your iCloud Drive files using Finder and your iCloud Photos through the Photos app.
- To use iCloud Drive, launch the Finder and choose "**iCloud Drive**" from the sidebar.
- To access your iCloud Photos, launch the Photos app, pick the "**Photos**" option, and then click "**All Photos**" to see them all.

Access Payment & Shipping Information

You can get Payment & Shipping Information as follows:

1. To access the Apple Menu, click on the **Apple logo** in the top-left corner of the screen.
2. Choose "**System Settings**" from the Apple Menu.

3. If you see an "**Apple ID**" option in System Settings, you should select it. You can manage many parts of your Apple account here.
4. Once you've accessed the Apple ID settings, you will see a selection for "**Payment & Shipping**" or something like such. You can modify or adjust your shipping details and payment options here.

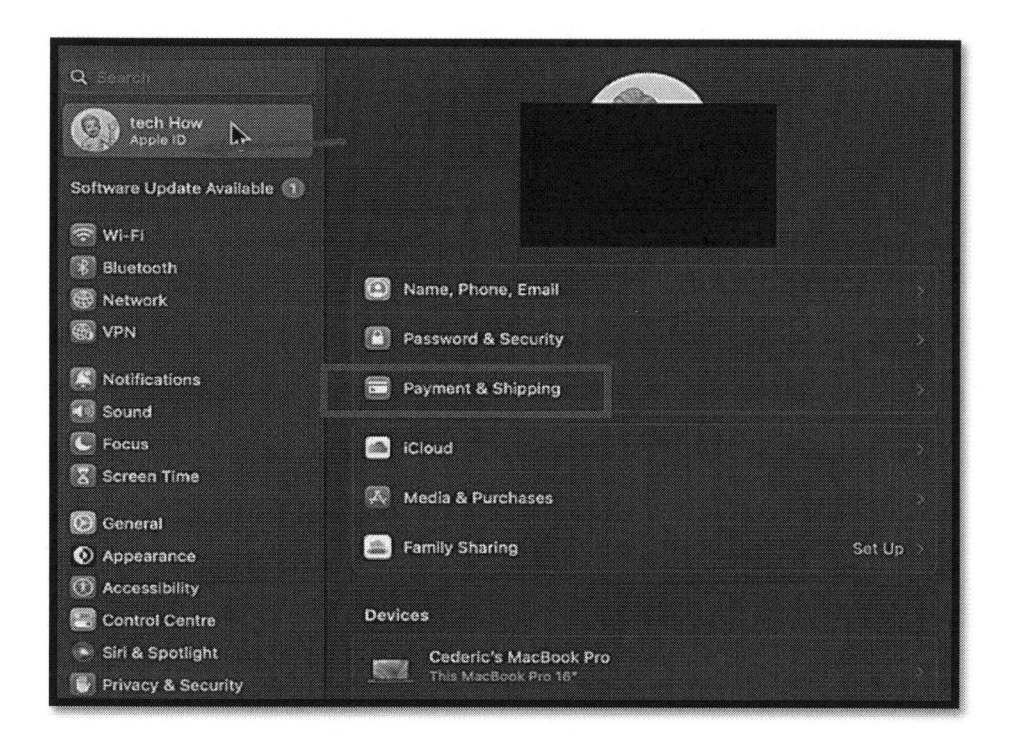

5. **Authenticate:** To authenticate and access your payment and shipping information, you may be asked to enter your Apple ID password or use your fingerprint Touch ID.

How to manage iCloud Sync Permissions

Managing iCloud sync permissions on your new MacBook Pro:

1. To begin, click the Apple menu in the top-left corner of your screen and choose **"System Settings."**
2. Find and choose "**Apple ID**" in the System Settings box. You can manage your iCloud settings here.
3. **iCloud Settings**: You'll find several categories, including Overview, Name, Phone, Email, and more, under the Apple ID preferences window. The left sidebar's "iCloud" link should be clicked.
4. **iCloud Sync Settings**: This page contains a list of the applications and services linked to your iCloud account. There will probably be a tick next to each app or service. The applications and services that sync with your iCloud account on your MacBook Pro may be managed using these checkboxes.

5. **Managing Permissions**: Simply tick or uncheck the box next to a particular app or service to manage sync permissions for it. An unchecked option means that the software or service won't sync with iCloud, whereas a ticked box means that it is permitted to do so.
6. **Advanced options:** Some apps or services come with advanced options. To discover whether there are any more settings you may configure, click on the application or service. This contains settings for what particular data is synced, how often it syncs, and other things.
7. **Review and Modify:** Review the list of applications and services linked to your iCloud account and modify the sync permissions following your preferences. Remember that certain applications may need an active iCloud membership and enough iCloud storage space to sync.
8. **Modifications and Confirmations**: Any modifications you make to the sync permissions must be implemented right away. When making changes to sensitive data, there may be alerts or confirmations.
9. **Syncing Procedure**: Once the permissions have been changed, iCloud will start syncing the data for the applications and services you have permitted. Depending on the volume of data being synchronized, this can take some time.

How to Sign Out of iCloud

Follow the below steps to sign out of iCloud:

1. Hover your cursor over the Apple logo in the top-left corner of your screen. In turn, a drop-down menu will appear.
2. Click the drop-down menu and choose "**System Settings**."
3. Look for a section in System Settings called "**Apple ID**" or "**iCloud**." To access the Apple ID options, click on it.
4. You will see many tabs reflecting various parts of your Apple ID settings in the Apple ID preferences window. Locate a tab or option that reads "**Sign Out**" or "**Manage**." Just click it.

5. You will be asked to confirm that you want to sign out of iCloud. If you want to maintain a duplicate of your iCloud data on your Mac, the system can ask you. Based on your preferences, choose the suitable one.

53

6. You will also need to enter your Apple ID password to finish the sign-out procedure. To protect your account from unwanted access, this security precaution has been put in place.

7. To finish the sign-out procedure, follow the instructions after entering your password. After that, your MacBook Pro will stop using your iCloud account.

iCloud Drive, iCloud Photos, Find My, and other features and services that depend on your iCloud account will all be disabled if you sign out of iCloud on your MacBook Pro. Before signing out, make sure you have backups of any crucial data.

How to use iCloud Private Relay

By passing your internet traffic across two different servers, the iCloud Private Relay function is intended to improve your online privacy and security by making it more difficult for websites to trace your surfing history.

Here are the steps:

1. **Update macOS**: Ensure that the most recent version of macOS, which enables iCloud Private Relay, is installed on your MacBook Pro. MacOS Ventura is the most recent version.
2. **Log in to iCloud**: On your MacBook Pro, open **System Settings** and choose "**Apple ID**." Use the Apple ID you want to use for iCloud Private Relay to log in.

3. **Enable iCloud Private Relay:**
- Open **System Settings**.
- Select "**Apple ID**."

- In the sidebar, click "**iCloud**."
- Locate and activate the "**Private Relay**" or a related option.

4. Depending on how iCloud Private Relay is implemented in 2023, you can change certain parameters. Options like whether to use Private Relay for all networks or only certain networks, etc., might be included here.

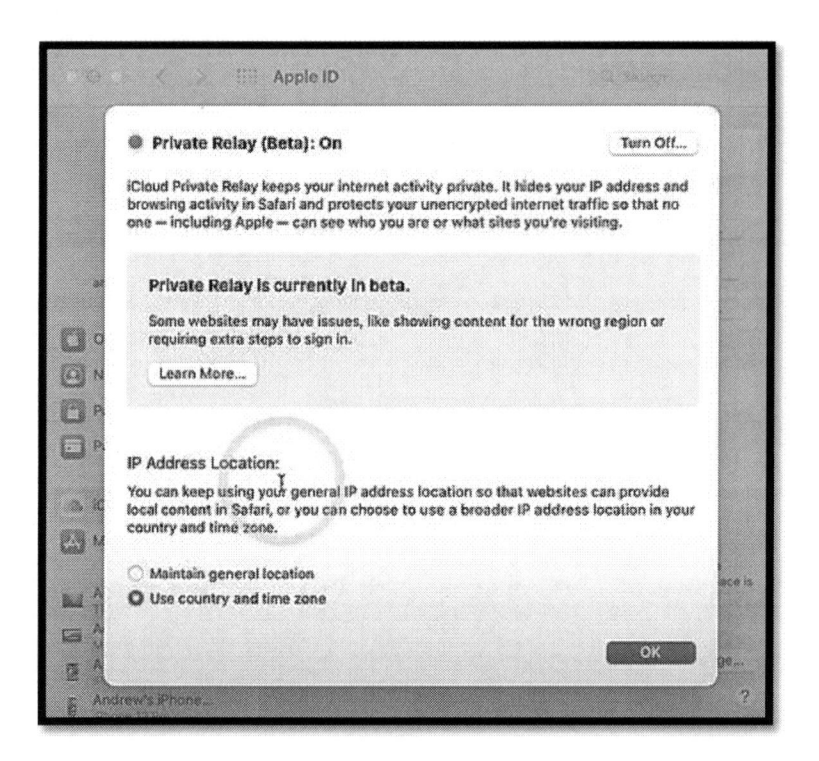

5. **Browsing**: After you activate iCloud Private Relay, all of your internet traffic will pass via Apple's servers, enhancing its security and privacy. The Private Relay function should operate in the background while you use your web browser as usual.
6. **Check Privacy and Security Settings**: To make sure that iCloud Private Relay is still active and to make any necessary adjustments to your preferences, it's a good idea to frequently examine your Privacy and Security settings in System Settings.
7. **Troubleshooting**: Check for updates, restart your MacBook Pro, or get help from Apple Support if you notice any problems with your internet connection or surfing after using iCloud Private Relay.

Activate and Deactivate iCloud Private Relay

To turn on iCloud Private Relay:

1. To open System Settings, click the **Apple logo** in the top-left corner of your screen and then choose **"System Settings."**
2. Find "**iCloud**" under System Settings and click it.
3. **Privacy and Security**: Depending on how the option is named, there may be a choice for "**Privacy**" or "**Security**." Just click it.
4. **iCloud Private Relay**: You could discover the option to activate or modify iCloud Private Relay under the Privacy or Security area. It could have its area or be included in more general privacy settings.
5. **Toggle the Switch**: If iCloud Private Relay is enabled, you'll probably notice a toggle switch that can be turned on or off. To turn on iCloud Private Relay, turn it on.
6. **Adhere to On-Screen Prompts**: Depending on how the function is used, you may have to adhere to more prompts to set up and customize iCloud Private Relay to your preferences.

How to turn off iCloud Private Relay

1. **Perform Steps 1-3 again**: Launch **System Settings** choose **iCloud settings** and go to the **Privacy or Security section**.
2. **Turn off iCloud Private Relay**: You should be able to see the toggle switch for iCloud Private Relay if it is on. To turn off iCloud Private Relay, flip the switch.
3. **Confirm Deactivation:** Depending on the function, you could be asked to confirm deactivation. Confirm your selection if asked.

Frequently Asked Questions

1. How do you set up and edit iCloud?
2. How do you access your iCloud account information?
3. How do you access payment and shipping information on your MacBook Pro?
4. How do you use iCloud Private Relay?
5. How do you sign out of iCloud?

CHAPTER FIVE
SCREEN TIME AND FAMILY SHARING

Overview

Screen time allows you to view contents or information on your screen for a limited or set time, after which it will not be available or suitable for you to continue. On the other hand, family sharing allows you to invite family members to watch or check out things you do on your end. This chapter emphasizes both and you can learn all about them below.

Set Up & Use Screen Time

The steps:

1. Firstly, click the **Apple logo** in the top-left corner of your screen and choose **"System Settings."**

2. In the System Settings window, select "**Screen Time**." It is in the top row of icons, or you may use the search bar to look for it.

3. To activate Screen Time for your user account, click the "**Turn On**" button on the Screen Time box.
4. **Create a Screen Time Passcode (Optional):** To prevent unauthorized access to your Screen Time settings, you can create a passcode. This is practical for preventing unauthorized alterations by others.
5. You have the option of selecting the content and privacy options you want to use. Pick content and privacy options. To suit your tastes, change these settings.

Using Screen Time

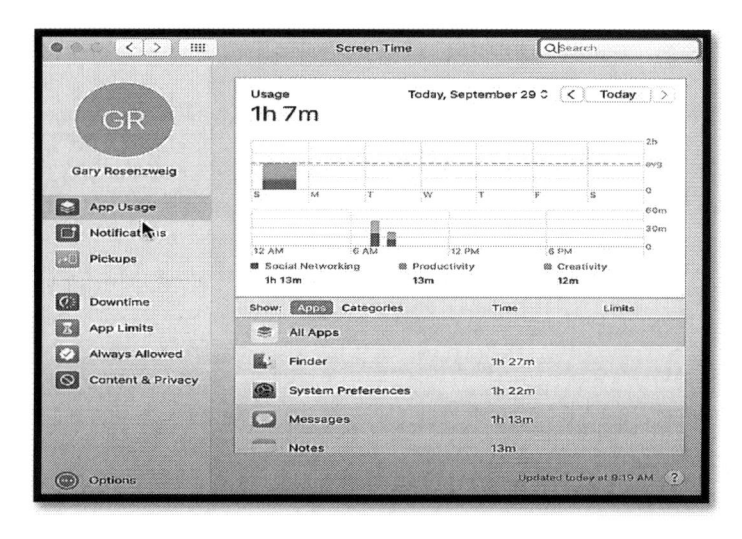

1. **Dashboard Overview**: After Screen Time is configured, you'll receive a summary of your daily screen time consumption. This includes pickups, notifications, and app use.
2. **App Usage**: You can view a breakdown of how much time you've spent on various app categories and specific applications under the "**App Usage**" section. You may use this to figure out which applications you use the most.
3. **Downtime**: When you plan "**Downtime**," just the applications you pick will be available for that amount of time. This can assist you in detaching and concentrating on other tasks at certain times, such as just before bed.
4. **App Limits:** Set daily time limitations for certain app categories or specific applications using the app limits feature. The app's icon will turn gray when the allotted amount of time has passed, and you will need to enter your Screen Time passcode to use it again.

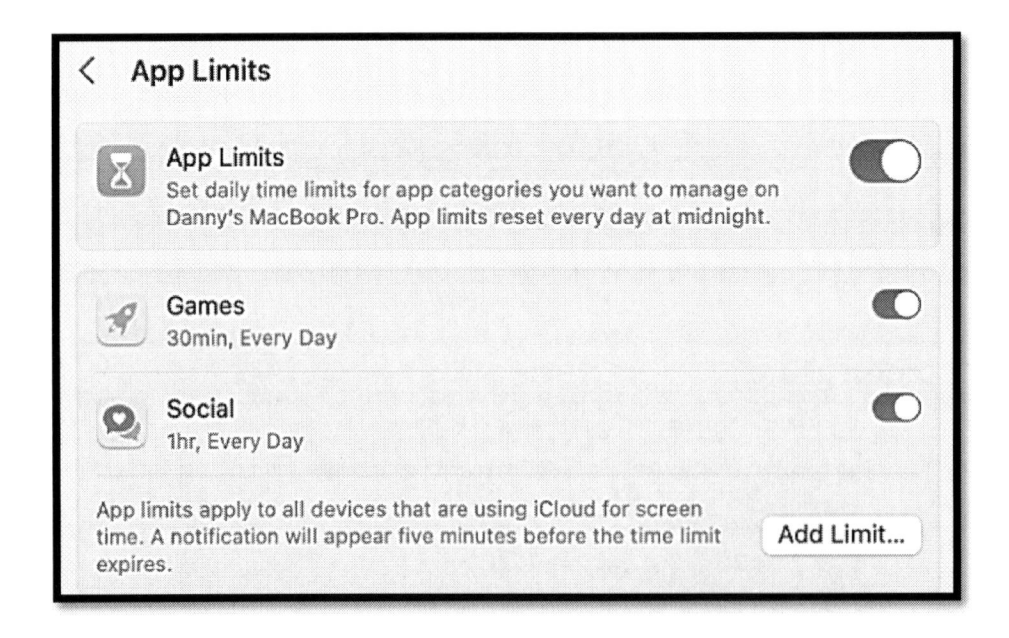

5. **Communication Limits**: Setting boundaries on whom you may receive calls from during downtime and which applications are authorized to give you alerts is one way to regulate communication.
6. **Notifications:** You can check which applications send you the most alerts in the "**Notifications**" section. To lessen distractions, change your notification settings.

7. **Usage Reports:** To examine thorough usage data for the previous week, choose **"See All Activity"** from the menu. You can also learn more about your consumption trends over time by doing this.

How to Enable Screen Time

Here are the steps:

1. Click the **Apple logo** in the top-left corner of your screen and select "**System Settings.**"
2. To access the Screen Time settings, click the "**Screen Time**" icon that should be visible in the System Settings window.
3. Toggle the option to "**Turn On Screen Time**" under the Screen Time settings. To make changes, you might need to click the padlock symbol in the lower left corner and input your administrator password.

4. **Set up Options:** After turning on Screen Time, configure many settings to limit your use. You can control downtime, app limits, and more. You can also control how much time you spend using certain programs on your MacBook by using these choices.

How to Monitor App Usage

Here's how you can approach it:

1. **Activity Monitor (Built-in Utility):** On macOS Ventura, the Activity Monitor is a built-in tool that lets you keep tabs on your computer's performance, including app use. To get to it:

- Look for "**Activity Monitor**" using Spotlight search (**Cmd + Space**), or look in the **"Applications" > "Utilities"** folder.
- Enable Activity Monitor.
- To see a list of currently operating processes and their resource utilization, click on the "**CPU**" or "**Memory**" tab.

- You may sort the processes using several criteria, such as CPU or memory use.
- If you want to track how different apps affect energy use, look for the "**Energy**" option.
2. **System Monitor Widgets:** Add a "**System Monitor**" widget to your Notification Center in certain versions of macOS. This widget shows real-time data on disk, network, CPU, and memory usage.
3. **Third-Party Apps:** The Mac App Store offers third-party programs that may provide more thorough information about your app activity. Several well-liked options include:

- **iStat Menus:** With this tool, your menu bar gets customized system monitors that let you keep an eye on things like CPU utilization, memory consumption, network activity, and more.
- **ActivityWatch** is an open-source application that monitors your computer use. It offers in-depth information on the programs and websites you use the most.
- **Timing**: This tool lets you assess your productivity by tracking the time you spend on different applications.
4. "**Screen Time**" that lets you monitor program use and set limitations can be present.
5. **Browser History**: You can review your browser history to see which websites you've visited and for how long if you're especially interested in keeping tabs on your online activity.

Impose App Limits

Using the built-in Screen Time function, which enables you to put restrictions on app use and total screen time, you can impose app limitations on your MacBook Pro.

Here's how you can go about it:

The steps:

1. Launch **System Settings**.
2. If you are unable to discover "**Screen Time**" in the System Settings window, you may easily find it by using the search bar in the top-right corner.
3. **Enable Screen Time**: If you haven't already configured Screen Time, you may need to click the "**Turn On**" button and adhere to the on-screen prompts to do so.
4. **App Usage Limits:**
- After you've enabled Screen Time, choose the "**App Limits**" option from the sidebar.
- If you want to add a new app limit, click the "**+**" button.
- Decide which applications or categories you want to restrict. For these applications, you may set daily time restrictions.

5. **Set Time Limits:**
- After choosing the applications or categories, choose the daily time limitations. If necessary, you can alter the restrictions on each day of the week.
- macOS Ventura will notify you when an app's time restriction is about to expire.

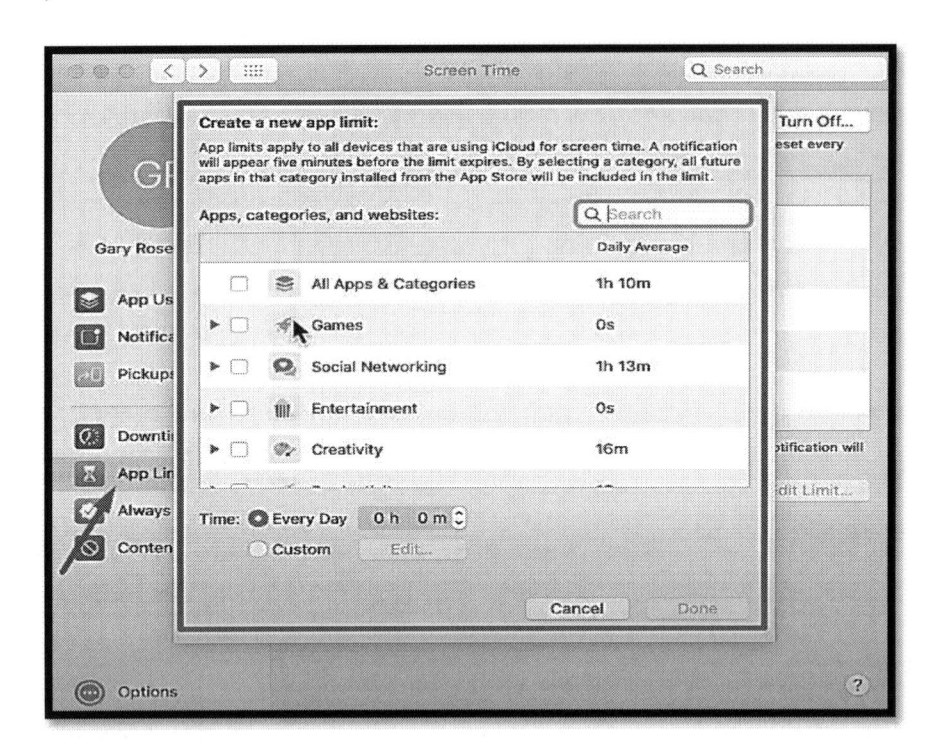

6. **Downtime and More:**
- Configure "**Downtime**" during particular hours when you wish to completely restrict app use, except for vital applications, in addition to app limitations.
- To control who you may speak with at certain times, you can also create communication limitations.

How to Set Downtime

The steps:

1. Open System Settings.
2. Find "**Screen Time**" in the System Settings menu and click it.

3. When asked, choose "**Turn On**" to activate Screen Time.
4. Click "**Downtime**" on the Screen Time window's left sidebar and enable it.

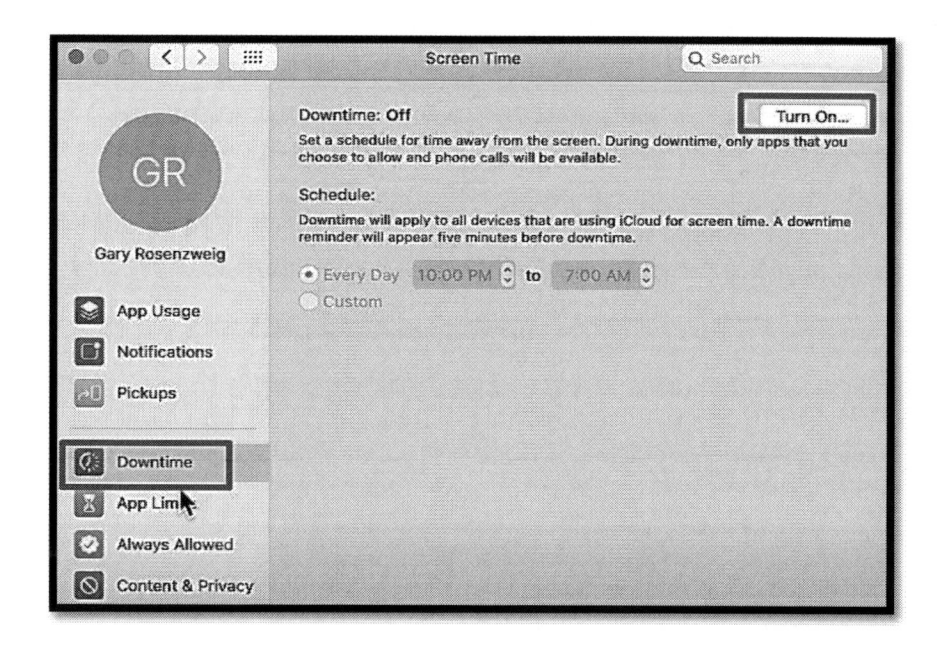

5. By selecting the checkboxes next to the days, you can choose the ones you want to apply downtime to.
6. Decide on the downtime's beginning and ending times. Certain applications and alerts will be disabled during this time.

Customize App Limits (Optional)

1. Use App Limits to restrict the use of certain applications during downtime. In the left column, choose "**App Limits**".
2. To add an app you want to restrict, click the "**+**" button.
3. Set the daily time limit you wish to give the app.
4. To restrict all the applications you desire, repeat this procedure.

Customize Communication Limits (Optional)

1. Set up Communication Limits to impose restrictions on communication during downtime. In the left sidebar, choose "**Communication Limits**".
2. Decide which people or organizations are permitted to contact you while you're offline.

Always Allow Apps

Here's how you can enable applications on your new MacBook Pro:

1. **Gatekeeper Settings:** The security function Gatekeeper in macOS manages which applications are permitted to execute on your device.
   - Select the Apple menu from the screen's top-left corner.
   - Then choose "**System Settings**."
   - Click "**Security & Privacy**."
   - Select the tab labeled "**General**".
   - Keep an eye out for the "**Allow apps downloaded from**" area.
   - If "**Anywhere**" is still an option in macOS Ventura in 2023, choose it to enable programs from anywhere. Use this option with caution as it can put your system at risk for security breaches.

2. **App-Specific Permissions**: Some applications may ask for particular access rights to specific functions or data on your MacBook Pro.

- If an application asks for authorization, a dialog box will often show up. You should carefully read the permissions before deciding whether to allow them.
- To adjust app-specific permissions, you may need to go to the "**Privacy**" page in the "**Security & Privacy**" settings.
3. **Developer Identification:** To verify the validity of their apps, Apple sometimes needs developers to sign them with a developer certificate.
- If an app is being prevented from starting because its creator is unknown, you may often right-click (or control-click) the app icon and choose "**Open**."
- A dialog box will ask you if you're certain you want to launch the unidentified developer's program. To continue, click "**Open**".
4. **Additional factors to consider:**
- Ensure that you only download apps from reputable places, such as the Apple App Store or the official developer websites. Unknown sources for program downloads might put your computer's security at risk.
- Update your operating system and applications to the most recent versions to take advantage of security fixes and enhancements.

Set Communication Limits

These procedures can be used to set communication limits:

1. Open **System Settings**.
2. Find and choose the "**Screen Time**" icon in the System Settings box by clicking on it. You can establish communication limitations with the aid of this function, which is intended to help you control your time spent on your devices.
3. **Enable Screen Time:** If you haven't already configured Screen Time, you may need to do so. To set up Screen Time for your user account, click the "**Turn On**..." button and adhere to the instructions shown on the screen.
4. **Communication Limits:** You should be able to locate a section on Communication within the Screen Time settings. You can restrict the functions and applications for communication here.
5. **App Limits**: "**App Limits**" or a comparable option should be selected. Here, you have the option to impose restrictions on a selected group of applications, such as social networking apps and messaging apps like Messages and FaceTime.

6. **Add Communication Applications**: Manually add the communication applications to the list if they aren't already present in the categories. Find the option to add certain applications, then choose the communication apps you wish to restrict.
7. **Set Time Limits**: After choosing your communication applications, you can give each one a daily or weekly time restriction. You can also specify a timetable for when these restrictions take effect, such as just during certain hours of the day.
8. **Notifications**: Your ability to reduce communication interruptions is further improved by the option to regulate alerts from certain applications at specific times in some versions of macOS Ventura.
9. **Password Protection**: Depending on the settings, you may be able to demand a password to modify these limitations, limiting simple evasion.
10. **Monitor Usage**: After establishing communication restrictions, you can return to the Screen Time area of System Settings to keep an eye on your use and make any necessary adjustments to the restrictions.

Manage Content and Privacy

The new MacBook Pro in 2023 requires a mix of system settings, software selections, and best practices to manage content and privacy.

The steps:

1. **System Settings:**
- **Security & Privacy:** Open System Settings and go to the "**Security & Privacy**" section for further information on security and privacy. You can control your privacy settings here, including whether apps may access your location, camera, microphone, and other features.
- **Screen Time**: You can set up Screen Time to better monitor your use and privacy. You can keep an eye on app use with this function and set time restrictions for certain applications.
2. **Software Updates:**
- Update your macOS regularly to ensure you get the most recent security fixes and privacy tools.

- **App Updates:** To make sure your applications have the most recent security updates, regularly update them from the App Store.
3. **App Permissions:**
- **App Store Apps:** When you first launch an app, macOS asks you to allow it a set of rights. Examine these permissions and only permit those that are required for the operation of the app.
4. **FileVault:**
- **Encrypt Your Data**: Launch FileVault to encrypt your hard drive's data. This guarantees that even if your MacBook Pro is stolen or lost, your data will still be kept private.
5. **Safari Privacy Settings:**
- **Enhanced Tracking Protection**: To increase your online privacy, turn on **"Prevent cross-site tracking"** and **"Ask websites not to track me"** in Safari's settings.
6. **Firewall:**
- **Enable Firewall:** In the Security & Privacy settings, activate the built-in firewall. This shields your MacBook Pro against inbound connections that are not allowed.
7. **Two-Factor Authentication(2FA):**
- **Enable 2FA**: Add a layer of protection to your Apple ID by configuring two-factor authentication to prevent illegal access.
8. **Privacy-Focused Software:**
- **Virtual Private Network (VPN):** To secure your internet connection and safeguard your online privacy, think about using a reliable VPN.
- **Password Manager:** Create and save secure, one-of-a-kind passwords for your accounts using a password manager.
9. **Backup:**
- **Time Machine**: Use Time Machine to regularly backup your MacBook Pro. This guarantees that, in case of unintentional data loss, you have a current backup of your data.
10. **Secure Online Behavior:**
- **Phishing Awareness:** Be wary when clicking on links or sending personal information in emails or texts, particularly if they come from an unexpected source.

- **Public Wi-Fi:** Unless you're using a VPN to safeguard your connection, avoid accessing public Wi-Fi networks for critical activity.
11. **Physical Security:**
- **Lock Screen:** To safeguard your MacBook Pro while not in use, configure a password, PIN, or biometric authentication (Touch ID).
- **Anti-Theft Measures**: To remotely monitor and lock your device in the event of theft, think about using apps like Find My Mac.

How to Setup Family Sharing

Here's how to set up family sharing:

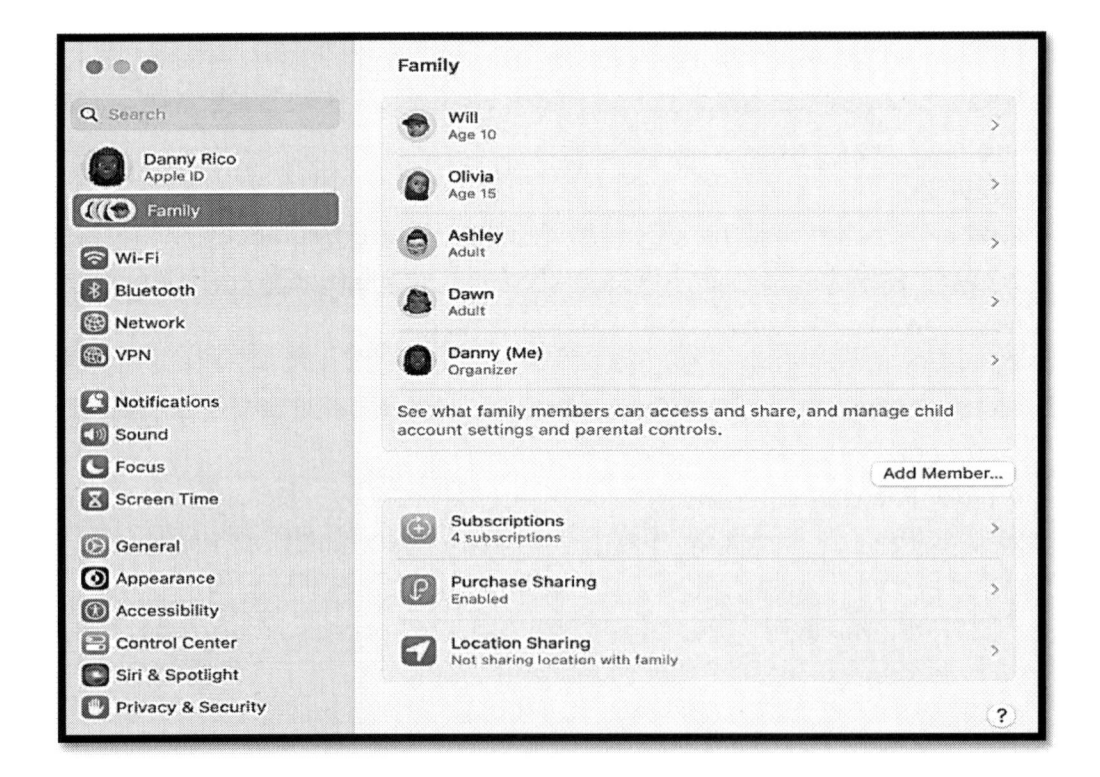

1. **Update macOS if necessary:** Verify that the most recent version of macOS is installed on your MacBook Pro. If updates are available, install them by selecting **"System Settings" > "Software Update"** from the Apple menu in the top-left corner of the screen.
2. **Proceed to Set Up Family Sharing:**
- Launch System Settings.

- Go to **System Settings** and choose "**Apple ID**."
- Click "**Family Sharing**" on the left-hand side of the Apple ID settings screen.
- Click the "**Set up Family**" button to create your family. You'll have to manage the family's planning.

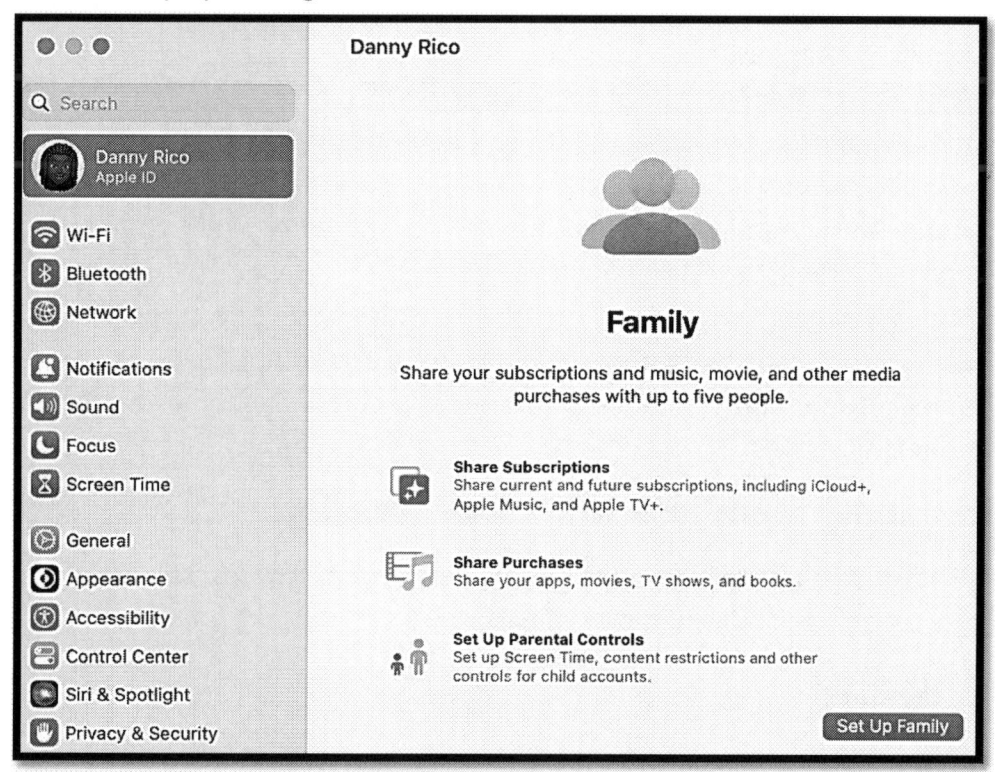

- To set up Family Sharing, adhere to the on-screen instructions. This entails extending an invitation to family members, selecting the information you want to share (such as App Store purchases, Apple Music, and iCloud storage), and, if necessary, controlling parental restrictions.
- The establishment of a payment option for usage on family purchases will be required. You have the option of letting your family members use your payment method or letting them use their own.

3. **Invite Family Members:**
- You can invite family members after you've configured Family Sharing. To send them an invitation, you'll need their email addresses or Apple IDs.
- An invitation will be sent to your family members through Apple devices. They must accept the offer to become a part of the family unit.

4. **Manage Family Sharing Settings:**

After your family members have joined the family group and accepted the invitation, you may modify many Family Sharing options, including:

- **Family Sharing Settings**: You can control shared purchases, shared iCloud storage, location sharing, screen time limitations for kids, and more under the Family Sharing settings.
- **App Store Purchases**: Family members can access applications, music, movies, and other material that has been bought by other family members via the App Store.
- **Apple Music**: Family members can use your shared Apple Music membership and make their playlists if you have one.
- **iCloud Storage**: Family members may effortlessly save pictures, movies, and other information by sharing an iCloud storage subscription.
- **Screen Time:** You can establish parental controls and time restrictions for your family's kids.

Invite Family Members in Family Sharing

Apple's Family Sharing function enables the sharing of purchases, subscriptions, and other services across family members' devices.

Here are the steps:

1. Launch **System Settings**.

2. To access Apple ID, find it in the System Settings window and select "**Apple ID.**"
3. **Family Sharing:** There should be a "**Family Sharing**" option in the sidebar of the Apple ID area. You will need to select it.
4. You'll get a list of services that may be shared with your family members after clicking "**Add Family Member**." There should be an "**Add Family Member**" button at the bottom of this window; click it.
5. You will be given the chance to invite a family member to your group. You may invite them by emailing a link or using their Apple ID email address. To finish the invitation procedure, adhere to the instructions.
6. **Accept the invitation**: The invited family member will get an email invitation to accept the invitation using their Apple ID. The request to join your Family Sharing group must be accepted.
7. **Configure Sharing Options**: Once they've agreed, you can choose the services you wish to share with each family member by configuring the sharing options. You may share items like iCloud storage, Apple Music, Apple TV+, and more.
8. **Authorize Purchases**: Enable "**Ask to Buy**" for family members' children. This implies that before they make purchases, you must permit them.

Invite People to Family Sharing

Invite others to Family Sharing in the following ways:

1. Open System Settings.
2. Find and choose "**Apple ID**" in the System Settings window by clicking on it.
3. **Family Sharing:** In the Apple ID window's sidebar, look for the "**Family Sharing**" area. Just click it.
4. **Add Family Member**: If you are already a member of the Family Sharing group, you will see a list of family members. Click on the "**+**" (plus) button in the bottom left corner to invite a new person.
5. **Enter Email Address:** You will be prompted to enter the email address of the person you wish to invite in a window that appears. Inputting the email address connected to their Apple ID.

6. **Send Invitation:** After entering the email address, click "**Continue**." A prompt will appear asking you to confirm that you want to send an invitation to the specified email address. To send the invitation, click "**Send**".
7. **Follow Invitation Link:** The person you invited will get an email with an invitation link. They must access the email and choose the link.
8. **Join Family Sharing:** The Family Sharing setup page may be accessed by clicking the invitation link. To join the Family Sharing group, they must follow the on-screen directions. This might include using their Apple ID to log in, verifying their information, and accepting the rules.
9. **Configure Sharing Options:** After joining, users can choose their sharing options for a variety of services, including App Store purchases, Apple Music, iCloud storage, and more.
10. **Approval for Child Accounts:** You may need to provide permission for a child's account to be included in the Family Sharing group if you're inviting them. Setting up parental controls and validating your payment method are required for this.

Each family member must have their own Apple ID to participate in Family Sharing; if they don't already have one, they must first establish one.

Join Family Sharing Group

Here's how to do so:

1. Click the Apple Menu and select **System Settings**.
2. You'll find an option for "Apple ID" in the System Settings; click on it.
3. Select the "**Family Sharing**" option located in the Apple ID settings box.
4. **Create Family Sharing**: To create Family Sharing, click the "**Get Started**" button.
5. You will be given the option to choose a family organizer. This individual will be in charge of overseeing the Family Sharing group. If you're the one setting up the group, you may do so by following the directions on the screen.
6. **Inviting Family Members**: You can send an invitation to family members through email or iMessage. The request to join the Family Sharing group must be accepted.

7. **Share Purchases:** After inviting family members to the group, you may decide what you want to share, including Apple Music purchases, iCloud storage, and App Store purchases.
8. **Manage Family**: In your capacity as the organizer, you can set up parental controls for kids and manage family member permissions as well as shared purchasing restrictions.

Set up App Store Purchase Sharing

Here are the steps:

1. Make sure your MacBook Pro is running the most recent version of macOS by updating it.
2. Launch the "**App Store**" app on your MacBook Pro, and then enter your Apple ID to log in.
3. To access your account settings, click on your profile photo or name in the bottom-left corner of the App Store window.
4. Look for "**Family Sharing**" or a similar option in the account settings. Then click it.
5. You can now add family members to your Family Sharing group by sending them an invitation. To invite them, you'll need their Apple IDs.
6. App Store Purchase Sharing can be enabled when family members accept your invitation and sign up for the group. You should be able to share the applications, music, movies, and other items you buy with your family as a result.

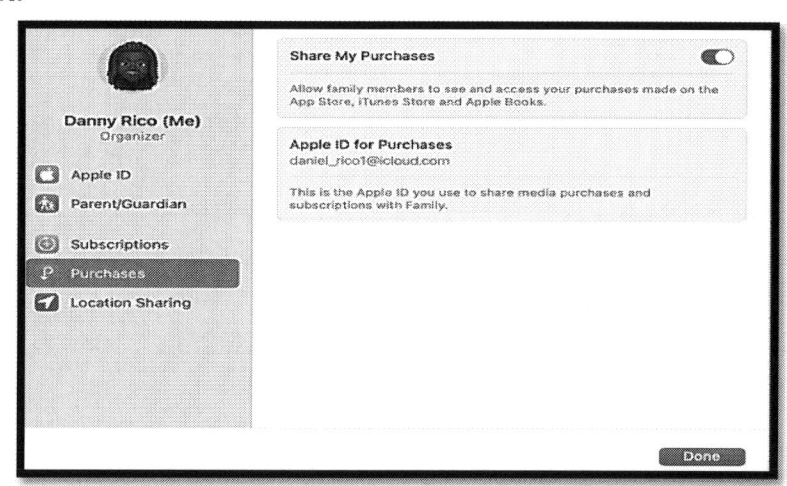

7. Depending on your preferences, you may need to sanction family members' use of the shared payment method for purchases.
8. Now that family members have their own Apple IDs on their own devices, they should be able to access the shared app purchases.

Set up iCloud Storage Sharing

Here's how to set up iCloud Storage Sharing:

1. Make sure your MacBook Pro is running the most recent version of macOS by updating it. This is crucial to guarantee that you have access to the most recent features and upgrades, including any adjustments to iCloud Storage Sharing.
2. **Sign in to iCloud:**
- In the upper-left corner of your screen, choose the **Apple menu**.
- Then, choose "**System Settings**."
- To access your iCloud settings, click "**Apple ID**".
- If you haven't already, log in with your Apple ID.
3. **Enable iCloud Storage Sharing:**
- Click "**iCloud**" on the left sidebar of the Apple ID settings window.
- Select the "**Manage...**" option under the "**iCloud Storage**" section.
- The "**Family Sharing**" area ought to be present in the iCloud Storage window. Select "**Set up Family**" from the menu.
4. **Set Up Family Sharing:**
- If you haven't already, set up Family Sharing by following the on-screen directions. To do this, use the Apple IDs of your family members to invite them to your family-sharing group.
- Once Family Sharing is configured, you can choose to share a variety of services with your family, including iCloud Storage.
5. **Select Storage Plan:**
- Return to the iCloud Storage section of the Apple ID options after setting up Family Sharing.
- Your iCloud storage plan should now include a "**Family**" option. Select "**Share Storage**" from the menu.
6. **Choose Family Members:**

- The iCloud storage plan that you want to share with your family can be chosen. You have the option of choosing your current plan or, if necessary, upgrading to a bigger plan.
7. **Choose Family Members:**
- Your Family Sharing group's family members will be listed on the screen. Choose the relatives you want to share your iCloud storage with.
8. **Confirm and Share:**
- Make sure your choice is correct, and then share the iCloud storage with the chosen family members.
9. **Notifications to Family Members:**
- The shared storage will be made known to your family members. They have the option to accept and begin using the shared storage immediately.

Setting up Screen Time for Kids in Family Sharing Group

This broad overview should get you started:

1. **Create a Family Sharing Group**:
- On your MacBook Pro, choose "**System Settings**".
- Click "**iCloud**" or "**Apple ID**."
- From the sidebar, choose "**Set up Family**" or "**Family Sharing**."
- To create your Family Sharing group, adhere to the directions shown on-screen. Using their Apple IDs, you may invite family members, including your kids.
2. **Set Up Screen Time:**
- You can control the Screen Time settings for your children's devices after creating the Family Sharing group.
3. **Setting up Screen Time:**
- On your MacBook Pro, choose "**System Settings**".
- Then choose "**Screen Time**."
- Type your Apple ID and password when requested.
4. **Add Child's Apple ID:**
- Select "**Options**" from the drop-down menu next to your child's name.
- In the "**Family**" section, click "**Add**".
- Type the kid's Apple ID, and then choose "**OK**."

5. **Customize Screen Time Settings:**

You can change many Screen Time settings after adding your child's device, including:
- **App time limits**: Establish time restrictions for certain app categories or specific applications.
- **Communication limits**: Control with whom your kid may communicate.
- **Downtime**: Establish a timetable for when your child can use their device.
- **Always Allowed**: Select applications that are always available, even when they aren't being used.

6. **Monitor Activity:**
- You can keep an eye on your child's screen time and gadget use.
- Click the "**Reports**" tab to get statistics for various applications and categories.

Set up Apple Music in the Family Sharing Group

You can share a variety of Apple services, including Apple Music, with up to six family members with Family Sharing.

Here's how to configure it:

1. **Set Up Family Sharing:**
- Select the Apple menu from your screen's top-left corner.
- Then choose "**System Settings**."
- Select "**Family Sharing.**"
- Select "**Get Started**" from the menu.

2. **Initiate Family Sharing:**
- Choose "**Set Up Family Sharing**."
- Log in using the Apple ID you want to use as your organizer.
- To set up payment options and iCloud sharing, click "**Continue**" and adhere to the on-screen directions.

3. **Invite Family Members:**
- You'll be requested to invite family members after setting up Family Sharing. They must provide their Apple IDs.
- To send the invitations, enter the Apple IDs of your family members and follow the on-screen directions.

4. **Enable Apple Music Sharing:**
   - You can activate Apple Music sharing if your family members accept the invites.
   - Under "**Shared Features**" in the "**Family Sharing**" options, select "**Add Music**".
   - Confirm you want to share your Apple Music membership by following the on-screen instructions.
5. **Access Apple Music on Family Member's Devices**:
   - Your family members can now use their devices to access Apple Music.
   - To see the music that is accessible to them as part of Family Sharing, they should launch the Apple Music app, sign in with their Apple IDs, and choose the "**For You**" option.

To use the shared services, keep in mind that each family member must be logged in with their own Apple ID. While Apple Music is shared, it's vital to keep in mind that each family member's library, playlists, and suggestions are kept private.

Set up Apple Arcade in the Family Sharing Group

How to set up Apple Arcade in a Family Sharing Group is as follows:

1. Click the Apple logo in the top-left corner of your screen and choose "**System Settings**" from the drop-down menu to get the System Settings window.
2. Choose "**Apple ID**" from the list of options in the System Settings window to see the settings for your Apple ID and Family Sharing.
3. In the left sidebar of the Apple ID settings, choose "**Family Sharing**." This is where you manage and set up your Family Sharing group.
4. To add a family member to your Family Sharing group if you haven't already, click the "**+**" button in the lower-left corner. Using their Apple ID email address, invite them by following the on-screen instructions.
5. Locate the family member to whom you want to provide access to Apple Arcade after adding them to the family. Check the box next to "**Apple Arcade**" in the list of available services after making sure their name is chosen. As a member of the Family Sharing group, this will provide them access to Apple Arcade.
6. Launch the **App Store** on your MacBook Pro after configuring Apple Arcade for the family member. The "**Arcade**" tab should be located at the bottom of

the App Store window. To explore and download Apple Arcade games, click on it.
7. **Play Games**: After installing them, you may start playing games right from your MacBook Pro's Launchpad or Applications folder. You can download and play the games that are accessible via Apple Arcade without making any extra payments.

Frequently Asked Questions

1. How do you set up and use Screen Time on your MacBook Pro?
2. How do you monitor app usage?
3. How do you impose app limits?
4. How do you set up Family Sharing?
5. How do you set up App Store purchase sharing?
6. How do you invite family members in Family Sharing?
7. How do you set up Apple Music and Apple Arcade in Family Sharing Group?

CHAPTER SIX
FOCUS MODE AND QUICK NOTES

Overview

Chapter six talks about focus mode and quick notes and how you can use them effectively on your new MacBook Pro.

How to Enable Focus Mode

The steps:

1. Select the **Notification Center Icon**.
2. **Enable Focus Mode**: You can do this straight from the Notification Center if a **"Focus Mode"** or related feature is available. Select the Focus Mode button or menu item.

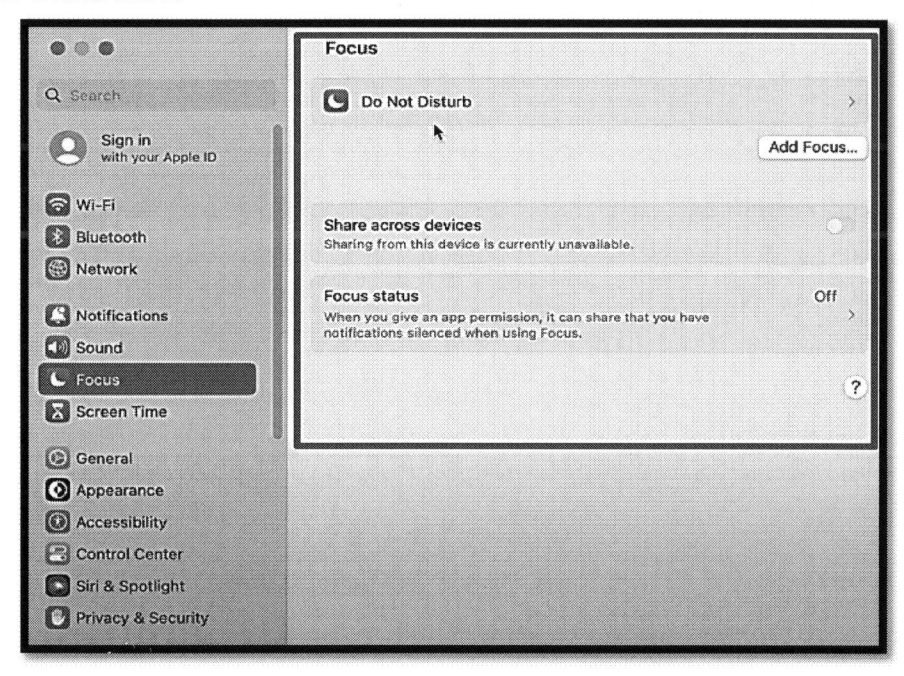

3. **Select the Type of Focus Mode**: Depending on how the function is designed, you can be given the option to select between several focus modes, such as **"Work," "Personal," "Sleep,"** etc.

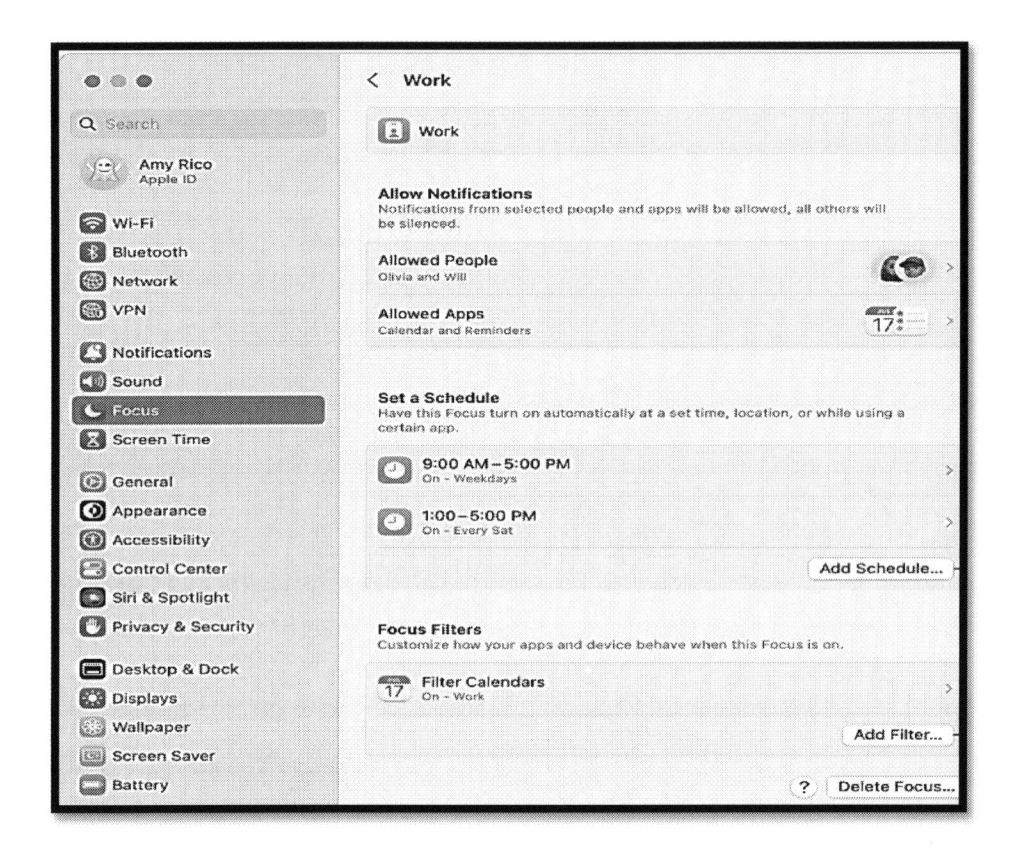

4. **Customize Settings**: After choosing a focus mode, you could have the option to alter its parameters. This might include setting up automatic message answers, selecting which applications can give you alerts, and more.
5. **Schedule**: The focus mode may also be engaged automatically based on a schedule that you create. For instance, you can program it to operate just while you are at work.
6. **Manual Activation**: Even if the focus mode isn't planned, you should be able to manually activate and deactivate it anytime you need to.

Activate Focus from the Control Center and System Settings

From the Control Center:

- In the menu bar, choose the **Control Center icon**. This symbol seems to be a collection of smaller icons.

- Keep an eye out for the Focus Mode icon, which may look like a bell or a crescent moon.
- Toggle between different focus modes by clicking on the Focus Mode icon.

From System Settings:

- In the top-left portion of the screen, click the **Apple menu**.
- Then choose "**System Settings**."
- Search for either the "**Notifications**" or "**Focus**" option window.
- You should be able to configure your focus modes under the Notifications or Focus settings.

Create a New Focus Filter

Here is how you can design and set up a "Focus Filter" function:

1. Open **System Settings**.
2. The focus settings are included in a section titled "**Focus**" or "**Notifications**," where you can establish preferences for controlling alerts and interruptions.
3. **Create a New Focus Filter**: You ought to be able to do this under the Focus settings. To add a new filter, use the button or menu item that says "**Add Filter**."

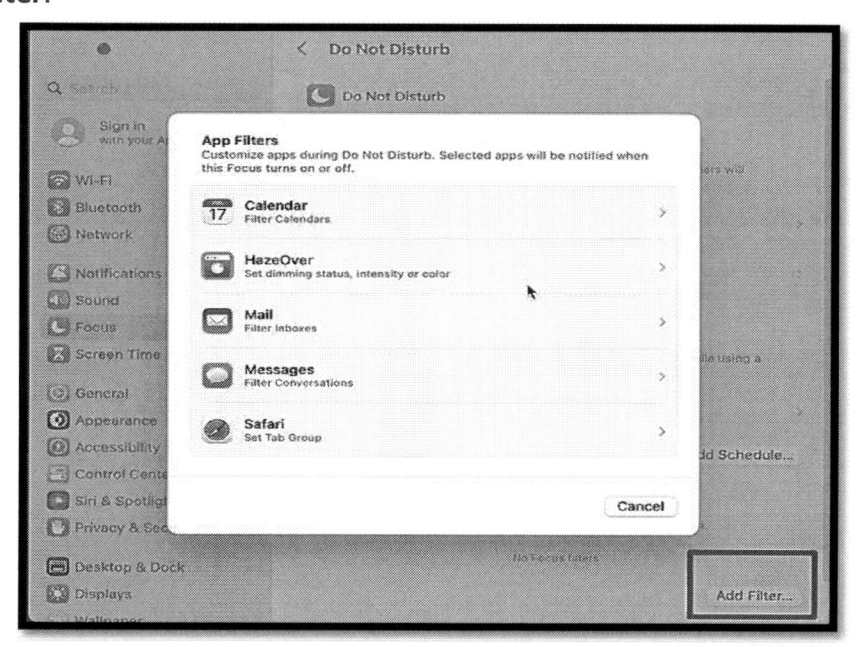

4. Give your focus filter a name that describes what it does. Something **like "Work," "Study," "Personal,"** etc. might be used here.
5. **Select Apps and Notifications**: Decide the apps and notifications you want to enable or disable when you're trying to concentrate. You can decide to enable alerts from some critical contacts or applications while deactivating or muting those from other sources.
6. **Change Settings:** Change how your MacBook Pro operates during this time of concentration. Changes the way alerts are presented, enable "**Do Not Disturb**" mode, or configure custom notification sounds.
7. **Schedule:** You can specify the times when this focus filter should be in effect. For instance, you could want it to turn on automatically while you're at work or during certain periods.
8. After you have finished configuring your focus filter's settings, be sure to turn it on. Your MacBook Pro will then enter the concentration mode you've established, assisting you in staying focused and minimizing distractions.
9. **Adjust as Necessary:** You can always return to the Focus settings and change your preferences, timetables, and filters under your changing requirements.

Edit an Existing Focus Filter

Focus Filters, previously known as Do Not Disturb, let you choose which alerts and notifications you get at certain times.

On a MacBook Pro, modify the focus filter as follows:

1. First of all, open **System Settings**.
2. To choose Focus, search for the "**Focus**" or "**Notifications**" option in the System Settings window. It might be found in the first row or the "**Notifications**" area.
3. **Choose the Focus Filter to Edit**: You should see a list of focus filters that are accessible, including Work, Personal, Sleep, and others. Pick the one you want to alter by clicking it.
4. **Edit the Focus Filter:** You can change how alerts operate inside the chosen focus filter to suit your preferences. This might include permitting or prohibiting alerts from certain contacts, applications, or categories. The timing and nature of warnings are also modifiable.

5. After making the changes you want, be sure to save them. Depending on the user interface, this could be done by pressing the "**Save**" or "**Done**" button.
6. Activate the Focus Filter: After saving your changes, turn on the focus filter. This can include manually turning it on or establishing a timetable for when it should turn on automatically.

Allow Notifications from Specific Persons & Apps

Here's how you can enable alerts on your new MacBook Pro from certain people and apps:

1. If you want to access your notification preferences, click the Apple menu in the top-left corner of your screen and choose "**System Settings.**"

2. Open Notifications by searching for and selecting the "**Notifications**" icon in the System Settings window. This should launch the preferences window for notifications.

3. **Change Notification Preferences:** On the left side of the Notifications preferences pane, you'll see a list of applications. Locate the app you want to customize by scrolling through the list.
4. **Configure App alerts**: Click on the app whose alerts you want to accept from certain people. This will display the app's notification settings.

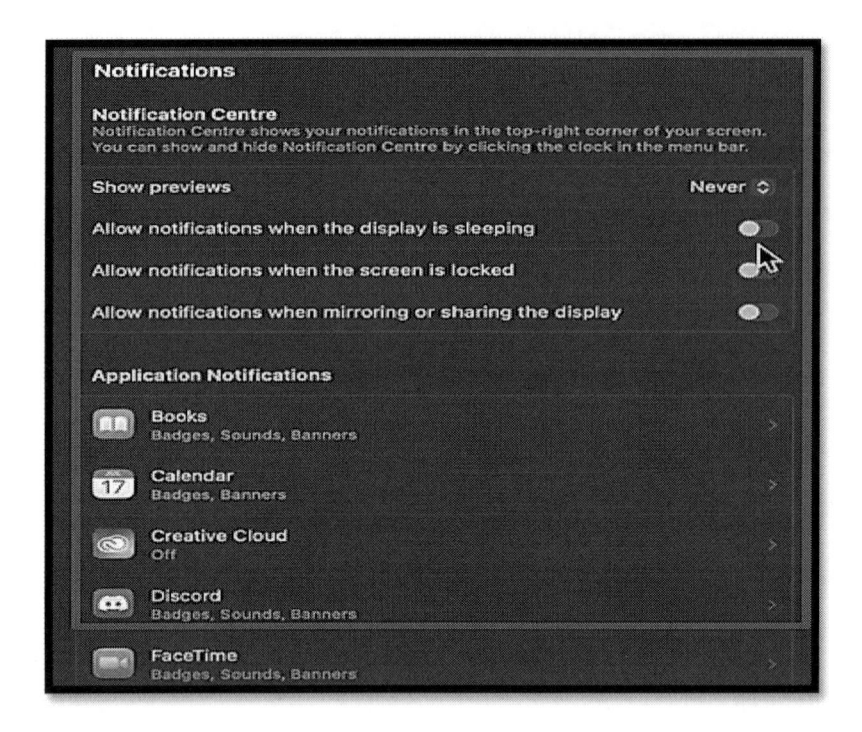

5. **Customize alerts**: You can typically change many different characteristics of how alerts are shown inside the app's notification settings. Search for options such **as "Alert Style," "Show Notifications,"** or alternatives. You could also find options to accept alerts from certain contacts or persons depending on the app.
6. **Allow alerts from Specific Persons**: If the app has this feature, you may be able to tailor your alerts to come from just certain people. Adding certain email addresses, names, or contacts to a whitelist might do this. Check the notification options in the app's settings to check whether this choice is there.
7. Close the Notifications preferences window after making the required adjustments to the app's notification settings.

Allow Time-Sensitive Notifications

On your MacBook Pro, you can enable time-sensitive alerts by following these steps:

1. To access the notification settings, click the Apple logo in the top-left corner of the screen and choose "**System Settings**."

2. Navigate to the "**Notifications**" icon in the System Settings window and click it. You can change all of your notification settings here.
3. **Choose App:** Select the app for which you want to activate time-sensitive alerts from the list of applications on the left side of the alerts pane.

87

4. **Change Notification Style**: After choosing the app, you'll find choices to change the notification style, such as "**Banners**" and "**Alerts**." Banners transiently show in the top-right corner of your screen before disappearing. Alerts are shown until you choose to dismiss them.
5. Make sure "**Show Notifications on Lock Screen**" is enabled if the alerts are time-sensitive and you want to be able to view them even while your MacBook's screen is locked.
6. **Set up Alerts**: Some applications let you set up extra options for their alerts. For instance, you could be able to decide whether to play a sound, how many alerts to display in the Notification Center, or whether to provide a sample of the notification's content.
7. While not directly connected to time-sensitive messages, you may also think about activating the "**Do Not Disturb**" function as necessary. This suppresses alerts for a certain amount of time. By selecting "**Do Not Disturb**" from the Notification Center menu (found in the top-right corner of the screen), you can access this option.
8. **Customize "Focus" Settings (if available):** Depending on the macOS version and upgrades, a feature called "**Focus**" is available that enables you to alter notification behavior depending on your current activity or time of day. You can control which alerts are sent out under certain circumstances.

Manage Apps to Display your Focus Mode Status

You can do the following actions on a MacBook Pro to manage apps and show your focus mode status:

1. Look for a "**Focus**" or "**Notifications**"-related area where you can manage which applications may inform you and how they can disturb you when you are trying to concentrate.
2. Locate the Focus Mode options and turn on the mode that best meets your requirements (such as Work, Personal, or Do Not Disturb). This setting blocks out unnecessary alerts and distractions to aid with concentration.
3. **Customize Focus Mode**: In the Focus Mode settings, choose which applications are permitted to notify you while you are in this mode. You can compile a list of applications that are necessary for your job and should continue to alert you while others are turned off.

4. **Status Display**: The menu bar, notification center or another readily accessible area may show your concentration mode status. It can be a little symbol that shows your mode at the moment.
5. **Third-Party applications**: If Apple's built-in capabilities fall short of your expectations; you could look into third-party applications with an emphasis on productivity and attention control. When downloading and installing software from unreliable sources, exercise caution and consider user reviews before selecting an app.
6. **Shortcuts and Automation**: Using applications like Automator or AppleScript, you may be able to create personalized shortcuts or automation processes to switch between focus modes or app alerts, depending on the capabilities of the macOS version installed on your MacBook Pro.
7. **Learning Resources**: Information on the precise features and procedures for controlling focus modes on the 2023 MacBook Pro may be found in Apple's official literature, user manuals, and online communities (such as Apple Support forums and Reddit).

How to use Quick Notes

With the help of the Quick Notes feature in macOS Ventura, you can rapidly make notes on your Mac from any location and view them later. It's intended to be a quick method to write down thoughts, facts, or reminders without needing to launch a different note-taking program.

How you may use Quick Notes is as follows:

1. **Creating a Quick Note:**
- Typically, you can launch Quick Notes using several techniques, including a keyboard shortcut, a gesture, or (if accessible) a button in the Control Center.
- When the feature is engaged, a little window or interface will show up on your screen so you may input or paste your notes.
- Depending on the capabilities of the Quick Notes function, you can also add other content to the note, such as links, photographs, or checklists.

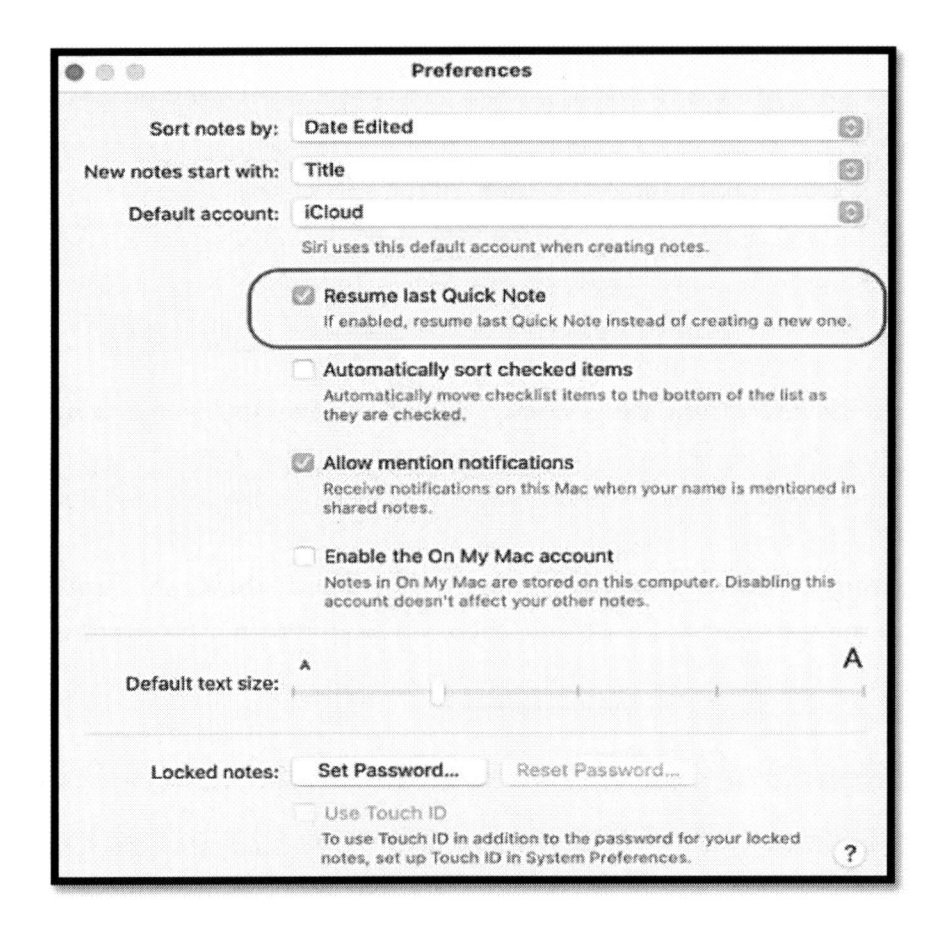

2. **Saving and Accessing Quick Notes:**
- Quick Notes are often stored automatically, and you may retrieve them in the Notes app at a later time.
- The Notes app on your MacBook Pro should be opened. Your Quick Notes should be posted in a distinct area that is often titled "**Quick Notes**" or something similar.
3. **Organizing and Editing:**
- After you've saved a Quick Note, you can arrange it in the Notes app by moving it to various folders, giving it tags, or changing how it looks.
4. **Syncing and Accessibility:**
- Using iCloud, macOS notes often sync across devices. This indicates that other Apple devices connected to the same iCloud account should be able to access your Quick Notes.

How to Access Quick Notes

You can quickly take notes from anywhere on the machine. You can attempt the following methods to open Quick Notes on a MacBook:

1. **Using the Control Center (if available):** The Control Center is a tool that offers rapid access to many system controls and features. You can access Quick Notes by selecting the Control Center symbol in the menu bar if Quick Notes are incorporated into the Control Center. There should be a note-taking or Quick Notes icon.
2. **Using the Notes App:**
- Launch the "**Notes**" app by selecting it from your Applications folder or by entering "**Notes**" into Spotlight (by pressing **Command + Space**).
- If the Notes app has a shortcut feature, you can open a new note fast by pressing a certain key combination (such as a function key).
3. **Gestures (if supported):** To access certain functionalities, Apple laptops often incorporate touchpad gestures. You can start a Quick Note by making a particular touchpad motion if Quick Notes are made to work with gestures.

4. If available, use a keyboard shortcut. Apple routinely adds keyboard shortcuts for fast access to numerous functionalities. Check to see whether the 2023 MacBook Pro has a new keyboard shortcut for opening Quick Notes.

5. If the MacBook Pro has sophisticated voice control features, you may be able to launch Quick Notes using voice commands.
6. **System Notifications**: You can make brief notes from widgets or system notifications in certain versions of macOS. To rapidly take notes, see if there is a widget or notification option available.
7. **Check the macOS Documentation:** The 2023 MacBook Pro's official user manual or documentation should have detailed instructions on how to access Quick Notes on that particular model.

Enable Hot Corners

When you move your pointer to a certain corner of your screen, Hot Corners lets you activate specific features or activities.

Here's how you can set them up:

1. The Apple menu is located in the top-left corner of your screen. Select "**System Settings**" from there.

2. Depending on the macOS version you are using, choose either **"Mission Control"** or **"Desktop & Screen Saver."**

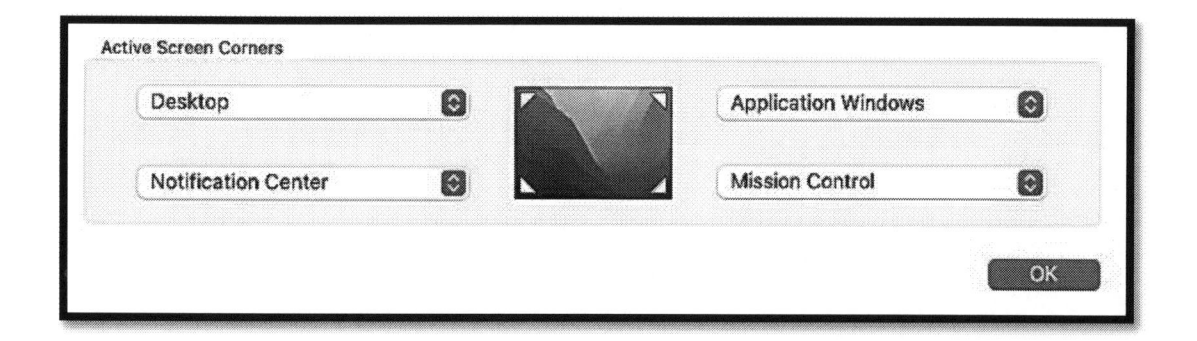

3. Look for the Hot Corners configuration option. You may call this "**Hot Corners**" or anything like that.
4. The four corners of your screen should be shown in a grid under the Hot Corners settings. Click the dropdown menu next to a corner to choose it.
5. Move your pointer to that corner to choose the action you want to do. This might include selecting options like **"Start ScreenSaver," "Show Notification Center,"** or other operations.

How to Create a Quick Note

The steps:

1. Check that your MacBook Pro is running macOS Monterey or a later version before trying to use Quick Note since it is a feature of these operating systems. Quick Note is accessible in a variety of ways:
- **Control Center**: To reach the Control Center, swipe downward from your trackpad's upper-right corner. The Quick Note icon (a pen in a circle) should be clicked.
- **Keyboard Shortcut**: Simultaneously press and hold the Control, Command, and Q keys.
2. **Creating a Note**: A little window will show on the screen as soon as you open Quick Note. There are many methods you can use to create a note:
- **Typed message**: Just begin writing your message. Your input will be recognized and converted to text by the MacBook Pro.
- **Handwritten Note**: If you prefer handwriting, you may write right on the screen using your trackpad or a compatible pen. For subsequent easier finding, your handwriting will be transformed into digital text.

- **Images and Links**: In the Quick Note box, you can drag and drop photos, links, or a selection of text from Safari.

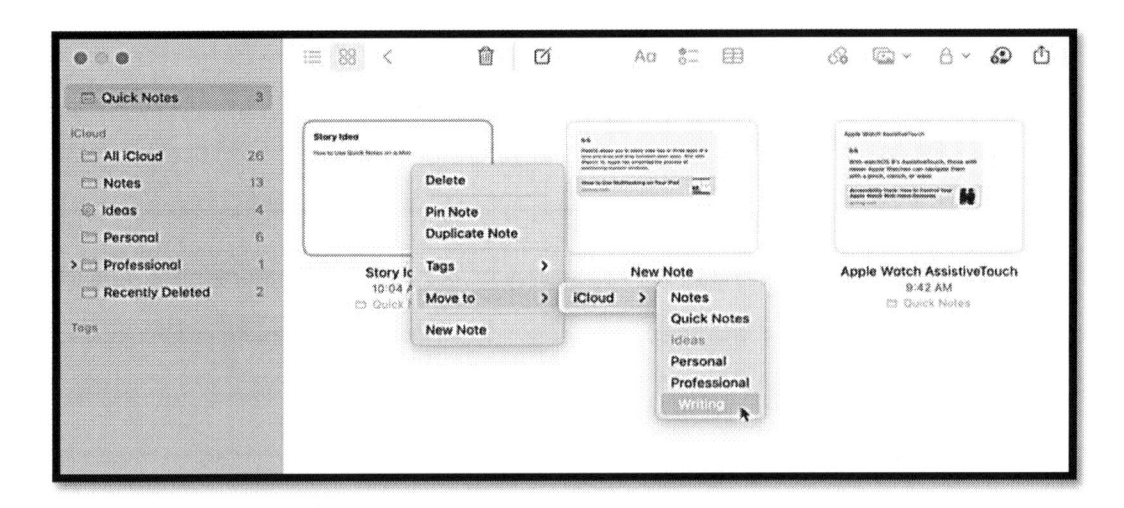

3. **Formatting Your Note**: To assist you in organizing your ideas, Quick Note offers several simple formatting options:
- **Headings:** make headers, use the '**#**' sign followed by a space.
- For lists containing bulleted or numbered items, start a line with a '*' for a bullet or a '1.' for a numbered item.
- **Checklists:** Type '- []' to add a new item to a checklist and '- [x]' to remove an item from a checklist.
4. **Adding Context** include links in your notes for rapid access:
- **Web Links:** Drag & drop URLs into the Quick Note window from Safari. A title and thumbnail will be shown beside the link.
- **App Links**: To make references, drag and drop links from applications like Messages, Mail, or Notes.
5. **Managing and Organizing Quick Notes**: As you create more Quick Notes, organization becomes more important.
- **Tagging:** To add pertinent tags to your note for simple classification, click the tag symbol in the Quick Note box.
- **Accessing Recent Notes**: In the Control Center, click the Quick Note symbol to go to your most recent notes.
- **Access All Notes**: Open the Notes app and search for the "**Quick Notes**" category in the sidebar to view all of your Quick Notes.

6. **Sync across Devices**: If you use iCloud, your Quick Notes will sync across all of your Apple ID-enabled devices:
   - **iPad and iPhone:** Use the Control Center or Notes app on your iOS devices to access Quick Notes.
   - **Mac:** Your other Mac devices will be able to access any Quick Notes you generate on your MacBook Pro.
7. **Advanced Features:** Quick Note provides sophisticated tools to improve your note-taking experience. These include:
   - **Highlight Text:** Choose the text and pick the highlight option to draw attention to certain passages in your note.
   - **Text Recognition in Images**: If you include text in an image attachment, Quick Note can search the text.
   - **Shared Notes**: Using the Share button, you can send Quick Notes to friends or coworkers.

Add Smart Links to Quick Note

Understanding Quick Notes and Smart Links

Similar to digital sticky notes, the MacBook Pro's Quick Notes feature makes it simple to record ideas and chores without navigating between programs. These notes are a flexible tool for note-taking on the move since they can be produced from anywhere on your device. These remarks get much more impact when Smart Links are included. Smart links are dynamic hyperlinks that instantly create connections to content previews. For instance, when you add a Smart Link to a website, the note will contextualize itself by displaying an image, title, and short description of the page. Your note-taking procedure is streamlined, and the notes' usefulness is improved thanks to this connection.

Add Smart Links to Quick Notes

1. To get started, launch Quick Note on your MacBook Pro. You can accomplish this by using your finger or, if you have one, the Apple Pencil, to swipe up from the trackpad's bottom right corner.
2. To create a new note, click the **"+"** icon in the Quick Note interface's bottom right corner. Alternatively, use your keyboard's **"Command"** and **"N"** keys.

3. **Add Text:** Fill out the text portion of your remark. This might be anything you wish to remember, such as an idea or a job. Highlight the words you want to connect if you want to create a smart link.
4. **Insert Smart Link:** Right-click (or Ctrl-click) on the required text while it is highlighted to display the context menu. Choose "**Add Link**" from the menu. You can then paste the link you want to go along with the selected text in the pop-up window that will emerge.
5. **Automatic Preview Generation:** The Smart Link capability will automatically create a preview of the connected content after the link has been pasted. The connected website or document's title, a thumbnail picture, and a succinct explanation may all be included in this preview.
6. **Customizing the Link:** Change the title or description of the Smart Link by clicking on the preview. This makes sure that even without clicking the link, the message accurately conveys context.
7. **Saving Your Note**: After adding the Smart Link and making any required customizations, you can either click outside the note interface or the "**Done**" button in the upper-left corner of the Quick Note window to save your note.
8. **Accessing Smart Links**: The Smart Links you've placed will instantly give context and a visual representation of the linked information whenever you return your Quick Note. The relevant website or document will be opened when you click on the Smart Link.

Quick Note Thumbnail

The Quick Note Thumbnail is one of the new MacBook Pro's most avant-garde features. The way we take notes and record information is changed by this capability, which makes it easier and smoother than before.

Think about yourself perusing the internet, viewing a movie, or studying a project. You have a thought or a small bit of information that you want to record right away before it disappears. The Quick Note Thumbnail reduces this procedure to a single motion. Think of it as a digital sticky note that's constantly available to record your ideas. A little note-taking window appears when you swipe your finger from the bottom corner of the touchpad.

Taking Notes Immediately

The Quick Note Thumbnail is a flexible tool that fits into your workflow; it's not simply a digital notepad. It allows you to make notes, copy and paste text, take screenshots, and even doodle ideas. Beyond words, the feature enables you to compile a thorough record of your ideas in many different forms. The Quick Note Thumbnails seamless integration with other programs and services is what stands out. When doing online research, you may swipe to enable the Quick Note Thumbnail, select some text on the page, and the highlighted content will be added instantly to your note. Other Apple applications are also integrated, which simplifies the process of gathering data from various sources.

Making organization simple

The Quick Note Thumbnails connection with Apple's Notes app is what gives it its true brilliance. You can quickly drag and drop your thoughts into your Notes for additional categorization once you've written them down in the thumbnail. You may designate notebooks specifically for certain tasks, add categories for quick classification, and even utilize the robust search engine to quickly find your notes.

Increased productivity and efficiency

The Quick Note Thumbnail is a productivity game-changer rather than simply a pretty touch. Having a tool that allows for fast capture without interfering with your workflow is crucial in a world where inspiration may strike at any time. The Quick Note Thumbnail is your one-stop solution for simple note-taking. No more switching between programs or looking for the correct tab. The usefulness of this function extends to experts in other disciplines. Researchers can swiftly compile information for their studies, designers may quickly sketch up thoughts for their next project, and content makers can quickly gather inspiration for their next video. Business executives may easily keep track of critical information during meetings, while students can easily assemble references for homework.

Insert Text or Photos from Safari to Quick Notes

The steps:

1. **Launch Safari and locate your content**

On your MacBook Pro, open Safari and go to the website with the text or image that you wish to include in Quick Notes. It can be a piece of writing, a picture, or any other piece of information that interests you.

2. **Enable Quick Notes**

You have a few alternatives for starting the process of adding the information to Quick Notes. The use of the Control Center is the fastest method. To display the Control Center on your MacBook Pro, you slide downward from the top-right corner of the screen. To create a new Quick Note, click the Quick Notes icon, which looks like a little pencil inside of a square. Another method is to simultaneously hit "**Control + Command + Q**" on the keyboard to access the shortcut. This will start a new Quick Note as well.

3. **Add text or a photo**

You can now begin inputting the material from Safari with the Quick Note open. Simply highlight the text on the website in Safari, right-click, and choose "**Add to Quick Note**" from the context menu to add it to the note. A reference link to the original website and the highlighted content will be immediately added to the Quick Note. Right-click the picture you want to add and choose "**Add to Quick Note**" from the context menu to add it to the note. The picture will be added to the Quick Note, enhancing its aesthetic appeal and illuminating its content.

4. **Edit and Organize**

You can change and format the text or image after it has been added to your Quick Note to suit your requirements. In addition to adding bullet points, numbering, and other formatting choices, you may alter the font style, size, and color of the text. Categorize information that you've contributed to a single Quick Note by adding headers, subheadings, or bullet points. This helps in organizing your notes for subsequent reference.

5. **Add Annotations (Optional)**

Additionally, Quick Notes lets you instantly annotate the information you've placed. Use the annotation tools in Quick Notes to highlight a particular passage of text, emphasize a certain region of a picture, or explain a point. These features include underlining, highlighting, and even free-hand sketching using your mouse or trackpad.

6. **Save and Sync**

Make sure to save your Quick Note after you're through with it. On your MacBook Pro, Quick Notes are instantly saved to the Notes app. They are also synchronized with all of your Apple devices that are connected to the same iCloud account. This ensures that your crucial information is always available and that you can access your Quick Notes from your iPhone, iPad, or other Mac devices.

View & Customize Quick Notes in the Notes App

Quick Notes is an easy-to-use tool for jotting down ideas as they come to mind since it can be accessible in just a few quick steps.

The steps:

1. Click the **Notes app**.
2. **Use the Keyboard Shortcut**: Using the keyboard shortcut will access Quick Notes even more quickly. A Quick Note window will display in the bottom right corner of your screen when you press **Control + Command + N**.
3. **Access via Control Center:** via the Control Center, click the **Notes symbol** to access Quick Notes.

Capturing your Thoughts

When you first use Quick Notes, you'll find a straightforward UI that is prepared for your ideas. The default look is a clear canvas with few obstructive elements. You may start composing your message right now. You may, however, customize your Quick Notes even further to meet your requirements.

Customizing Quick Notes

1. **Formatting Options**

While Quick Notes is intended for quick note-taking, plain text is not your only option. You can format your text, create lists, and even add photos with this software. When you highlight the text you wish to style, a menu bar will appear where you may access formatting options. To make your notes aesthetically beautiful and simple to comprehend, you can choose the font style, size, color, and more.

2. **Adding Attachments**

A note can sometimes need more than simply words. Attach anything like pictures or documents to your notes using Quick Notes. You can drag and drop files into the note or add photographs from your Photos collection by clicking the **"+"** symbol inside the note.

3. **Organizing with Tags**

Additionally, Quick Notes includes tags, which may be used to effectively classify and arrange your notes. By selecting the **"Tag"** symbol in the note's upper-right corner, you may add tags. Create categories for your content that are relevant, such as **"Work," "Personal," or "Ideas,"** and afterward you can quickly filter and locate notes based on these tags.

4. **Sketching and Drawing**

Quick Notes has a sketching feature that enables you to sketch or draw immediately within your notes if you prefer visual communication. To use this function, click the pen symbol on the toolbar. This may be very helpful for concept-illustration workshops or brainstorming sessions.

5. **Customizing Appearance**

You can also change Quick Notes' look to suit your tastes. To access the modification options, click on the three dots in the top-left corner of the message. You can change the note window's opacity, switch between light and dark modes, and even change the accent color.

6. **Syncing Across Devices**

The Notes app's seamless connectivity with all of your Apple devices is one of its best features. Your MacBook Pro's Quick Notes application will immediately sync any notes you write with your other devices, including your iPhone and iPad. You will always have access to your ideas and thoughts thanks to this.

Saving and Closing Quick Notes

You can quickly save and dismiss a Quick Note after you've done writing in it:

1. **Save**: Your note is automatically saved as you write, but you can also save it manually by clicking the check mark symbol in the toolbar or holding down the Command key and S.
2. **Close**: Click the "**x**" symbol in the top-left corner of the note window to dismiss the Quick Note. By selecting the yellow "**Minimize**" button, you can also make the note smaller.

Frequently Asked Questions

1. How do you enable Focus Mode on your MacBook Pro?
2. How do you create and edit a new focus filter?
3. How to you allow time-sensitive notifications?
4. How to access and use Quick Notes?
5. How do you add smart links to Quick Note?
6. How do you use Quick Note Thumbnail on your MacBook Pro?

CHAPTER SEVEN
FOLDERS AND NOTES

Overview

Chapter Seven discusses folders and notes in your MacBook Pro 2023. Here, you will get to see how you can arrange notes with folders, how to add checklists to notes, how to share your notes, and a whole lot more.

Arrange Notes with Folders

The steps:

1. **Launch the Notes app**

Find the Notes app on your MacBook Pro to get started. You can look for it in the Applications folder or by using Spotlight (click **Command + Space** and type "**Notes**" to search for it). Clicking on the app will start it after you've found it.

2. **Create a New Folder**

Your current notes are shown on the left when you first start the Notes app. It's time to create a new folder so you can begin organizing your notes. Use the keyboard shortcut **Shift + Command + N**, or click the "**File**" menu in the top-left corner of the screen and choose "**New Folder**." You will be prompted to name your new folder in a pop-up window. Specify a meaningful name for your folder and click "**OK**."

3. **Move the Notes to the Folder**

It's time to begin transferring your notes into your new folder now that you have one. Simply drag and drop the individual notes into the newly formed folder from the left-hand side's main list. As an alternative, you can right-click on a note, choose "**Move To**," and then choose the folder you want to place it in. For every note you want to arrange, just repeat this procedure.

4. **Create Subfolders (Optional)**

Add subfolders within your primary folders if you have more notes and wish to better organize them. If you are working on many distinct categories or projects, this might be extremely helpful. Give your new subfolder a name, right-click the main folder, and choose "**New Folder**," then begin adding pertinent notes to it.

5. **Rename and Rearrange Folders**

Change the names of your folders and subfolders as necessary to make your arrangement more understandable. To rename a folder or subfolder, choose "Rename" from the context menu when you right-click on it. Additionally, inside the sidebar, you may click and drag individual folders up or down to change their arrangement.

6. **Look for the Notes**

You may need to look for certain notes even if you have a well-organized folder arrangement. This is simple using the Notes app. There is a search box in the top-right corner of the app. You may use the app to find the note you're searching for by simply typing in keywords linked to it.

7. **Sync with iCloud**

Consider turning on iCloud syncing to guarantee that your notes and folders are available from all of your Apple devices. No matter what device you use, this will maintain the organization and updating of your notes. Make sure the "**Notes**" option is selected when configuring this by going to **"Apple Menu" > "System Notes" > "Apple ID" > "iCloud."**

How to Create a Folder

The steps:

1. **First, look for the Finder icon**

On your MacBook Pro, you can manage and organize your files using the Finder. Find the Finder icon on your Dock to get started. It's usually found on the Dock's far left side and looks like a blue-and-white smiling face.

2. **Open a New Finder Window**

To launch a new Finder window, just click the **Finder** icon once. You may see a list of all of your files, directories, and running programs in this window. This window allows you to browse the file system on your computer.

3. **Choose a Location**

Choose the location where the new folder will be created. On your desktop, in the Documents folder, or inside of other folders already there, you can create new ones. Select the place where you wish to create the new folder by navigating there.

4. **Right-click and choose "New Folder"**

Right-click on a blank area of the Finder window once you're at the desired place. Then a context menu will show up. Alternatively, you can create a new folder by heading to the "**File**" option at the top of the screen and choosing "**New Folder**" from that menu.

5. **Name the Folder**

Once you've chosen "**New Folder**," a new folder icon will appear in the place you specified. The name of the folder will be highlighted so that you can quickly create a new name for it. Pick a name for the folder that accurately describes its contents. When you have finished entering the folder's name, hit "**Return**" on your keyboard.

6. **Drag and Drop**

Additionally, you can create folders by dragging and dropping files into them. Simply choose the folders or files you want to combine, and then drag them to a free area of the Finder window. You'll see a translucent rectangle following your mouse as you move the objects. The objects you've chosen will be placed in a new folder when you let go of the mouse button.

7. **Customize the Folder's Look**

Change how folders look on the MacBook Pro. Right-click the freshly formed folder and choose "**Get Info**" from the context menu to do this. You can choose from several choices to change the folder's icon, color, and more in the new window that will open. This may make folders simpler to find and help you visually distinguish between them.

8. **Organize your Folders**

Keep your file structure logical and well-organized as you add new directories. To better organize your data, think about creating subfolders inside bigger directories. Your **"Documents"** folder, for instance, may have subfolders for **"Work," "Personal,"** and **"Projects."**

How to Rename a Folder

One simple thing you can do to manage your data and keep your digital workplace neat is rename folders.

The steps:

1. **Locate the Folder**

To achieve this, launch the Finder, which is macOS' built-in file manager by default? You can open the Finder by clicking on its icon in your dock, which is a blue and white happy face, or by using Spotlight Search by pressing **"Command + Space "** to start typing **"Finder"** and pushing Enter.

2. **Select the Folder**

Navigate to the location of the folder you want to rename while you're in the Finder. To quickly access popular areas like Documents, Downloads, and Desktop, use the sidebar on the left. Once you've located the folder, select it by clicking on it.

3. **Start the Renaming Process**

There are many methods to start the renaming process after selecting the folder:

Option 1: Hit Enter

- On your keyboard, press the **"Enter"** key (also known as **"Return"**). By doing this, you'll enable editing of the folder name, enabling you to enter a new name immediately.

Option 2: Click with the right mouse button and choose "Rename"

- Right-click the chosen folder (or use two fingers to navigate the touchpad). Select "**Rename**" from the context menu that pops up to make the folder's name changeable.

Option 3: Use the Menu Bar

- Keep an eye on the screen's top when the folder is chosen. You'll notice the "**File**" option in the menu bar. To change the name of the folder, click "**File**" and then choose "**Rename**" from the drop-down menu.

4. **Type the New Name**

Regardless of the option you choose, a text box will show up next to the folder name where you may enter a new name. Type in the folder's new name of choice. Although macOS does not have the same restrictions on special characters as some other operating systems, it is nevertheless wise to avoid employing characters like "/", "", and ":" to avoid any possible compatibility problems.

5. **Confirm the Renaming**

Once you've given the folder a new name, confirm it by pressing the "**Enter**" key on your computer or by clicking anywhere else except the name box. The folder will then be given the new name you specified when your MacBook Pro has processed the modification.

6. **Check the Renamed Folder**

Make sure the folder's name has been changed appropriately by checking it twice. In the Finder window, the revised name ought to be shown next to the folder icon.

How to Rearrange Folders

The steps:

1. **Launch Finder**

Find the Finder icon in your Dock or click on the desktop to launch Finder before you can start arranging your files. On macOS Ventura, managing files and folders is done via the Finder.

2. **Navigate to the Folder**

Navigate to the location of the folder you want to reorder using Finder. You have access to many places, including your desktop, documents, downloads, and other specially created folders.

3. **Arrange Folders**

The folder you want to organize may be started after you've found it. There are several methods for doing this:

- **Drag-and-Drop**: Click on the folder and move it to a different folder or a new position within the same directory. As you drag the folder, a visual indication will show you where it will go when you let go of the mouse button.
- **Cut and Paste:** Another option is to use cut and paste. Move the folder to the new place by right-clicking the folder, choosing "**Cut**," then selecting "**Paste**."
- **Context Menu:** Right-click on the folder you want to transfer, pick "**Move to**" or "**Copy to**" from the context menu, and a popup enabling you to choose the destination folder will appear.
- **Keyboard Shortcuts**: Move folders with the use of keyboard shortcuts. Press "**Command + X**" to cut and "**Command + V**" to paste the folder in the new place after selecting it.

4. **Organize within Folders**

You can organize the files within the folder after transferring them to the appropriate location:

- **Sort Files:** After opening the folder in Finder, you can sort the files according to several factors, including name, date changed, size, and more. To choose your chosen sorting option, click on the toolbar's sorting choices.
- **Create Subfolders**: Within the main folder, you may want to create subfolders to better organize the contents. Within the folder, use the right-click menu to choose "**New Folder**," then give it a meaningful name. Files may then be dropped into these subfolders using drag-and-drop.
- **Rename Files and Folders**: Either choose "**Rename**" from the context menu when you right-click on a file or folder or click once on the file or folder name, then wait a second before clicking again. You can directly alter the name by doing this. For simple identification, give your files and folders distinctive names.

5. **Customize Folder Icons**

You can change folder icons to provide a more unique touch:

- **Get Information**: From the context menu, choose "**Get Info**" when you right-click on the folder you want to change. Choose the folder instead, and then press "**Command + I**."
- **Customize Icon**: In the top-left corner of the Info window, there is a little folder icon. To copy the icon, select it by clicking it and then pressing "**Command + C**".
- **Paste Icon**: Find a picture or icon that you want to use as the new folder icon and paste it in. It could be a bespoke design or a web picture. To paste the folder icon, select the picture and click "**Command + V**".

How to Delete a Folder

The steps:

1. **Find the Folder:** You must first find the folder on your MacBook Pro to remove it. Finder, mac Os file management program, is where folders can be located. Either click the happy face icon on your dock or open the Finder by hitting **Command + Space** and entering "**Finder**."
2. **Open the Finder:** You can browse through your files and folders after you have the Finder open. In the sidebar on the left, look for the folder you want to remove. If you don't see the folder there, you may look it up using the search box in the top-right corner.
3. Click once to choose the folder that you wish to remove. The folder will be highlighted, indicating that it is currently chosen. Before moving on, make sure you've selected the proper folder.
4. **Move to Trash:** After selecting the folder, you have a few choices. Drag and dropping the folder into the Trash is the quickest approach to get rid of it. At the end of your dock is an icon called "**Trash**" that resembles a trash can. Simply drop the chosen folder onto the Trash icon by dragging it there.
5. **Empty the Trash**: The folder has only been temporarily erased by being transferred to the Trash. Consider the Trash as a holding location for delete-worthy objects. You must empty the Trash to permanently remove the folder.

To empty the trash, just right-click (or two-finger press) on the trash icon and choose "**Empty Trash**."

6. **Confirm Deletion:** A pop-up window requesting your confirmation will show before permanently deleting the things in your Trash. Make sure you haven't unintentionally deleted anything significant by going through the items. The folder and all of its contents will be permanently removed from your MacBook Pro if you choose to "**Empty Trash**."
7. **Using a Keyboard Shortcut**: To transfer a folder to the Trash, select the folder, then press Command + Delete on your keyboard. To empty the trash, right-click on the trash symbol while holding down Control and choosing "**Empty Trash**."
8. **Recovery of Deleted Items:** Use caution while removing directories since once the Trash is empty, it is difficult to retrieve the items. If you have a backup or are using a cloud storage service with version history, you can restore anything crucial if you find you've accidentally destroyed it.

Working with Notes

Notes has developed into a flexible tool that lets you easily record, catalog, and collaborate on your thoughts. Whether you're a professional, a student, or a creative person, using Notes' features may greatly improve your productivity and creativity.

Getting Started with Notes on MacBook Pro

Simply find the Notes app in your Applications folder or use Spotlight search to quickly open it to start using Notes on your new MacBook Pro. You'll be welcomed with a simple and clear UI once it's opened.

Creating and Formatting Notes

The **"+"** button is found in the bottom left corner of the program, and you can add a new note by clicking it or by typing **"Command" + "N."** You can also click on an existing note to begin altering it. To assist you in efficiently structuring your content, Notes provides a choice of formatting options. Your notes will be more aesthetically pleasing and well-organized if you use the formatting toolbar to change the fonts, styles, and text sizes.

Collaboration in Notes

The collaborative capabilities of Notes make collaboration simple. By selecting the **"Collaborate"** option in the toolbar and inputting the email addresses of your collaborators, you can share a message with others. This makes it possible for many people to simultaneously edit the same note. The message is instantly updated across all devices, and you can see who made modifications. For group assignments, brainstorming sessions, or just simply exchanging ideas with coworkers or students, this function is immensely helpful.

Search and Organization

The search feature becomes essential as your collection of notes expands. With the help of Notes' robust search feature, you can easily locate certain words, phrases, or even handwritten text within your notes. When you need to find a key piece of information hidden inside a large database of notes, this capability is helpful. Additionally, the Notes app for the MacBook Pro has a function called **"Pin"** that allows you to move critical notes to the top of your list for quick access.

Privacy and Security

Notes on MacBook Pro make sure that your notes stay private and safe since your privacy and data protection are very important. The content of your notes can only be accessed by you and the people you choose to share them with since Notes uses end-to-end encryption. When working with sensitive information, this degree of protection is very crucial.

Syncing and Accessibility

The seamless iCloud integration of Notes on your MacBook Pro is one of its most important benefits. Your notes will be instantly synchronized across all of your Apple devices, including iPhones and iPads, thanks to this connection. You have access to your notes whenever and wherever you need them thanks to this function. You may continue working on a note you began on your MacBook Pro even if you're on the run and just have your iPhone with you.

Markup and Sketching

Including visual components in your notes helps improve communication and comprehension. To collaborate on projects or provide comments, use the Notes' Markup function, which enables you to annotate photos and PDFs. Additionally, the sketching tool gives you the option to doodle freely inside your notes, which is very helpful for designers, painters, and other people who need to depict ideas.

How to Create a Note

Access the Notes App

Make sure your MacBook Pro is turned on and logged in before you begin. The Dock, a row of icons generally seen at the bottom of your screen, is where you may find the Notes app. A notepad and a pen are shown in the Notes symbol. Alternatively, to find and launch the program, press **Command + Space** and type "**Notes**" into the Spotlight search box.

Create a New Note

1. If you have any existing notes, they will be shown when you first launch the Notes app. simply click the "**+ New Note**" button in the upper-left corner of the program window to start a new note. The identical outcome may also be obtained by pressing **Command + N** on the keyboard.

2. **Add Content:** The note window will now be available for you to begin entering content. Using the keyboard, you can enter your notes or paste content from another document. Additionally, by selecting the plus button that displays while your cursor is above the note area, you may add pictures, doodles, and even scanned documents.

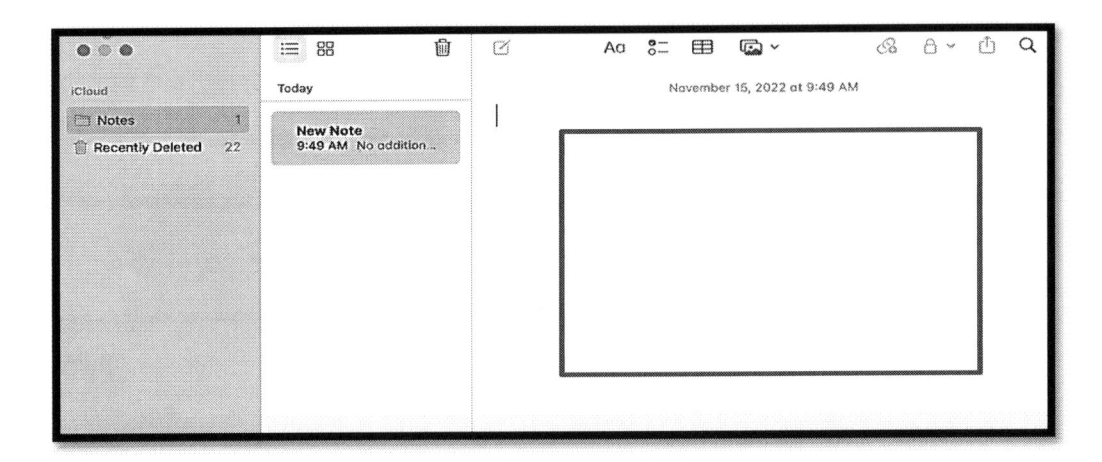

3. **Formatting Options:** Basic text formatting options are available in the Notes app, enabling you to change how your note appears. Font sizes, colors, and styles are all customizable. Additionally possible are lists, alignment changes, and underlining significant information.
4. **Adding Attachments:** Add files directly to your note by dragging them into the note and dropping them there. Using this, you can easily include papers, pictures, or other pertinent resources in your message.
5. **Organizing Your Notes**: As your collection of notes expands, organization is crucial. To organize similar notes, you can create folders. Click **"File"** in the menu bar, choose **"New Folder,"** and then give the folder the name of your choice to create a folder. To organize your notes effectively, just drag & drop them into these folders.

Syncing with iCloud

The seamless iCloud integration of the Notes app on your MacBook Pro is one of its many noteworthy benefits. You may now access your notes from any Apple device linked to your iCloud account thanks to this feature.

1. Sign in to iCloud: Make sure you are logged in to iCloud on your MacBook Pro to sync your notes across devices. Enter your Apple ID and password by going to **"Apple Menu" > "System Settings" > "iCloud"**.
2. After logging into iCloud, make sure the "**Notes**" option is selected. This will enable Notes Sync. It also makes sure that all of the devices connected to your iCloud account instantly sync your notes.

Searching for Notes

Finding particular information becomes more important as your collection of notes expands. With the help of the powerful search function provided by the Notes app, you can easily find notes using keywords, phrases, or even the contents of attachments.

1. **Using the Search Bar:** The Notes application window has a search bar at the top. You just click on it and enter the search terms. Your notes will be automatically filtered by the app to only show those that meet your search parameters.
2. **Advanced Search:** The search bar's magnifying glass symbol, when clicked, displays advanced search possibilities. Here, you may add further criteria, such as searching inside certain folders or looking for notes containing attachments.

Additional Tips

- **Use Keyboard Shortcuts:** To make taking notes easier, use keyboard shortcuts. To bold, italicize, or underline text, for instance, use **Command + B, Command + I, or Command + U.**
- **Checklists:** Create interactive checklists in the Notes app. **Command + Shift + L** can be used to add a checklist item. For making grocery lists, to-do lists, and other lists, this tool comes in useful.
- **Instant Formatting**: The Notes app often preserves the original formatting when copying and pasting text from the internet or other sources. Right-click the copied information and choose "**Paste and Match Style**" to match the note's formatting.

Move a Note

The steps:

1. **Launch the Notes App**

Start by selecting the "**Notes**" icon from your MacBook Pro's dock or by typing "**Notes**" into Spotlight (press "**Command + Space**" to search for the app). When the Notes app opens, your current notes are shown in the main pane.

2. **Select the Note to Move**

Within the Notes app, find the note you wish to relocate. By using the search box at the top or the list on the left-hand side, you may browse through your notes. When you locate the note you wish to move, click on it to make it a selection.

3. **Drag and Drop**

Drag and drop operations are all that are required to move a note in the Notes app. To choose a note, click and hold it on the mouse or trackpad. Drag the note while holding it to the appropriate spot in the list of notes in the left sidebar. A visual cue will show you where the note is in the list as you move it around.

4. **Select the Ideal Location**

Carefully move the message to the desired location by dragging it there. Other notes may move slightly as you hover over them to create a place for the note you are moving. You can place your note precisely where you want it thanks to its dynamic rearrangement.

5. **Drop the Note**

Release the mouse button or take your finger from the trackpad after you've located the best spot for your message. The other notes will reposition themselves when the note is deposited into its new location. A note has been successfully moved within the Notes app!

6. **Check the Move**

Look through your list of notes in the sidebar to make sure the note has been placed in the proper spot. The message should now be visible in its new location. Open the note to ensure that everything on it has survived the transfer.

Tips to organize notes:

1. **Create Folders:** Think about building folders to further improve note organizing. This enables you to put relevant notes together, making it simpler to manage a huge collection of notes. To accomplish this, click on "**File**" in the top menu bar and pick **"New Folder."**
2. **Use Tags**: Using tags to classify and organize your notes is a good idea. When writing or modifying a note, you may add tags by selecting the "**Add Tag**" option. Later, you can quickly access particular information by searching for notes based on their tags.
3. **iCloud sync**: If you have many Apple devices, check sure they are all signed into the same iCloud account. As a result, your notes are synchronized seamlessly across all of your devices, allowing you to make changes on one device and see them immediately on all of the others.
4. **Smart Search:** The Notes app offers an effective search function. Use terms associated with the note's text or title in the search box at the top of the app window to find it fast.
5. **Use Formatting Options**: The Notes app lets you format text, add photographs, make checklists, and even draw with the trackpad or Apple Pencil (if appropriate). Make use of these tools to enhance the aesthetic appeal and informational content of your notes.

Pin a Note

The steps:

1. Open the Notes app on your MacBook Pro to get started. You can look for it in Spotlight (by pressing **Command + Space** and entering "**Notes**") or on the Dock at the bottom of the screen.
2. After opening the Notes app, you have the option of opening an existing note that you want to pin or making a new note by selecting the "**+**" button in the top-left corner of the app window.

New Note	⌘ N
New Folder	⇧ ⌘ N
Manage Shared Note	
Close	⌘ W
Import from iPhone	>
Import to Notes...	
Export as PDF...	
Share	>
Pin Note	
Lock Note	
Duplicate Note	⌘ D
Print...	⌘ P

3. If you want to open an existing note, click on its title in the list on the app window's left side. Simply put your stuff into the note editor to create a new note.
4. With the note chosen, you'll see a little thumbtack icon in the note preview or editing window's upper-right corner. To pin the note, click on this thumbtack symbol. When a note is pinned, it rises to the top of the list and stays there as you navigate through your other notes.
5. Open the Notes app to easily view your pinned note. The top of the list will prominently feature your pinned message. This eliminates the need to look up crucial information and makes it simple to refer to it.
6. Open the Notes app and look for the pinned note if you want to unpin it at any time. To unpin the message, click the thumbtack symbol once again. It will then revert to the list's previous position.
7. You can edit pinned notes the same way you edit any other note. To access the pinned message, make any required adjustments, and save your changes, click on it. The note's content will be updated and kept pinned.

8. iCloud is used to sync pinned notes across all of your devices, which is great news if you own other Apple products like an iPhone or iPad. To provide consistent access to your crucial information, each note you pin on your MacBook Pro will likewise show up at the top of your Notes app on your other devices.
9. As you collect more pinned notes, you may wish to arrange them. To do this, create folders in the Notes app. You can name the folder, drag and drop pinned notes into it to keep relevant content together, and build a folder by clicking "**File**" in the menu bar and choosing "**New Folder**."
10. Pinned notes are a terrific method to keep important information close at hand. You may want to use them for fast references, continuing to-do lists, project summaries, or any other information you constantly want. Your workflow might be streamlined and your total productivity increased with the aid of this function.

Lock a Note

The steps:

1. **Launch the Notes App**

Start by tapping the Notes app icon in your MacBook Pro's dock or by putting "**Notes**" into Spotlight Search (by pressing **Command + Space**). This will launch the Notes app and show any current notes you have or let you start a new one.

2. **Create or Select a Note**

Find the note in the list of notes if you already have one that you wish to lock. If not, click the "**New Note**" button in the top-left corner of the app window to start a new note. Enter the text you want to safeguard and give your note a title.

3. **Lock the Note**

Click the "**Lock**" icon in the top-right corner of the app window while your note is open. This symbol resembles a padlock.

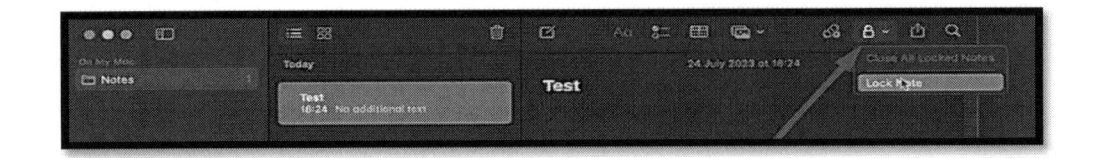

When you click the button, a pop-up box asking you to secure the note with a password will appear.

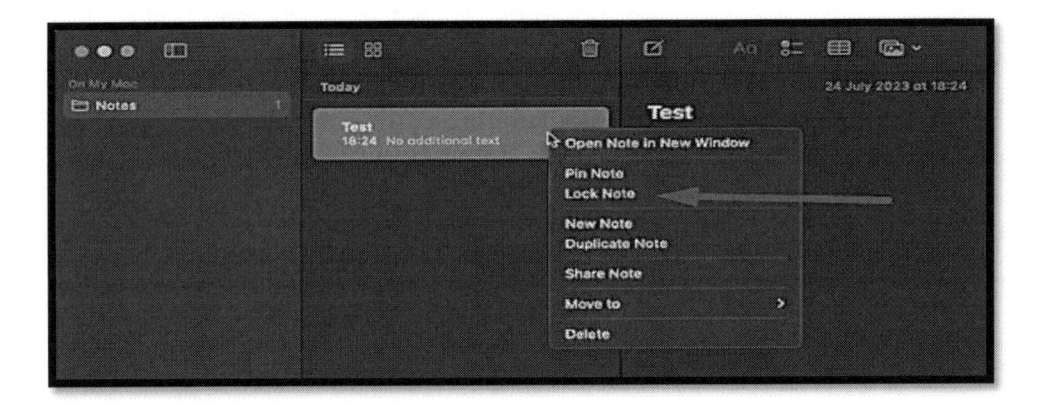

4. **Set a Password**

Enter the note's preferred password in the pop-up box. For increased protection, be sure you use a strong password that incorporates letters, numbers, and special characters. The password should also be easy for you to remember but difficult for others to guess. Keep this password private; you'll need it each time you wish to access the restricted note.

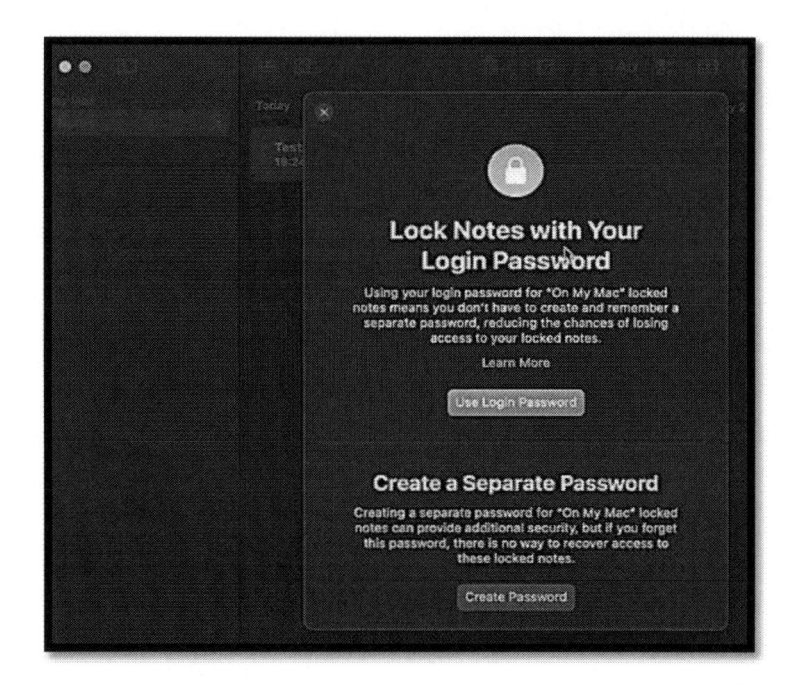

5. **Add a Hint (Optional)**

Add a clue to the password to aid with memory retention if you forget it. The tip needs to be a nuanced indication that only you can grasp. Although it shouldn't reveal the real password, it should bring up memories. This step is optional, so if you'd rather not provide a clue, you may omit it.

6. **Confirm Password**

Click the **"Set Password"** button after the password and, if desired, the clue has been entered. You will be prompted to enter the password again in a confirmation popup asking for confirmation. This confirms that you entered the password correctly the first time.

7. **Successfully Locked**

The note will be successfully locked after you enter the password, at which point a padlock symbol will show up next to its title in the list of notes. This symbol denotes that the message is now password-protected.

8. **Accessing a Locked Note**

Simply click on a locked note in the list of notes to open it. The password you previously established will be required when requested. Enter the password, and then hit "**OK**."

Delete a Note

The steps:

1. **Launch the Notes app**

Find the "**Notes**" app on your MacBook Pro to get started. You can simply discover it in your Applications folder or by using Spotlight by hitting "**Command + Space**" and entering "**Notes**."

2. **Choose the Note to Delete**

When the Notes app is launched, a list of all your notes is shown in a straightforward layout. You just need to click the note you want to erase. This will reveal the note's contents and open it.

3. **Select the Thrash Icon**

You will see a little trash can symbol in the note window's upper-right corner. The "**Delete**" action is symbolized by this icon. To begin the deletion procedure, click the trash can symbol.

4. **Confirm Deletion**

A confirmation dialog box will show up when you click the trash can symbol, asking you to confirm that you wish to remove the note. To avoid inadvertent deletions, it is essential to do this step. Make sure the note you plan to delete is the one you have read the contents of. Click the "**Delete**" button in the dialog box if you are certain.

5. **Check the Recently Deleted Folder (Optional)**

A note is not instantly and permanently deleted after deletion. Instead, information is transferred to the Notes app's "**Recently Deleted**" section. This enables you to retrieve unintentionally deleted notes within a certain window of time (often 30 days). You can enter the **"Recently Deleted"** section and retrieve a deleted note from there if you're not sure you deleted it or want to. Click on the **"Back"** button (seen as an arrow) in the upper-left corner of the Notes app to open the **"Recently Deleted"** folder. You will then land on the primary Notes screen. There is a list of folders on the left side. To examine the notes you've recently erased, click **"Recently Deleted."** Simply click on a note to select it, and then choose the **"Recover"** icon that appears.

6. **Fill the "Recently Deleted" Folder (Optional)**

Empty the **"Recently Deleted"** folder to clear up space on your MacBook Pro if you're convinced that you want to permanently erase a note. To do this, go to the **"Recently Deleted"** folder and choose the **"Delete All"** option, which is often found at the folder's base. Confirm the action in the ensuing dialog box.

Format your Notes

The steps:

1. **Launch the Notes App**

Locate and launch the Notes app on your MacBook Pro to begin. You can either use the **"Spotlight"** search feature (press **Command + Space**, then enter **"Notes"**) or the **"Notes"** icon in your Dock to accomplish this.

2. **Create a New Note**

Clicking the **"New Note"** button in the top-left corner of the Notes window will allow you to start with a new note. By selecting the **"Untitled Note"** option and entering a name that briefly describes the contents of your note, you will give your note a descriptive title.

3. **Text Formatting**

To assist you in organizing your material and creating a visually pleasing presentation, the Notes app provides a variety of text formatting options.

To format text:

- **Bold**: To bold text, select it and either click the "**B**" symbol in the formatting toolbar at the top of the note or hit **Command + B** on your keyboard.
- **Italic**: Similarly, to italicize a passage of text, first highlight it. Then, either click the "**I**" button in the toolbar or press **Command + I.**
- **Underline**: Text can be highlighted and underlined by clicking the "**U**" button or by pressing **Command + U**.
- **Font Styles and Sizes**: Using the formatting toolbar, you can modify the font style and size of your text. To access the font selections, click the "**A**" symbol.

4. **Lists and Bullets**

Your content and information will be more effectively organized if you make lists and use bullet points.

To format a list with bullets:

- In the top menu bar, choose the "**Format**" menu.
- Select "**Lists**" and then "**Numbered List**" or "**Bulleted List**."

5. **Headings**

To organize your notes into parts or to draw attention to key ideas, use headings. Applying headings

- Highlight the text you would like to change into a heading.
- Select "**Style**" from the "**Format**" menu, then "**Style**," then the appropriate heading level.

6. **Checkboxes**

You can add checkboxes to your notes if you're using them for task lists or to-do lists so you can monitor your progress.

Add a checkbox here:

- Select "**Format**" from the menu.
- To add a checkbox, choose "**Add Checklist Item**".

7. **Images and Attachments**

Occasionally, using photos or files may improve your remarks. To add a photo or attachment:

- In the top menu bar, choose the "**Insert**" menu.
- Add a file by selecting "**Add Attachment**" or "**Add Photo**" and then choosing the file.

8. **Tables**

You can make tables in your notes if you need to arrange data in a tabular format:

- Select "**Table**" from the formatting toolbar's menu.
- Determine the number of rows and columns your table will have.

9. **Links**

To add email addresses or web URLs to your notes:

- Highlight the text you want to turn into a link
- Press the **Control or Right buttons** to choose the text.
- Select "**Add Link**" and provide the email address or URL.

10. **Sync and Save**

Through iCloud, the Notes app on your MacBook Pro syncs with your other Apple devices. This implies that you can access your notes using an iPad, iPhone, or other Mac-compatible device. You may manually save your notes by clicking the "**Done**" button in the top-left corner of the note, but they are automatically saved as you work.

11. **Export Options**

You can export your notes in many formats if you need to share them with someone who might not be using the Notes app:

- In the top menu bar, choose the "**File**" menu.

- Choose **"Export as Text"** or **"Export as PDF"** and a location for the file.

Sort your Notes

Keeping your notes organized may greatly increase your productivity and creativity, whether you're a student, professional, or simply someone who loves to write down thoughts.

The steps:

1. **Choose a Note-Taking App**

You must choose a note-taking app before you can begin organizing your notes. Thankfully, the Apple Notes software that comes pre-installed on your MacBook Pro provides a variety of tools for generating and managing notes. Depending on your interests and requirements, you can also think about using third-party note-taking applications like Microsoft OneNote or Evernote.

2. **Create Folders and Categories**

The first step after selecting your favorite note-taking program is to establish folders or categories to organize your thoughts. The basic organizing framework for your notes will be these folders. Follow these basic procedures to establish a folder, for example, **"Work," "Personal," "Project Ideas,"** and **"To-Do Lists."**

- Select a note-taking app and launch it.
- Look for a feature that allows you to add a new folder or category.
- Give your folder a name that adequately describes what is within.

3. **Create and Label Notes**

Now that you have your folders organized, you can begin adding notes to them. Make sure to give your notes names that are both informative and obvious as you generate them. Later on, it will be simpler to locate certain notes as a result. Remember to make your notes succinct and orderly, since crowded notes might negate the goal of organizing. For instance, if you're writing down meeting minutes, use headings like "Meeting with Team A - August 10, 2023."

4. **Use Tags and Labels**

You can add tags or labels to your notes in a lot of note-taking programs, including Apple Notes. Your notes may be further organized using tags, which makes them simpler to look for and sort. You can label notes as **"Urgent," "Important," "Research,"** etc., for instance.

To give your notes tags:

- Launch the note you would like to tag.
- Search for the label or tag addition option.
- Select or create appropriate tags for the message.

5. **Search and Filter**

The capacity to swiftly search for particular notes is one benefit of adopting a digital note-taking system. The majority of note-taking applications offer a search bar with options to look for information by tag, date, or phrase. As your note collection expands, this function proves to be quite useful.

To efficiently browse and sort your notes:

- Find the search field in your note-taking program.
- Type any pertinent keywords, dates, or tags here.
- Examine the search results, and then choose the desired note.

6. **Regular Maintenance**

Your collection of notes will keep growing over time. Reviewing and cleaning up your notes regularly is crucial for maintaining an orderly structure. Delete any notes that are no longer relevant or timely, and make sure any new notes are appropriately classified and categorized. By doing routine maintenance, you can keep your organizational system from getting too complex.

Search Notes

Knowing how to search for notes successfully becomes essential due to the enormous quantity of data that might be gathered over time.

1. **Become familiar with the Notes App**

It's essential to get familiar with the Notes app's user interface before beginning the search process. Explore the app's functionality by launching it from the Dock or the Applications folder. You may add attachments like files and photographs to your notes as well as arrange them into folders.

2. **Use Descriptive Tiles and Tags**

Adding descriptive names and pertinent tags to your notes is one of the easiest but most efficient methods to make them readily searchable. Pick a title for your new note that concisely summarizes the content. You may add tags by clicking on the note and choosing the tag symbol, which enables you to attach phrases that are pertinent to the note's content, such as **"Q3 Sales Projection Update,"** rather than using the title **"Project Update."**

3. **Use the Search Bar**

The Notes app on the MacBook Pro has a robust search feature that makes it easy to find certain notes. Simply click the magnifying glass icon in the upper right corner of the Notes app window to open the search bar. After you click, a search box will show up where you may enter your question.

4. **Use Keywords and Specific Phrases**

It's crucial to use particular terms and phrases related to the material you're searching for while searching. This specific method can limit your results and boost the probability of finding the relevant note, for example, if you're looking for a note on a meeting, enter keywords like **"meeting minutes," "conference call,"** or **"agenda."**

5. **Filter Search Results**

The Notes app lets you use filters to further hone your search results. Following a search, you will see a **"Filter By"** option to the right of the search box. To see a variety of filtering options, including attachments, checkboxes, and more, choose this option. Finding the information you need is made simpler by selecting a filter, which limits the results to notes that fit the given criteria.

6. **Search within Folders**

You can search inside a certain folder if you've separated your notes into other folders to speed up the procedure. To achieve this, use the folder's search field after navigating to the folder where you think the note could be. This stops you from looking up notes that aren't relevant to your interests.

7. **Use Advanced Search Operators**

The Notes app offers advanced search operators for customers who need even more detail in their searches. With the help of these operators, you can combine keywords, omit certain words, and look for precise phrases.

Several typical operators are:

- **AND:** When searching for notes that include two keywords, use "**AND**" between the keywords. For example, **"project AND timeline."**
- **OR**: You can use "OR" to search for notes that include either of the given keywords, for example, **"budget OR expenses."**
- **NOT**: You can use the term "NOT" to exclude a keyword from your search, such as **"presentation NOT draft."**

8. **Sort Search Results**

The most essential information should be at the top of the search results after you've located the pertinent note. To pick your chosen sorting technique, click on the "**Sort By**" option at the top right corner of the search results. The Notes app offers sorting options like **"Date Modified," "Date Created,"** and **"Title."**

Add Media to Notes

Your notes can become more interesting and educational by using media.

1. **Launch the Notes App**

Locate the Notes app on your MacBook Pro and open it. It is located in the Dock or by using Spotlight Search by hitting "**Command + Space**" and entering "**Notes**."

2. **Create a new note or open an existing one**

If you're already in the Notes app, you can open an existing note by tapping on it in the list of notes or add a new one by hitting the "**+**" button in the bottom left corner.

3. **Add Text Content**

It could be a good idea to include any required written information in your remark before adding any media. To begin typing on the note, click it. Using the formatting toolbar at the top of the note, you may format the text by altering the font, style, and color.

4. **Add Media**

Follow these procedures to include media in your note:

- **Drag & drop**: Moving files right into the note using this method is the quickest way to add media. You can drag things from your Finder window into the note where you want them to appear, including photos, movies, audio files, and even PDFs.

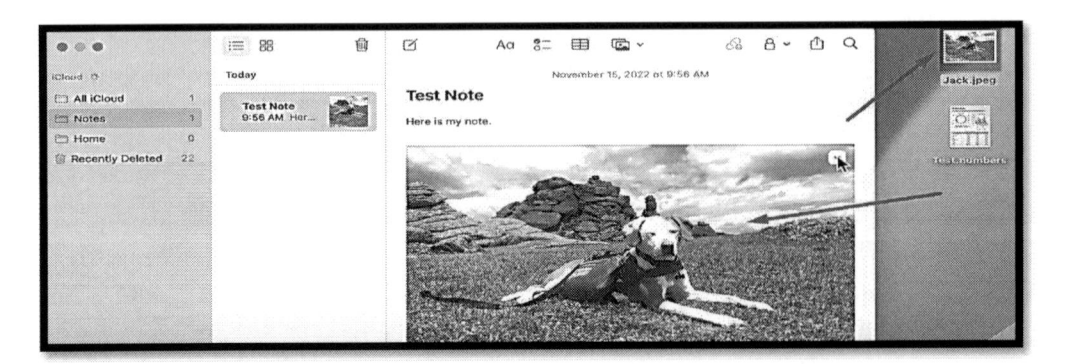

- **Hit the "+" button:** Alternatively, choose to click the "**+**" button that shows in the note when your mouse is over it. You may choose from a variety of alternatives, such as uploading a picture or video, scanning documents, or contributing sketching, using the dropdown menu that will display.

- **Insert from Menu:** Select "**Insert**" from the drop-down menu under "**Format**" to get choices for including media in your note. If you wish to integrate media while maintaining a precise formatting style, this might be quite helpful.

5. **Resize and Format Media**

Change the note's size and orientation once you've uploaded any accompanying media. Clicking the media element will reveal resize handles that you may drag to change the element's dimensions. Use the alignment options in the formatting toolbar to align the media.

6. **Organize Your Note**

You may arrange the content to make your note both aesthetically beautiful and simple to interpret. The content may be organized using headers, bullet points, and numbered lists. Media assets can be positioned according to how well they fit within the note's overall context.

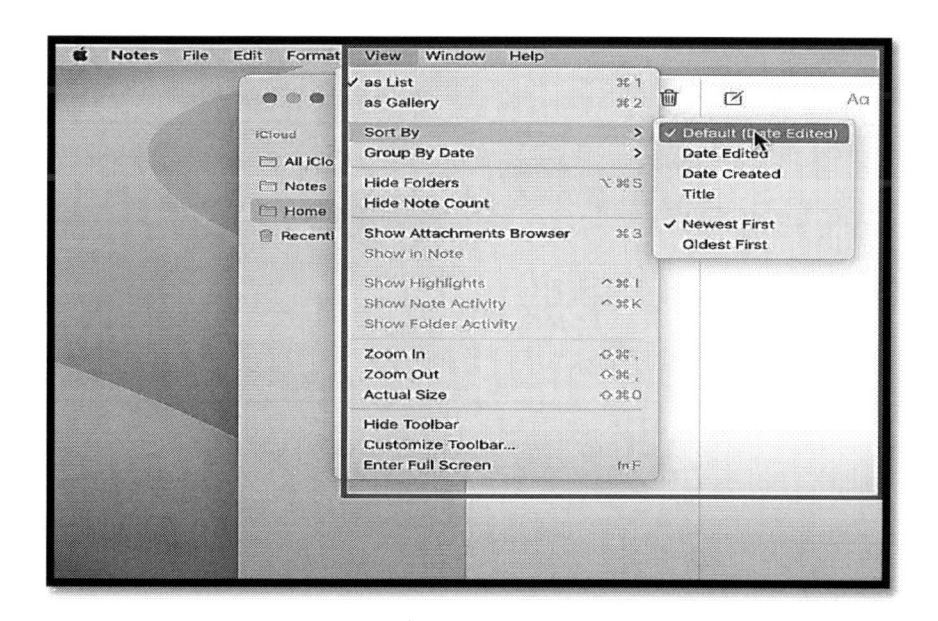

7. **Add Markups and Annotations**

Your new MacBook Pro's Notes software now enables you to annotate pictures and PDFs right within the note. Clicking on an image or PDF after adding it will display the toolbar for annotations. You may highlight certain sections as well as create shapes, lines, and text.

8. **Sync and Access Across Devices**

The Notes app's flawless synchronization across all of your Apple devices is one of its best qualities. Your iPhone or iPad, for example, will instantly sync any notes you add or modify on your MacBook Pro. You will always have access to your notes and media thanks to this.

9. **Collaboration and Sharing**

You can quickly share your notes with someone if you're working on a project with others or just want to. To share a note through email, messaging, or AirDrop, click the "**Share**" button in the upper right corner of the note. You can also create a link that can be shared so that other people may see or work on the note with you.

10. **Save and Secure your Notes**

Your MacBook Pro's Notes software automatically saves changes as you make them. However, you might think about turning on iCloud sync for Notes in your System Settings if you want to guarantee that your notes are backed up. Additionally, you can protect private notes by adding a password or authenticating with Touch ID.

Add Attachments to Notes

The ability to add attachments is one of the Notes app's most helpful features. Attaching pertinent items to your notes, whether it is a PDF file, a picture, or a file, may increase productivity and keep everything in one place.

The steps:

1. **Launch the Notes app**

Click the "**Notes**" icon on the dock of your MacBook Pro to begin, or use Spotlight to search for "**Notes**" (type **Command + Space** and start typing "**Notes**").

2. **Create a new note or open an existing note**

The "**New Note**" button, which is shaped like a pencil inside of a square, is located in the top-left corner of the Notes app. You can either click it to make a new note or double-click it to access an existing note.

3. **Select the body of the note**

Open a note and click anywhere in the body of the note to make sure the cursor is active and flashing. You should put your attachment here.

4. **Attach a File**

There are several methods for adding a file to your note:

Method 1: Drag and Drop

- Launch the Finder by clicking on the desktop or the dock's Finder icon.
- Find the document you want to attach.
- Click and hold the file and then drag it to the note's active note.
- Insert the message and the file. You'll see the file's name and a thumbnail of it.

Method 2: Use the Menu Bar

- In the Notes app's top menu bar, choose the "**Edit**" option.
- From the dropdown menu, choose "**Add Attachment**..."
- In the file selection box that displays, go to the file you want to attach.
- Select "**Choose File**" to add it as an attachment to your letter.

5. **View and Interact with Attachments**

You'll see the file's thumbnail and file name after it has been added to your message.

You can engage with an attachment in several ways depending on its type:

- **PDFs and Documents:** You can examine a PDF or document you've attached online by clicking on the attachment. This indicates that you may read the document's contents within the Notes app.

- **Images:** To see an image in a bigger size for attachments with images, click on the thumbnail. To examine and modify the picture in more detail, double-click it to open it in the Preview app.

6. **Save and Sync**

You don't have to be concerned about losing your connected files since the Notes app on your MacBook Pro automatically saves your modifications. Additionally, if you have iCloud enabled and are logged in with your Apple ID, your notes and attachments will sync across all of your Apple devices so you can view them from anywhere.

7. **Organize Your Notes**

It's crucial to keep your notes with attachments organized as you gather more of them. You may organize your notes into categories by creating folders and subfolders in the Notes app.

Take the following actions to create a folder:

- Select "**File**" from the top menu.
- From the dropdown menu, choose "**New Folder**".
- Choose your folder's name and location (on My Mac or in your iCloud account).

8. **Look for Attachments**

With its powerful search functionality, the Notes app makes it easy to find certain notes or attachments. Simply type terms about the file or note you're searching for in the search box located in the top-right corner of the app. Real-time relevant results will be shown via the app.

Browse Attachments in Notes

Attaching files can help you retain all your important information in one place, whether it's a PDF, picture, or text.

The steps:

1. To launch the Notes app, click on its icon in the Dock of your MacBook Pro. You can also discover it by using Spotlight (key **Command + Space** and type "**Notes**" to search for it).
2. When the Notes app is launched, the left sidebar displays all of your previously created notes. Select the message that has the attachment you want to see by clicking on it. By selecting the "**New Note**" button (a square with a pencil icon) in the top-left corner, you may create a note with attachments if you haven't already.
3. Depending on the kind of attachment, you can discover it inside the chosen note by looking for a little icon or thumbnail. Documents, pictures, and PDFs are common attachment types.
4. **Preview the Attachment**: Simply click the attachment once to receive a brief preview of it. For instance, if it's a picture, it will open in a preview window where you may move through different images that are linked to the note and zoom in and out. If the attachment is a PDF or document, your MacBook Pro's default reader will launch when you click on it.
5. **Open the Attachment:** By opening the attachment in the appropriate app, you can fully interact with it or make changes to it. If the attachment is a PDF, for instance, you may open it with any PDF viewer you have installed, such as Preview. Simply double-click an attachment to open it.
6. Use the left and right arrow icons that display when you hover your cursor over an attachment in the note to effortlessly browse through any multiple attachments that the note may have. When you have many photographs or documents attached and want to examine each one without leaving the letter, this is quite helpful.
7. **Save Changes:** After making any required adjustments to the attachment, remember to save your changes before quitting the program that opened the attachment. This makes sure that the message has the most recent copy of the attachment.
8. **Adding New Attachments**: The attachment icon in the note interface, which is often represented by a paperclip symbol, can be clicked to add new attachments to your note. This will launch a dialog box where you can choose the file you wish to connect from the storage on your MacBook Pro.

9. **Removing Attachments**: Attachments can be deleted from a note by clicking on them to select them and then using the "**Delete**" key on your keyboard. If asked, confirm the deletion. Keep in mind that removing an attachment from a note just deletes the reference to the attachment inside that note and does not erase the file from your MacBook Pro's storage.
10. **Syncing Across Devices**: Your notes and their attachments will sync across all of your devices if you use the same Apple ID and iCloud account on different ones. This implies that your notes and any attachments may be accessed easily from your MacBook Pro, iPhone, iPad, and other Apple devices.

Add Tables to Notes

The steps:

1. **Launch the Notes App**

Make sure your MacBook Pro is turned on and unlocked before anything else. Locate the "**Notes**" app on your dock or by entering "Notes" into Spotlight (by pressing **Command + Space**). To open the app, click the Notes icon.

2. **Create a New Note or Launch an Existing Note**

You can opt to start a new note or open an existing one once you're in the Notes app. Click the "**New Note**" button, which is often found in the upper left corner of the app, to start a new note. Simply click on the note's title in the list of notes if you want to add a table to an existing note.

3. **Inserting a Table**

It's time to add a table once you've opened a message.

This is how:

- Select "**Table**" from the menu.
- Select "**Insert Table**" from the dropdown menu that will show when you click "**Table**."
- **Adjust Table Dimensions**: A pop-up window letting you alter the table's proportions will appear. You can choose how many rows and columns to

have. Your table will be built on this, and you may always make changes afterward.
- **Insert Table**: After specifying the dimensions, just click "**Insert**." Your note now includes your table.

4. **Populating the Table**

Now that your note has a table, you can begin adding content to it:

- To navigate between cells, exactly as you would in a conventional spreadsheet, use the Tab key.
- **Text Formatting**: Just as in any other text document, the table cells' text may be formatted. Modify the font's sizes, colors, and styles as desired.
- **Adjusting Table Size:** Click on the table to expose little handles on the corners and edges. If you discover that your table needs extra rows or columns, just click on the table. To change the table's size, click and drag these handles.
- **Merge Cells (Optional):** You can combine cells to make your table's sections bigger. Right-click on the cells you want to combine, then choose "**Merge Cells**" from the context menu.
- **Adding Images and Attachments**: You can also insert photos and attachments into the table cells in the Notes app. Click within a cell, and then choose the "**Add Attachment**" button that appears to accomplish this.

5. **Save Your Changes**

The Notes app will automatically store any changes you make to your notes and table as you work on them. However, periodically manually saving your notes is usually a smart idea. To complete this, click the "**Done**" button in the note's upper-right corner. Once your changes have been saved, you can either close the note or keep editing.

6. **Sync Across Devices**

One advantage of using the Notes app on a MacBook Pro is that all of your Apple devices, including iPhones, iPads, and other Macs, will instantly sync with your notes. As a result, your notes are easily accessible and editable on any device that is connected to your Apple ID.

Add Checklists to Notes

The steps:

1. Locate the Notes app on your MacBook Pro and open it to get started. You can search for it in the Applications directory or Spotlight by hitting **Command + Space** and searching "**Notes**."
2. Create a new note or open an existing one in the Notes app once you're there if you want to add a checklist.
3. **Access the Formatting Toolbar**: A formatting toolbar with many options is located at the top of the note. The "**Show Markup Toolbar**" button may be used to display more formatting options.
4. **Turn on the Checklist Option**: You'll see a checkbox symbol among the formatting choices. To enable the checklist function for your note, click on this symbol.
5. **Begin Adding Items to the Checklist**: As soon as you enable the checklist function, a checkbox will appear at the start of each new line in your note. Enter the items or tasks you wish to include on your checklist in text form.
6. **Check and Uncheck Items:** To mark jobs as finished, all you need to do is click the checkboxes next to them. Click on the checkbox once more to uncheck an item if you need to.
7. **Formatting Your Checklist**: Just as with ordinary text, you can format the items on your checklist. The font, size, color, and alignment may all be changed in this manner. This might assist you in graphically categorizing activities or highlighting certain objects.
8. **Adding additional Items to Your Checklist:** After the last item on your checklist, hit "**Return**" to add additional items. You can add more tasks by clicking the checkbox that will immediately appear on a new line.
9. **Checklist Organization**: Within the Notes app, you can arrange your checklists by creating folders for various tasks or categories. This may keep your checklists and notes organized.
10. **Sync across Devices**: You'll be happy to hear that your checklists and notes will sync across all of your Apple devices that are connected to the same

Apple ID if you own additional Apple devices. By doing this, you may access your sorted information from anywhere.

11. **Easily change and Rearrange things**: You can quickly change and rearrange the things on your checklist. To reorder things or edit the wording, click and drag the relevant elements.
12. **Delete Items from Checklist:** To delete an item from your checklist after finishing it all, just highlight its text and hit the "**Delete**" key on your keyboard.
13. **Personalize Checklist Symbols**: By default, your checklist's checkboxes are blank. You may alter it to use a different symbol if you'd like. You can switch a checkbox between being empty, ticked, or dashed by right-clicking on it and choosing "**Change to...**"
14. **Print Your Checklist**: Print your checklist straight from the Notes app if you prefer a hard copy. To modify print options and print a physical copy of your checklist, pick "**File**" from the menu and then "**Print**."

Share your Notes

The steps:

1. First, launch the Notes app. Make sure your MacBook Pro is first logged into your iCloud account. This will allow your notes to sync seamlessly across all of your Apple devices. Using Spotlight search or the Dock launches the Notes app.
2. **Choose the Note to Share:** Select the note you want to share from your list of notes. To open it, click on it. The "**+**" button on the app's UI may be used to add a note if you haven't already.
3. **Select the "Share" option:** Share a note by clicking the share button, which is shown as a square with an upward-pointing arrow in the upper-right corner of the note window. This button must be clicked to start the sharing procedure.
4. **Select a Sharing Method**: A menu with numerous sharing options will be displayed. You have a variety of options, depending on your interests and the kind of content you're sharing:
   - **Message**: Clicking on this choice will launch the Messages application, enabling you to send the message to a specific contact or group of contacts in

your Messages. Before sending, you can choose the recipients and add a message.
- **Mail**: Send the message as an email attachment using this option. The message will be linked to a new email draft that opens in the Mail app. If necessary, enter the email address of the recipient, the topic, and the message before clicking send.
- **Add People:** This option is excellent for instantaneous note-taking collaboration. You can invite people to see and modify the message by choosing "**Add People**." An invitation will be sent using Mail or Messages. Participants may edit and contribute material to the note, and you can all see modifications as they happen.
- **AirDrop:** Use AirDrop to send the note to a nearby Apple device user who is also using AirDrop. You may wirelessly transmit the note to their smartphone using this capability. Just make sure Bluetooth and Wi-Fi are turned on both devices.
- **More Sharing Options**: Selecting this option will offer you extra sharing options, including the ability to share notes via third-party applications or by saving the note in a PDF or other appropriate format.

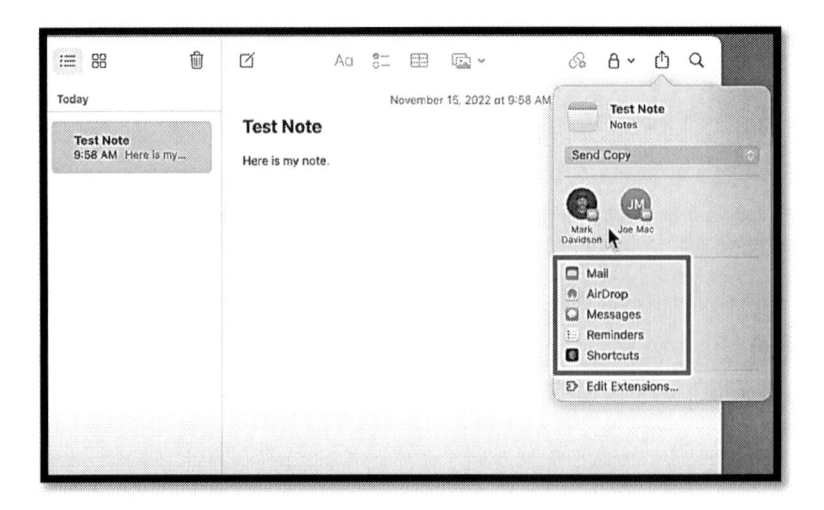

5. **Verify and Change Sharing Settings**: You may need to confirm recipients, modify the message, or specify sharing options depending on the sharing method you choose. You may provide collaborators the ability to read or

modify the note by setting permissions for them when using the "**Add People**" option.
6. **Share or Send:** Click "**Send**" or "**Share**" to start the sharing procedure after customizing the sharing options and adding any relevant details.
7. **Collaborate and Sync**: An invitation to view the note will be sent to collaborators if you have shared it with them using the "**Add People**" option. Once they agree, you may all edit the message at the same time, and any changes one person makes will be immediately reflected for everyone.

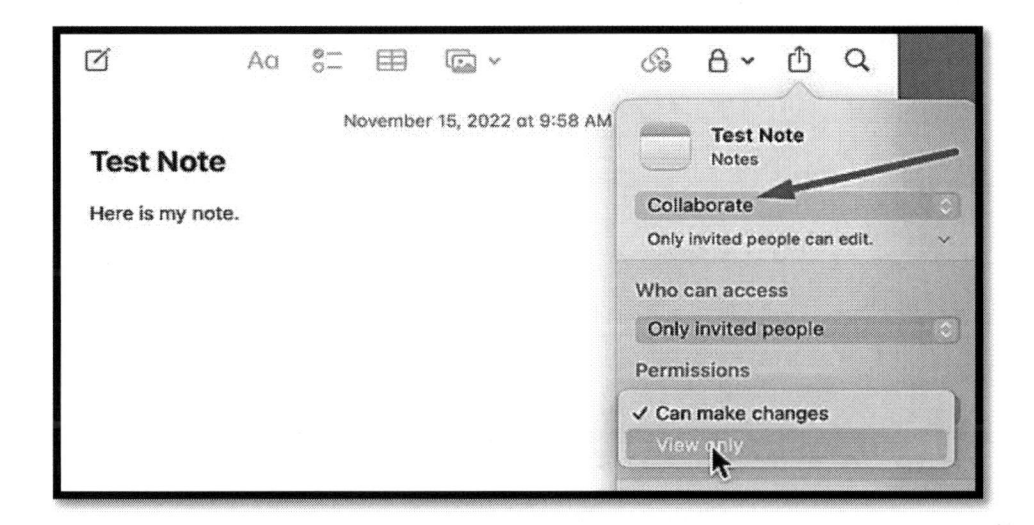

8. **Manage Sharing**: You can stop sharing the note at any time by going back to the note and clicking the share icon once more. From there, you may modify rights, delete colleagues, or control sharing settings.

Frequently Asked Questions

1. How do you arrange Notes with Folders?
2. How do you create and rename a folder?
3. How do you work with Notes?
4. How do you move, pin, and lock a Note?
5. How do you add media to Notes?
6. How do you share your Notes?
7. How do you add tables and checklists to Notes?

CHAPTER EIGHT
FACETIME

Overview

Keep in touch with friends, family, and coworkers has become essential thanks to FaceTime, Apple's exclusive video and voice calling tool. The new MacBook Pro's strength and beauty elevate the FaceTime experience to a whole new level.

How to Set Up FaceTime on a MacBook Pro

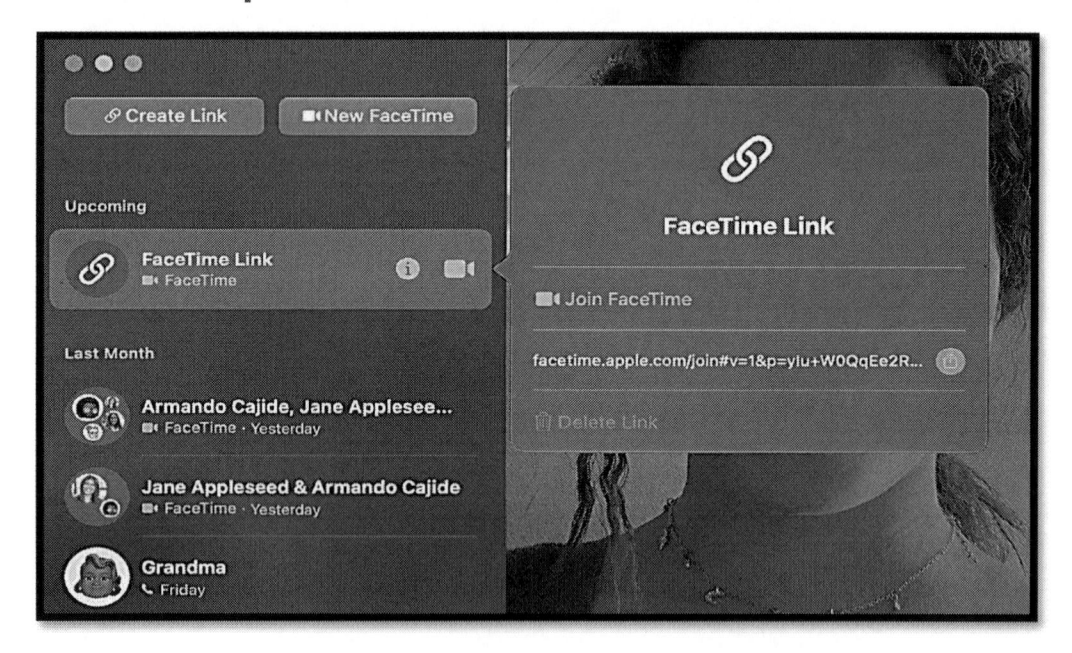

1. **Ensure your MacBook Pro is Ready**

Make sure your new MacBook Pro is fully configured and connected to the internet before you start configuring FaceTime. Keep your MacBook Pro up to date to guarantee you have the most recent FaceTime features and security enhancements by clicking on the Apple menu in the top-left corner of your screen, selecting **"System Settings,"** and then selecting **"Software Update."**

2. **Sign In with your Apple ID**

You must sign in with your Apple ID to use FaceTime on your MacBook Pro. If you don't already have an Apple ID, you can create one by going to the Apple ID website.

Once you have an Apple ID, sign in using these steps:

- Open "**FaceTime**" by clicking on the icon in your Dock or selecting it from the Applications directory.
- There will be a greeting screen. Simply choose "**Use your Apple ID for FaceTime**."
- After providing your Apple ID and password, choose **"Sign In."**

3. **Configure FaceTime Settings**

You should now set up your FaceTime settings to guarantee that your calls are customized to your preferences after signing in.

This is how:

- Click "**FaceTime**" in the top menu bar of the FaceTime app and choose "**Preferences**."

- Configure your caller ID in the Preferences box. When you call someone, they will see this phone number or email address. You have the option of using your Apple ID email address as your caller ID or adding another email address.

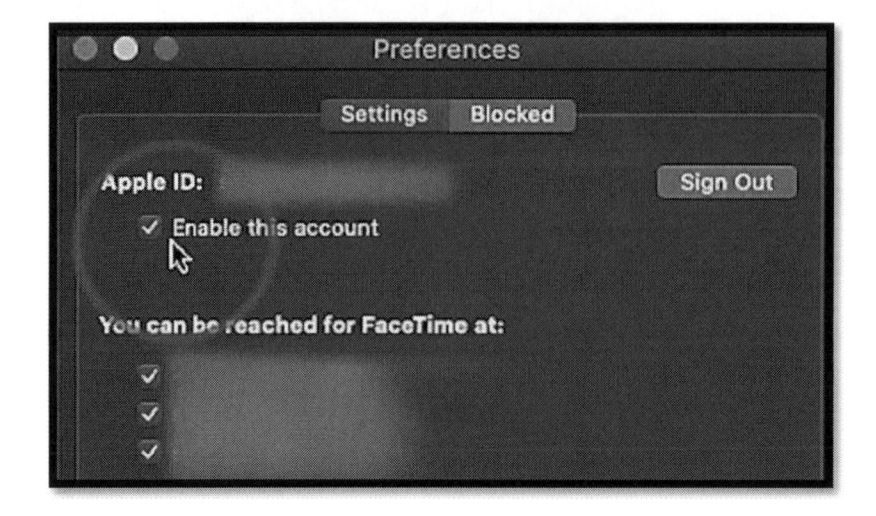

- Decide whether to enable FaceTime to make calls using your mobile data. You can decide to deactivate this option if you have a restricted data plan.

4. **Add Contacts to FaceTime**

You must add contacts to your FaceTime list before you can begin making FaceTime calls. This list includes individuals who have their Apple IDs set up and use FaceTime.

To add contacts, adhere to the following steps:

- Launch the **FaceTime** app.
- In the top-right corner of the app window, click the **"+"** symbol.
- Add someone to FaceTime by entering their name, phone number, or email address.
- To invite someone to join your FaceTime contacts, click "**Add**".

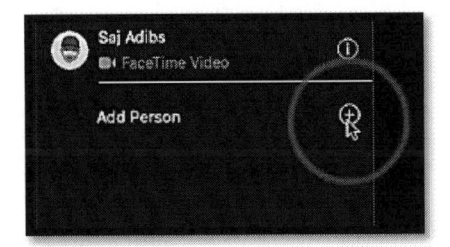

5. **Make Your First FaceTime Call**

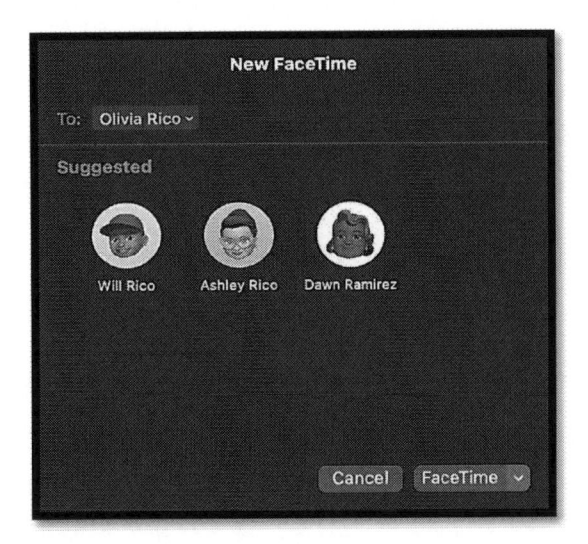

145

It's time to make your first FaceTime call now that everything is set up:

- Launch the **FaceTime app**.
- Enter the name, email address, or phone number of the person you want to call in the **"Search"** field.

- When the contact's name shows in the search results, click on it.
- To start a video call, click the camera symbol, and to start an audio call, click the phone icon.

6. **Managing FaceTime Calls**

You can improve your FaceTime call by choosing from many options:

- Mute your microphone by clicking the microphone.
- By pressing the camera icon, you can switch between the front and back cameras.
- Use the volume controls on your MacBook Pro or the call window to change the call volume.
- Simply click the red phone symbol to stop the call.

Make a FaceTime Audio Call

The steps:

1. **Set up FaceTime**

Make sure FaceTime is configured correctly on your MacBook Pro before you begin making audio calls.

If you haven't already, do these easy steps:

- Open "**FaceTime**" by clicking on the icon on your dock or selecting it from the Applications directory.
- You'll need to create an Apple ID if you don't already have one to use FaceTime, so do so when asked.
- Choose how you want to be contacted on FaceTime after you've logged up. This is crucial because your contacts will use your phone number or email address connected with your Apple ID to contact you.

2. **Make a FaceTime Audio Call**

Making a FaceTime audio call is relatively simple once FaceTime is set up:

- Open the "**FaceTime**" app from the Applications folder or your dock.
- Enter the name, email address, or phone number of the person you want to contact in the search box at the top of the FaceTime window. As you write, FaceTime will automatically search your contacts.
- Click on the name of the individual once you find it in the search results to choose it.
- Click the "**Audio**" button to start a FaceTime audio call. You now have two options: "**Video**" and "**Audio**."

3. **During the Call**

Once the phone has been answered, you will be engaged in a crystal-clear audio chat. You have access to various helpful features while on the call:

- **Mute/Unmute**: Mute your audio by clicking the microphone icon if you need to be silent for a short period. When you are ready to talk, click it one again to unmute.
- **Speaker/Headphones**: Choose between using the built-in speakers on your MacBook Pro and an external audio source, like headphones. This may come in particularly helpful if you're in a loud setting.
- **End Call:** Simply click the red phone symbol with an "**X**" in the middle to end the call. The FaceTime audio call will cease at this point.

- **Volume Control**: Using the volume keys on your MacBook Pro or the slider in the FaceTime call window, you can change the call volume.
- **Add Call:** By selecting the "**Add Call**" option, you can add a second caller. As you dial the new number, your existing call will be placed on hold. You may combine the calls into a conference after they have responded.
- **Change from Audio to Video**: Change from an audio call to a video call at any time by selecting the "**Video**" option while on the call.

4. **Ending the Call**

Simply click the red phone symbol with the "**X**" in the middle to stop the call when you're ready. By doing so, you'll end the FaceTime audio call and return to the FaceTime app window.

Make a FaceTime Call via Messages App

Here are the steps:

1. Open the Messages app on your MacBook Pro. The Applications folder, the dock, or Spotlight search (by pressing **Command + Space** and entering "**Messages**") can all be used to locate it.
2. If you haven't already done so, the Messages app may ask you to sign in when you begin it. Sign in to Your Apple ID before you can conduct FaceTime audio calls using Messages; you must make sure that you are logged in with your Apple ID. If not, sign in using your Apple ID by navigating to **Messages > Preferences > iMessage**.
3. After logging in, the Messages app's left side will display your list of contacts. It is simple to call individuals you usually connect with since this list is linked with your contacts from your other Apple devices.
4. Click on the contact's name in the list to choose them for a FaceTime audio call. The discussion window for that contact will now be accessible.
5. Start an audio or video call by selecting the icons in the discussion window's upper right corner. Click on the symbol for audio calls, which resembles a phone, to start a FaceTime audio call. The audio call on FaceTime to the chosen person will begin right away.

6. After you place the call, the other party will hear a notice and ringing sound. They will be given the choice of accepting or rejecting the call. You'll be able to speak with them clearly through audio after they accept.
7. You have many controls available to you while in the conversation. The name of the caller, a microphone mute button, and a hang-up button are all shown in the call window. Using your MacBook Pro's volume settings, you may also change the call volume.
8. When you're done talking, just hit the red "**Hang Up**" button to put the call to a stop. You will return to the chat window in Messages once the call window closes.

Additional Tips

1. **Notifications**: If a FaceTime audio call comes in while you're not actively using the Messages app, you'll get a notice in the upper right corner of your screen. Without opening the Messages app, you may answer the call by clicking "**Accept**" on this notice.
2. **Recent Calls**: If you've recently made or received a FaceTime audio call, you can discover it in the Messages app's recent calls area. It is now simple to phone back somebody you've just talked to.
3. **Group FaceTime**: FaceTime group calls are also supported through the Messages app. By opening a group chat and selecting the audio call icon, you may start a group call.
4. **Call Quality**: FaceTime audio calls have a reputation for having excellent sound. However, depending on the speed of your internet connection and the intensity of your Wi-Fi signal, the call quality may change.

Start a Group FaceTime Call

The steps:

1. **Open the FaceTime App**

Make sure you're signed into your MacBook Pro before you start, then look for the FaceTime app. The Applications folder is usually where you can locate it, or you can just use Spotlight by hitting **Command + Space** and entering "**FaceTime**."

2. **Sign In and Grant Permissions**

If you're using FaceTime for the first time on your MacBook Pro, you'll need to sign in with your Apple ID and provide access to your camera and microphone, which are required for both video and voice conversation.

3. **Select the "+" button**

You will see a **"+"** symbol in the upper-right corner of the window once you're in the FaceTime app. To start a new call, click this symbol.

4. **Add Contacts**

A panel will show up on the right side of the FaceTime window after hitting the **"+"** symbol. Enter the name or phone number of the first person you wish to add to the group call in the **"Add Person"** area. FaceTime will offer related people from your address list as you enter. To include the contact in the call, click on their name.

5. **Add More Contacts (Optional)**

Simply click on the "**Add Person**" option once again and keep entering the names or phone numbers of the individuals you want to invite. Continue doing this until you've added everyone you want to the group FaceTime session.

6. **Customize the Call (Optional)**

You have the option to modify the call before you place it. You have the option of starting the call with video enabled or not. Additionally, you may decide whether to use FaceTime features like Animoji or Memoji while in the conversation.

7. **Start the Call**

Depending on whether you want to start an audio-only or video call, click the **"Audio"** or **"Video"** option after you are happy with the participants and settings. Following then, FaceTime will begin calling the participants and establishing the connection.

8. **Manage the Call**

You have several choices for controlling the discourse during the call. By clicking on the respective icons, you may turn off your camera and mute your microphone. You may also choose between several views layouts while on a video conference in order to zoom in on the speaker or watch everyone in a grid.

9. **End the Call**

Simply click the red "**End**" button at the bottom of the FaceTime window when you're ready to stop the conversation. By doing this, you will end the call and dismiss the FaceTime window.

Tips for a Smooth Group FaceTime Experience

1. **Stable Internet Connection**: For a seamless group FaceTime chat, you'll need a reliable, fast internet connection. Ensure that the Wi-Fi network you are using is reputable.
2. **Device Orientation**: If you're using a MacBook Pro, be sure that it is oriented such that it catches your face clearly and reduces background noise.
3. **Lighting and Background**: For crystal-clear video quality, your face has to be lighted well. Pick a well-lit setting, and think about a plain, unobtrusive backdrop.
4. **Notifications and Disturbances**: Setting your MacBook Pro to "**Do Not Disturb**" mode before the call-in order to avoid incoming alerts from interfering with it is a smart idea.
5. **Test Call**: Make a test call to a friend or member of your family if you're new to FaceTime or using a new device to make sure your camera, microphone, and internet connection are all functional.

Answer/Decline a FaceTime Call

Answering a FaceTime call

Your MacBook Pro will notify you when a FaceTime call is received.

The steps:

1. Look in the top-right corner of your screen, in the notice Center, for the notice of an incoming call. Along with the "**Accept**" and "**Decline**" buttons, it will also show the caller's name or phone number.
2. **Accept the Call:** Press the "**Accept**" button to accept the call. By doing so, you will be immediately connected to the caller's video stream and be able to start conversing.
3. Once the connection is established, you can change many options, including the audio input and output devices, the camera settings, and more. The FaceTime call interface's control panel provides access to these choices.
4. **End the Call:** To end the call, click the red "**X**" button in the call window's top left corner. The "**End Call**" button in the call interface is another option.

Declining a FaceTime Call

You can sometimes be unable to respond to a FaceTime call.

The steps:

1. **Notification Center:** The top-right corner of your screen will display a notice for an incoming call, much as when you answer a call.
2. **Decline the Call:** Select the "**Decline**" button to end the call. This will let the caller know that you are now unable to answer.
3. **Options**: If you choose not to answer the call, you will be given other options, such as sending a brief message informing the caller of your decision. You can choose from pre-written messages like "**Can't talk right now**" or "**Call you later.**"
4. **Send Message (Optional):** Select the message icon next to the refuse button if you want to send a message. The message you choose to send will be sent automatically to the caller.
5. **Quiet alerts:** You can activate "**Do Not Disturb**" mode if you don't want to be disturbed by alerts when in a certain circumstance. Toggle the "**Do Not Disturb**" option by selecting the Notification Center icon in the top-right corner of the screen. When you're ready to start receiving alerts again, remember to shut it off.

Additional Tips

1. **Change Notification Settings:** You can change how FaceTime call notifications are displayed. Find the FaceTime app in the list of notifications by going to **"System Settings" > "Notifications"**. You can change the notification banners, audio, and other settings from here.
2. **Use Siri:** Use Siri to accept or reject FaceTime calls if you'd rather go hands-free. Just say "**Hey Siri, answer the FaceTime call**" or "**Hey Siri, decline the FaceTime call**."
3. **Enable/Disable Camera**: Turn off your camera before answering a FaceTime call if you'd rather not instantly turn on your camera. If you're not ready to appear on camera at that particular time, this might be useful.

Add another Participant to a Group FaceTime Call

Method 1: Start a Group FaceTime Call

1. Make sure you have a reliable internet connection before you do anything else. For effective conversation during group FaceTime sessions, a strong internet connection is necessary.
2. On your MacBook Pro, launch the FaceTime app. It can be found in the Applications folder or by using Spotlight (press **Command + Space** and enter "**FaceTime**" to search for it).
3. Click the "**+**" button in the top-right corner of the FaceTime app.

Method 2: Add Participants to the Call

1. Your existing contacts will appear in a new window that appears. The search box is located at the top of the window, where you can input the name, email address, or phone number of the person you wish to add.
2. FaceTime will offer related people from your address list as you enter. When you see the name of the contact in the list of recommendations, click on it.
3. Manually input the email address or phone number of the person you want to add if it's not already in your address book in the search field.
4. After choosing the contact, choose them by clicking the "**Add**" option next to their name. They will be added to the list of attendees for the Group FaceTime call as a result.

Method 3: Confirm the Addition

1. After selecting "**Add**," a message inviting the contact to the Group FaceTime call will be delivered to them. A notification stating that an invitation has been issued will appear on your screen.
2. You can easily add more participants by carrying out the same procedure for each additional person you want to include in the call.

Method 4: Managing Participants

1. Participants' video feeds will show up on your screen once they accept the invitation and join the session. Everyone on the call will be visible to you at once, and you may communicate with them.
2. Resize, rearrange or arrange each participant's thumbnail window in any way you want. To move a participant's thumbnail across the screen, simply click and drag.
3. Click the microphone symbol next to a participant's name to mute or unmute them. This is helpful when you want to reduce background noise while on the phone.
4. Similarly, by clicking the camera symbol next to a participant's name, you may start or stop filming for that specific person. If someone has to move away from the camera for a moment, this is useful.
5. Click the red "**End**" button at the bottom of the window to stop the call for everyone.

Share Your Screen on FaceTime

The steps:

1. **Start a FaceTime Call**

You must start a FaceTime call with the person you want to connect with before you can start sharing your screen. Select the person you want to call from your contacts list by opening the FaceTime app on your MacBook Pro. To begin the call, click the video call button after clicking the other person's name or phone number.

2. **Enable Screen Sharing**

A set of controls can be found at the bottom of the call window after your FaceTime call has begun. The screen-sharing icon may be found among these controls. It seems to be two rectangles that are overlapping. To allow screen sharing, click this symbol.

3. **Select What to Share**

When you click the screen sharing button, a new window will open with sharing choices for you to choose from. You have the option of sharing your full screen, a particular program window, or even just a fraction of it. Depending on your demands, choose the best solution. You must provide the FaceTime app with the required rights to share a particular app window or section of your screen.

4. **Start Sharing**

Click the "**Start Sharing**" button after you've decided what to share. The individual with whom you are on the call will now be able to see the content you have chosen. On the shared screen, they will be able to view anything you do in real-time.

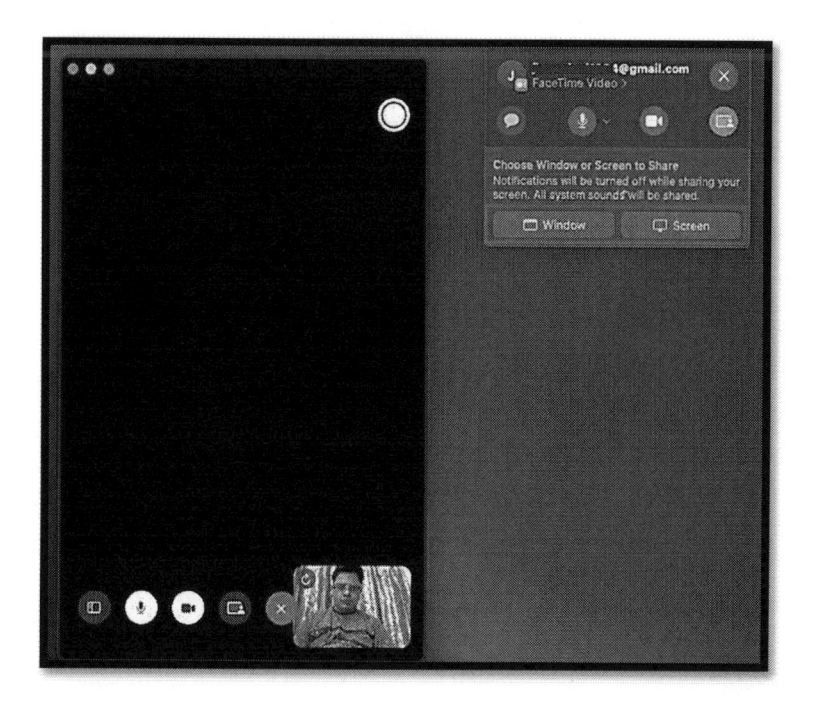

5. **Interact and Communicate**

You can carry on your FaceTime call as normal while sharing your screen. Your face will be shown in a smaller window, along with the information you're sharing with your discussion partner. This is your chance to explain what you're displaying, draw attention to important details, or walk the audience through certain actions on your screen.

6. **Stop Screen Sharing**

Simply click the "**Stop Sharing**" button in the screen sharing box when you're ready to stop sharing your screen. You can alternatively click the screen-sharing icon in the call window once again and choose "**Stop Screen Sharing**" as an alternative. By doing this, the connection will return to a standard FaceTime video call.

Tips for Successful Screen Sharing

1. **Clear Communication**: Be careful to explain your activities properly while sharing your screen. Describe the information you are displaying to your discussion partner in your own words.
2. **Reduce Distractions**: Close any superfluous programs or tabs that you don't want your discussion partner to view before you begin screen-sharing. This will assist in maintaining attention to the topic you are presenting.
3. **Prepare in Advance**: Before starting the call, have the app or presentation open and prepared if you want to share it. You won't have to fumble about throughout the call thanks to this.
4. **Test Ahead of Time**: If this is your first time using screen sharing, you may want to give it a try with a friend or relative before a crucial call. This will guarantee that everything goes according to plan and help you get comfortable with the procedure.
5. **Respect Privacy:** Always keep in mind that you are using someone else's screen while you respect privacy. Share only information that you would want others to view, such as private or sensitive information.

Activate & Use Screen Sharing

Using FaceTime's Screen Sharing feature:

1. **Ensure Current Software**: Before you start, check that the FaceTime app and operating system on your MacBook Pro are current. You will get access to the most recent features and advancements thanks to this.
2. **Check FaceTime Settings**: Open the FaceTime application on your MacBook Pro to check the FaceTime settings. Click "**FaceTime**" in the menu bar at the top of the screen and choose **"Preferences."** Make sure the "**Enable screen sharing between you and another FaceTime user**" checkbox is selected in the Preferences window. The Preferences window must be closed.
3. **Sign In to FaceTime:** Use your Apple ID to check in if you aren't already. This ID will be used by FaceTime to recognize you and make calls and screen-sharing sessions possible.

Using FaceTime's Screen Sharing feature

1. **Making a FaceTime Call**: Open the FaceTime app first. You can accomplish this by clicking the FaceTime icon in your dock or by using Spotlight (press **Cmd + Space** and then type "**FaceTime**" to search for it).
2. **Choose a Contact:** A list of your contacts will be shown in the FaceTime app. To start a FaceTime call, choose the person you wish to contact and click on their name.
3. **Launching Screen Sharing:** After the call is established, the person you are speaking to will appear in a video window. Place your pointer over the FaceTime window to begin screen sharing. Several icons will start to show up on the screen. The screen-sharing symbol resembles two overlapping rectangles.
4. **Select the Icon for Screen Sharing**: The screen sharing icon should be clicked to reveal a drop-down option. You have two options here:
- **Ask to Share Screen:** This choice will ask the other person whether you may share your screen with them.
- **Share Screen**: If the other person has already shared their screen with you, you may do the same by selecting this option.

5. **Asking for Screen Sharing**: If you choose "**Ask to Share Screen,**" the other person will get a notice asking for their consent to share their screen. They have the option of approving or rejecting your request.
6. **Sharing Your Screen**: If the other party has given their consent, their screen will appear on your screen in a different window. This capability is perfect for troubleshooting, group projects, and presentations since you can interact on their screen as if it were your own.
7. **Ending Screen Sharing**: Place your cursor at the very top of the window that is now being shared. When a menu appears, choose "**Stop Sharing**" from the options. As an alternative, you can choose "**Stop Sharing**" by clicking the screen-sharing button in the FaceTime call window.

Change Shared Window in FaceTime

Here are the steps:

1. **Starting a FaceTime call**

You must start a FaceTime call before you can begin sharing your screen. Follow these steps to do this:

- Launch the FaceTime app from the Applications folder on your MacBook Pro or by putting "**FaceTime**" into Spotlight Search (**Command + Space**).
- To begin a new call, click the "**+**" button in the top-right corner.
- Type in the person's name, email address, or phone number, and then click the video camera button to begin the call.

2. **Activating Screen Sharing**

Screen sharing is available once you are on a FaceTime call. Take these actions:

- To access the call controls while on a call, move your mouse cursor over the FaceTime window.
- Look for the green "**Share Screen**" button with a rectangular symbol and click it.

- A menu will show up with choices for what you can share. If you're using a web browser, you can decide whether to share the full screen, a particular application window, or a particular tab.
- Select the one that best meets your requirements.

3. **Change the Shared Window**

Let's look at how to modify the shared window now that you've enabled screen sharing and chosen what you want to share:

- Your FaceTime call will continue in a smaller window while your screen is being shared.
- To switch the shared window, just go to the app or window you want to share in its place.
- To bring a window to the front of your display, click on it. FaceTime's shared window will instantly be updated to show the information from the recently chosen window.

4. **Adjusting Shared Window Settings**

Customize the shared window in FaceTime using a few parameters to suit your needs:

- To access the screen-sharing controls when screen sharing, move the mouse cursor to the top of the screen.
- To access the shared window's options, click the "**Options**" button (depicted by three dots).
- Choose whether to highlight clicks performed throughout the session and whether to display or hide your mouse pointer from the settings menu.

Share Sharing Screen in FaceTime

The steps:

1. **Make Sure You're Running macOS Ventura**

Make sure your new MacBook Pro is running a suitable macOS version (macOS Ventura) before you start screen sharing on FaceTime. Click the Apple logo in the top-left corner of your screen, choose "**About This Mac**," and the version information will appear.

2. **Start a FaceTime Call**

Open the FaceTime app on your MacBook Pro to begin. You can do this by using Spotlight to search for it or by looking in your Applications folder. Once the app is launched, choose a person from your contact list or use the search box to locate someone to start a FaceTime conversation with.

3. **Begin the Video Call**

To initiate a video call with a contact you've chosen, click the video call button (camera symbol). Watch for the caller on the other end to pick up.

4. **Access the FaceTime Controls**

When your call is connected, the FaceTime call window will appear. There are many controls, such as buttons to mute your microphone and turn off your camera, at the bottom of this window. The button with two overlapping rectangles is the one we're interested in for screen sharing; this is the button.

5. **Share Your Screen**

Two overlapping rectangles that say "**Share Screen**" when clicked bring up a menu with the choices "**Your Entire Screen**" and "**A Window.**" According to what you wish to share, choose the relevant choice. Your discussion partner will be able to view all that is visible on your MacBook Pro screen if you choose "Your Entire Screen." You can pick a particular program window to share by selecting "**A Window**."

6. **Confirm Screen Sharing**

After making your decision, pick "**Start Sharing**" from the menu. FaceTime will request your consent before taking a screenshot. In the permission window, choose "**Start Recording**". At this point, the information you've decided to share will be visible to your chat partner.

7. **Interact and Collaborate**

Communicate and work together in real-time now that your screen is being shared. Your discussion partner will be able to see your movements while you surf the web, view files, or use your programs. This is very helpful when giving presentations, solving problems, or directing someone through a procedure.

8. **End Screen Sharing**

Move your pointer to the top of the screen to show the FaceTime controls when you're ready to end the screen-sharing session. A red button with the word "**Stop Sharing**" will be shown. To stop the screen-sharing session, click this button. You can also instantly halt screen sharing by using the "**Option + S**" keyboard shortcut.

9. **Continue your Call**

You can carry on your FaceTime call normally after you've finished sharing your screen. With the extra advantage of sharing visual information, you may converse, trade ideas, or just enjoy the discussion.

10. **End the FaceTime Call**

Click the **red phone button** to stop your FaceTime call when you're ready to do so. You've mastered the steps necessary to use your new MacBook Pro to share your screen through FaceTime.

Frequently Asked Questions

1. How do you set up Face Time on your new MacBook Pro?
2. How do you make a FaceTime audio and video call?
3. How do you start a group FaceTime call?
4. How do you share your screen on FaceTime?
5. How do you answer or decline a FaceTime call?

CHAPTER NINE
UNIVERSAL CONTROL AND CONTINUITY CAMERA

Overview

Chapter nine discusses universal control and continuity cameras. In this chapter, you will learn how to set up and use universal control, how to use the continuity camera, how to scan a document using the continuity camera, and so much more.

How to set up & Use Universal Control in MacBook Pro

With Universal Control, you can easily drag and drop data across devices as if they were one, integrated system.

Setting up Universal Control

Make sure your equipment complies with the Universal Control compatibility standards before you start. A MacBook Pro running macOS Ventura, an iPad running iPadOS 15 or later, and an additional Mac that satisfies the macOS Ventura requirements are required. Check to see whether all of your devices are signed in with the same Apple ID and are connected to the same Wi-Fi network.

How to set up Universal Control

1. Make sure your devices are updated to the most recent versions of the supported operating systems, namely macOS Monterey or later and iPadOS 15 or later, for your MacBook Pro, iPad, and other Macs.
2. Make that all devices are connected to the same Wi-Fi network by checking the Wi-Fi connection. A reliable network connection is necessary for Universal Control to operate without interruption.
3. **Turn on Bluetooth and Wi-Fi:** Make sure Bluetooth and Wi-Fi are switched on in all of your devices.
4. Enable Handoff by selecting **"Allow Handoff between this Mac and your iCloud devices"** in **"System Settings"** > **"General"** on your MacBook Pro.
5. **Sign in to iCloud**: Use the same iCloud account to log in across all devices. iCloud is used by Universal Control for device connectivity.

6. Turn on continuity by selecting "**System Settings**" > "**General**" on your MacBook Pro and making sure "**Allow Handoff between this Mac and your iCloud devices**" is checked.

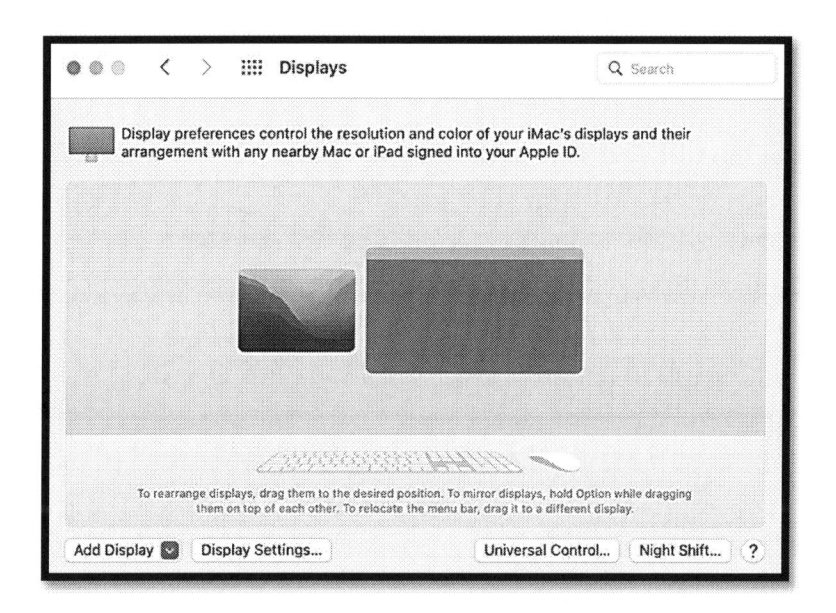

7. **Authorize device access**: You can be asked to provide permission to access other devices on each device. Give the necessary permissions by following the instructions.

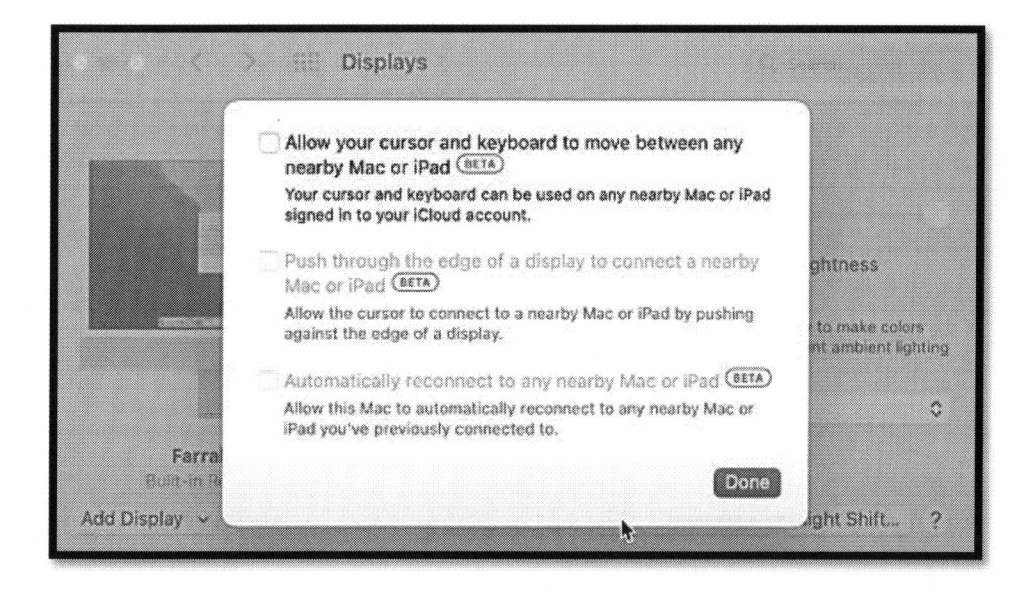

Using Universal Control

Using Universal Control is fairly simple after you've set it up. This is how:

1. **Position devices:** Set up your iPad, MacBook Pro, and additional Mac (if applicable) close to one another. Make sure the displays of your devices are facing one another and are visible.
2. **Move the cursor:** The pointer can be moved by smoothly gliding it from one device's screen to the opposite one by moving it to the edge of the first screen. The next device will be seamlessly selected with your pointer.
3. **Drag & drop**: Easily move files, text, photos, and more across devices by dragging them there. For instance, to add a picture from your iPad to a project you are working on on your MacBook Pro, just drag the image over to the document and put it there.
4. **Keyboard Input:** Type on the linked iPad or another Mac using the keyboard from your MacBook Pro. The target device's input field will automatically switch to your MacBook Pro's keyboard when you click it.
5. **Multi-touch Gestures:** Universal Control is compatible with multi-touch gestures. Like a single system, you can use motions like pinch-to-zoom, two-finger scrolling, and others on all of your devices.
6. **Access Dock and Menu Bar:** On your connected devices, you can also reach the Dock by dragging your mouse to the bottom of the display. Moving your pointer to the top of the screen will also give you access to the Menu Bar.

Adjust/Turn off Universal Control

Apple launched a feature called Universal Control that makes interacting across devices simple. You can drag and drop files across devices with Universal Control and move your cursor fluidly between your MacBook Pro, iPad, and other adjacent Macs. This function connects through Bluetooth and Wi-Fi, making it a useful tool for multitasking and increasing productivity.

Changing the settings on a universal control

Follow these instructions to change Universal Control's settings on your new MacBook Pro if you discover that it isn't functioning as you would want it to or if you

Just want to personalize its behavior:

1. To reach the **Apple menu**, click on the Apple logo in the top-left corner of your screen.
2. From the dropdown menu, choose "**System Settings**".
3. Find "**Displays**" in the System Settings box and click it.
4. Go to the "**Arrangement**" tab in the Displays options.
5. Your linked devices will be represented visually. The displays may be moved around and positioned here to suit your tastes. The operation of Universal Control is impacted by this configuration.
6. As long as the "**Show displays in menu bar**" option is selected, you can activate or disable Universal Control for a given device.
7. Once you're happy with your edits, close the System Settings window.

Disabling Universal Control

Even though Universal Control is a powerful tool, there may be instances when you wish to momentarily disable it. **To remove Universal Control from your MacBook Pro, follow these steps:**

1. In the menu bar at the top of your screen, choose the Universal Control symbol. This symbol resembles a little display with a left-side cursor arrow.
2. You can view a list of nearby devices that are presently linked through Universal Control in the drop-down menu that displays.
3. Simply click on the name of the device you want to disconnect from Universal Control to deactivate it. It will no longer be possible to share files or use a cursor on that device.
4. Click on the same device's name once again in the menu to re-enable Universal Control. Use Universal Control as usual as the connection is re-established.

Fixing Universal Control Problems

If you have any problems using Universal Control, such as difficulties connecting devices or sluggish cursor movement, think about trying the following troubleshooting techniques:

1. **Check Connectivity:** Ensure that Bluetooth is turned on and that all devices are logged into the same Wi-Fi network.

The efficient operation of Universal Control depends on a strong connection.
2. **Device Restarts**: Restarting your MacBook Pro and the other affected devices will sometimes fix connection problems.
3. **Update Software**: Make sure your MacBook Pro, iPad, and other devices are running the most recent software upgrades by updating them. Compatibility issues may occasionally be caused by outdated software.
4. **Toggle Bluetooth and Wi-Fi**: To reset the connections, try turning off Bluetooth and Wi-Fi on all of your devices, and then turning them back on.
5. **Reset SMC and NVRAM:** Resetting the System Management Controller (SMC) and non-volatile random-access memory (NVRAM) on your MacBook Pro may sometimes be able to assist you in fixing hardware-related problems.

How to Use the Continuity Camera

What is a Continuity Camera?

Apple's Continuity suite includes a feature called Continuity Camera. You can use your iPhone or iPad as a live camera feed for your MacBook Pro thanks to this feature. When you need to rapidly capture papers, photographs, or even QR codes and have them immediately accessible on your MacBook without having to go through emailing or other file-sharing processes, this capability is quite helpful.

Requirements

Here are the following requirements:

1. A MacBook Pro model from 2016 or later running macOS High Sierra or a later version. You have no problems using the MacBook Pro 2023 since it is running the most recent version of macOS Ventura.
2. iOS 12 or later must be installed on an iPhone, iPad, or iPod touch. The devices also need to be logged into the same iCloud account and connected to the same Wi-Fi network.
3. On both devices, Bluetooth and Wi-Fi must be turned on.

Using Continuity Camera

1. **Getting Started**: Verify that your iOS device and MacBook Pro are both logged into the same iCloud account and are connected to the same Wi-Fi network. Make sure both devices have Bluetooth switched on as well.
2. Opening an app that allows picture insertion, like Pages, Keynote, or Notes, will allow you to use the feature. To insert a picture or document, right-click (or control-click) on the document you wish to use.
3. To turn on the continuity camera, choose **"Insert from iPhone or iPad"** from the context menu that opens. There will be a submenu that appears with the options **"Take Photo," "Scan Documents,"** and **"Insert from iOS Device."**

4. **Taking Pictures:** From the submenu, choose **"Take Photo"** to launch the camera on your iOS device. The camera app for your iOS smartphone will launch and let you set up your shot. As soon as you capture the picture, your MacBook Pro will instantly add it to the document.
5. **Document Scanning**: From the submenu, choose **"Scan Documents"** to begin document scanning. The camera app on your iOS device will open with a live preview. Your iOS device will automatically recognize the edges and capture the document if you position it within the frame. The document will be added to your MacBook Pro document after scanning.
6. **Inserting Existing Photos**: Choose **"Insert from iOS Device"** from the submenu to insert a picture from your iOS device's photo library. The most recent pictures on your smartphone will appear in a new window. Your MacBook Pro document will now include the image you choose to include.
7. **QR Code Scanning:** The capacity to read QR codes right from your MacBook Pro is another useful function. You can put a QR code into a document by right-clicking it, selecting **"Insert from iPhone or iPad,"** and then choosing **"Scan QR Code"** from the submenu. The camera on your iOS smartphone will launch, and if it spots a QR code, it will instantly add the relevant data to your MacBook Pro document.

Take an Image with a Continuity Camera

1. **Ensure Compatibility**

Make sure your equipment is suitable before you start. Your iPhone or iPad must be running iOS 12 or later, and your MacBook Pro must be running macOS High Sierra (10.13) or a more recent version like the macOS Ventura. Additionally, confirm that both devices are logged in with the same Apple ID and are connected to the same Wi-Fi network.

2. **Prepare your Devices**

Open the app on your MacBook Pro where you wish to put the picture. This may be a Mail message, a Pages document, a Keynote presentation, or any other compatible software. Unlock your iPhone or iPad and make sure it is awake. Place the object so that the viewfinder of the camera is aimed towards the object you wish to photograph.

3. **Access the Continuity Camera**

On your MacBook Pro, choose "**Edit**" from the application's menu. Alternatively, you can right-click (Ctrl-click) on the document and choose "**Import from iPhone or iPad**," then pick "**Take Photo**" from the dropdown menu.

4. **Take a Picture**

The live camera feed from your iPhone or iPad will appear in a little window that appears on the screen of your MacBook Pro. You can see precisely what your device's camera is viewing thanks to this feed, which also serves as a viewfinder. On your iPhone or iPad, change the focus and position to compose your photo. Click your MacBook Pro's on-screen shutter button once you are happy with the composition. The camera on your smartphone will start taking pictures once you issue this command.

5. **Review and Insert**

A thumbnail preview of the photo will show up on your MacBook Pro's screen once it has been taken. You can examine the photo and decide on its use. When you are happy, press the "**Use Photo**" button. Click "**Retake**" to take another picture if you're not happy with the first one.

6. **Inserting the Image**

The picture you've selected will be automatically added to the cursor's position in your document, presentation, or email. Like every other element in the program, you may resize, move, or otherwise alter the picture.

7. **Additional Options**

Beyond only taking pictures, the Continuity Camera function also gives users other possibilities. Instead of selecting "**Take Photo**" when entering the Continuity Camera menu, you can choose "**Scan Documents**" to scan paper documents or receipts and import the scanned image into a MacBook Pro application.

Take a Picture in Finder

The steps:

1. Make sure your MacBook Pro and iOS device satisfy the requirements listed above before preparing your devices. Ensure that the Wi-Fi network is the same and that both devices are turned on.
2. Check sure Bluetooth is turned on in your MacBook Pro before you activate it. Make sure the Bluetooth switch is switched on by clicking on the Apple logo in the top-left corner of the screen, choosing "**System Settings**," and then "**Bluetooth**."
3. **Access the Finder:** On your MacBook Pro, click the blue and white smiling face icon in the Dock or press **Command + N** to launch a Finder window.
4. Choose the spot in the Finder where you wish to put the photo by right-clicking or using the menu bar. Right-click on a blank space or choose "Import from [the name of your iOS device]" or "**Take Photo**" from the "**File**" menu in the top-left corner.
5. **Use your iOS smartphone**: A pop-up showing the camera feed from your iOS smartphone will appear on your MacBook Pro. The camera on your iOS smartphone will launch immediately. Put it to use by framing the object you wish to photograph.
6. **Take the Picture**: Press the shutter button on your iOS smartphone once you have the subject properly framed. If it is more convenient, you may also activate the camera by pressing the volume-up button on your iOS smartphone.
7. **Accept the Picture:** The picture will appear on the screen of your iOS device once it has been taken. If you like the picture, choose "**Use Photo**"; otherwise, you'll have the alternatives to "**Retake**" or "**Use Photo**."
8. **Insert the Image:** The recently-captured image will now be put in the Finder window of your MacBook Pro at the location you specified. The picture may also be resized and modified inside the Finder as necessary.

9. Save your changes before moving on if you're working on a project or document. You may then go on with your job while also using the additional photograph that was taken with your iOS smartphone.

Scan a Document using the Continuity Camera

Here are the steps:

1. **Verify Setup and Compatibility**

Make sure your equipment complies with the Continuity Camera specifications before you start. You'll need an iPhone or iPad with iOS 12 or later and a MacBook Pro with macOS High Sierra (10.13) or later (macOS Ventura). The same Apple ID should be used to sign into both devices, and they should be linked to the same Wi-Fi network.

2. **Configure Wi-Fi and Bluetooth**

Make sure that both your MacBook Pro and your iPhone/iPad have Bluetooth and Wi-Fi turned on. These wireless technologies provide a flawless connection between the devices, which is necessary for Continuity Camera.

3. **Taking Position**

The physical document you desire to scan should be placed on a level surface, ideally against a backdrop that contrasts. This will make it easier for the iPhone's camera to precisely detect the borders of the page.

4. **Open the File on your MacBook Pro**

Open the app you want to use to add the scanned document to your MacBook Pro. This may be a Notes app note, a Pages document, a PDF, or even an email.

5. **Access the Continuity Camera**

Choose "**Import from iPhone**" or "**Insert from iPhone**" from the contextual menu that displays when you right-click or control-click anywhere inside the document. This will reveal a submenu.

6. **Choose your Device**

The name of your iPhone or iPad is given in the submenu, along with the choices for document scanning. To continue, click the name of your device.

7. **Choose the Document Type**

Now on your MacBook Pro, choose "**Scan Documents**" from the pop-up menu. This will launch the camera app on your iPhone.

8. **Take a Document Photo**

The paper you want to scan should be held over by your iPhone or iPad. The edges of the paper will be automatically detected by the camera, and they will be highlighted in yellow. Tap the shutter button on your iPhone's camera interface after you're happy with the framing to take the scan.

9. **Adjust the Scan**

A preview of the picture will show up on your iPhone's screen once you've taken the scan. If required, you can modify the corners of the scan using the buttons on the screen. To continue, choose "**Keep Scan**" when you're pleased.

10. **Save the Scan**

You can now trim, rotate, or retake the scan if necessary after seeing the scanned page on your iPhone. To confirm, hit "**Save**" when you are ready.

11. **Insert the Scan**

The program you just launched will now show the scanned document on your MacBook Pro screen. To insert the document, either click or drag it to the correct spot inside the document.

12. **Finishing up**

At this stage, you need to make a few small tweaks to make the imported scan fit smoothly into your document, such as scaling or moving it.

13. **Save and Share**

Remember to save your document after making any required edits. Depending on your requirements, you can now share your digital document through email, messaging applications, or cloud storage services.

Frequently Asked Questions

1. How do you set up and use Universal Control in MacBook Pro?
2. How do you use the continuity camera?
3. How do you scan a document using the continuity camera?
4. How do you take an image with a continuity camera?
5. How do you take a picture in Finder?

CHAPTER TEN
SAFARI

Overview

Safari is a web browser that allows you to visit web pages and do online research. In this chapter, you will learn everything about Safari including how to visit a website, how to bookmark a site, how to rearrange tab groups, how to create a tab group in Safari, and others.

How to Visit a Website

Our lives would not be complete without navigating the internet world, and the new MacBook Pro's strong features make this process easy and fun. Apple's web browser, Safari, is suitable for your new MacBook Pro and offers a variety of features in addition to speed and security.

Here are the steps to visit a website:

1. **Open Safari**

Find the Safari icon on the dock of your MacBook Pro or in the Applications folder to begin exploring the web. Clicking on the symbol, which looks like a blue compass, launches the Safari web browser.

2. **Type the URL of the website**

You'll see a search bar at the top of the browser window once Safari is launched. The web address (URL) of the website you wish to view may be entered here.

3. **Examine Favorites and Bookmarks (Optional)**

Save or add websites to your Favorites list if you often visit them for easy access. You can categorize your bookmarks into folders and even sync them across your Apple devices using iCloud by clicking on the **"Bookmarks"** button in the Safari menu bar and then choosing **"Add Bookmark"** or **"Add to Favorites."**

4. **Navigate backward and Forth**

You may want to go back to a previous page or move on to a page you've already seen while you browse various websites. Click the left arrow in the upper-left corner of the browser window to return. Click the right-pointing arrow adjacent to the back arrow to go ahead.

5. **Use Tabs to Multitask**

With Safari's tabbed browsing feature, you may have many websites open in different tabs simultaneously in the same browser window. Click the plus (+) sign in the top-right corner of the browser window, or use your keyboard to hit **"Command" + "T"** to launch a new tab. The keyboard keys **"Command" + "["** (to move left) and **"Command" + "]"** (to move right) may also be used to swap between tabs.

6. **Zoom In or Out**

You can zoom in or out to change the scale of the information on a website. To zoom in or out, use the keyboard shortcuts **"Command" + "+" and "Command" + "-"**. As an alternative, you can use the trackpad's pinch-to-zoom motion.

7. **Search Within a Page**

Use Safari's search feature to locate particular material while you're on a long site. Open the search bar by pressing "**Command**" and "**F**" on your keyboard, then input the term you're searching for. All of the keyword's appearances on the page will be highlighted by Safari.

8. **Refresh the Page**

Refresh a website if it's having trouble loading or if you want to see whether the content has been changed. In the address bar, click the round arrow symbol or press "**Command**" + "**R**."

9. **Adjust the Reader View**

The Reader View in Safari offers a clear and uncluttered reading environment for articles and blog entries. On the left side of the address bar, there will be a little symbol if the website supports Reader View. By clicking on this button, the website will change to a cleaner layout without any adverts or other distractions, making it simpler to read.

10. **Close Tabs and Safari**

To completely dismiss Safari, click the red "**X**" button in the top-left corner of the browser window or use the keyboard shortcut "**Command**" + "**Q**." To close a tab, click the "**X**" symbol on the tab or use the keyboard shortcut "**Command**" + "**W**."

How to Bookmark a Site

The steps:

1. **Launch Safari**

Find the Safari icon on your MacBook Pro's Dock or look for it in Spotlight to get started. Clicking on the symbol will open the Safari web browser after you've located it.

2. **Navigate to the Website**

Enter the URL of the website you want to bookmark in the address bar at the top of the Safari window. As an alternative, you can use a search engine to look for the website by entering relevant keywords. To open the webpage, use the "**Return**" key on your keyboard.

3. **Select "Add Bookmark"**

Once the page has loaded, look at the Safari window's top. You will see many options. Select "**Bookmarks**" from the menu bar. By doing so, a dropdown menu with numerous bookmark-related choices will be shown.

4. **Choose "Add Bookmark"**

The "**Add Bookmark**" option can be found in the "**Bookmarks**" dropdown menu; choose it to continue.

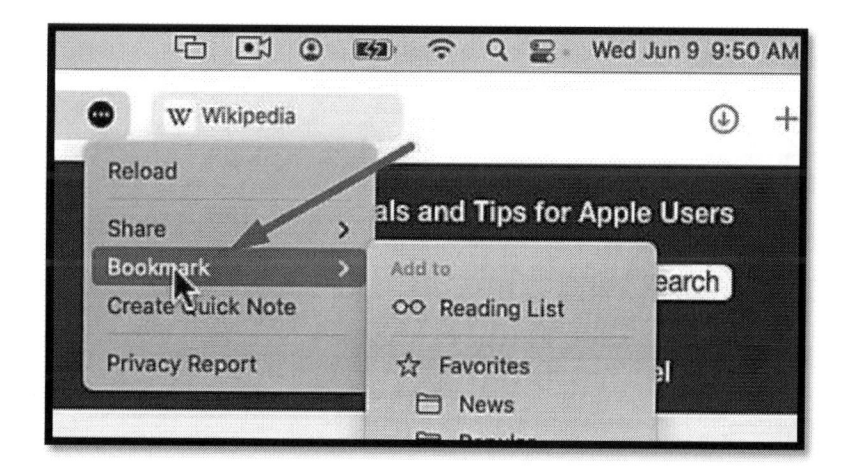

5. **Configure Bookmark Details**

You can now customize the settings for the bookmark you're going to make in a little window that will appear.

What you can accomplish in this window:

- **Name**: The bookmark's name. Safari will automatically propose a name for the site, but you can change it to something more evocative if you'd like.

- **Locate** the bookmark where you want it to be saved. From the dropdown menu, you can choose a particular bookmarks folder to use, or you can leave it in its default place, which is often the Bookmarks Menu.
- **Folder**: Use this dropdown menu to choose the folder where you want to store the bookmark if you've made that decision.

6. **Finalize the Bookmark**

You're ready to save the bookmark after you've customized its details to your liking. Simply choose the "**Add**" button in the window's bottom right corner. Your bookmark will be placed at the specified spot.

7. **Accessing Bookmarks**

Click on the "**Bookmarks**" option in the Safari menu bar to view your recently generated bookmark as well as any other bookmarks you store in the future. See a list of your bookmarks and any folders you've made for organizing them from the dropdown menu.

How to use Tab Groups in Safari

Understanding Tab Groups

The innovative Tab Groups feature in Safari is a game-changer for efficient tab management. Tab Groups lets you group relevant tabs so that you don't have a long list of open tabs, which makes it simpler to navigate between browsing contexts. Tab Groups have you covered whether you're doing research for a project, organizing a trip, or just want to keep work-related tabs distinct from personal ones.

Creating a Tab Group

Here are the instructions to create a tab group:

1. **Open Tabs**: Open a few tabs in your Safari browser to get things going.
2. To create a group, choose the "**Tab Groups**" icon in the upper right corner of the browser window. This symbol resembles a compact stack of tabs.
3. **New Tab Group**: A menu showcasing your open tabs will appear. Select "**New Tab Group**" from the option at the bottom.

4. **Name Your Group**: You can give your Tab Group a name in the dialog box that will display. Select a name that accurately describes the content of the tabs you are grouping. If you're looking for recipes, you can call the group **"Cooking Ideas."**
5. Click **"Create"** to complete the creation of your new Tab Group.

Managing and Customizing Tab Groups

After creating a Tab Group, you should investigate the numerous management options and methods to tailor it to your requirements:

1. **Adding Tabs:** Drag and drop tabs from the open tabs bar to the selected group to add them to a tab group. To pick the group you want to add a tab to, you can also right-click on the tab and choose **"Add to Tab Group"**.
2. **Rearranging Tabs**: Rearrange the tabs in a group by clicking and dragging them to the new place. This enables you to order tabs according to your workflow.
3. **Renaming Groups:** Quickly rename a Tab Group if you decide to modify its objective. Your organization will stay adaptable if you right-click on the group's title and choose **"Rename Tab Group."**
4. **Merging Groups:** Combine two Tab Groups if you discover that they are connected or should be united. To combine two groups, right-click on one group, pick **"Merge Tab Groups,"** and then choose the other group.
5. To reopen a closed group, click the **"Tab Groups"** button, choose the closed group from the list, and then right-click the group and choose **"Close Tab Group."**

Rename a Tab Group in Safari

The steps:

1. **Open Safari on your MacBook Pro**

Make sure your MacBook Pro is running macOS Monterey or a later version before you start. In the dock, click the Safari icon, or look for it in your Applications folder. Once Safari is launched, the new tab bar features, such as Tab Groups, will be visible.

2. **Create a Tab Group**

You must have at least one Tab Group established before you may rename one. It's an easy step to follow if you haven't previously. Give your new Tab Group a name that accurately describes its contents by right-clicking (or controlling-clicking) on any tab in Safari and choosing "**Add to Tab Group.**" You can subsequently alter this name, which will act as a placeholder.

3. **Open the Tab Groups**

There's a little symbol that resembles stacked squares on the tab bar. This icon may be clicked to see your Tab Groups. Every group will appear as a set of tabs with the temporary name you choose.

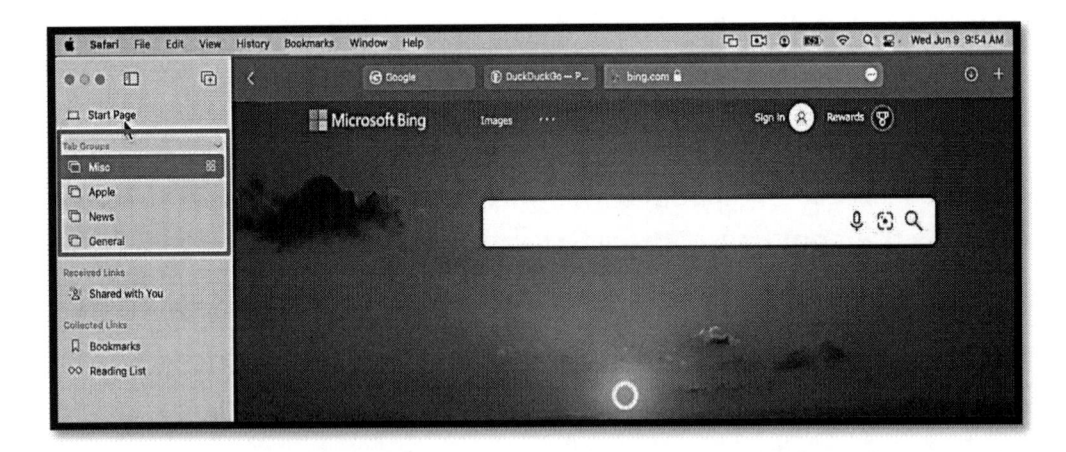

4. **Rename the Tab Group**

Place the pointer over the Tab Group that needs a new name. To the right of the group, the name should emerge as a little pencil icon. To begin the renaming procedure, click on this pencil symbol.

5. **Enter the New Name**

The current name of the Tab Group will be covered by a text area after clicking the pencil symbol. Enter the brand-new name you want. Make sure the name is sufficiently evocative to enable you to recognize the group's focus right away.

6. **Hit Enter or Return**

Press the **Enter** or **Return key** on your keyboard once you've typed in the new name. The name of your Tab Group will be changed to the new name you specified.

Move Safari Tabs from one Group to Another

Here are the steps:

1. **Launch Safari and Create Tab Groups**

Make sure Safari is open on your new MacBook Pro first. Observe these procedures to build tab groups:

- In the top menu bar, choose the "**Window**" menu. It will then display a dropdown option.
- To create a new group, click "**New Tab Group**" from the submenu that appears after choosing "**Tab Groups**" from the dropdown menu.
- Give the tab group a name. Consider giving it a name like "**Work,**" "**Research,**" or "**Shopping.**"

2. Organize Tabs into Tab Groups

It's time to arrange your tabs now that your tab groups are established:

- The websites you want to add to the tab group should be opened. A separate website should be shown by each tab.
- To add a tab to the tab group you already made, click and drag it there. To add the tab, just drop it inside the group.

3. **Switching Group Tabs**

The methods below should be followed if you need to shift tabs from one group to another:

- To begin, make sure the tab groups are visible. Through the "**Window**" option in the top menu bar, you can get to them.

- Choose the tab that you want to move. Your cursor should click and hold the tab.

4. **Drag and drop to Another Group**

Move the tab that is now being held by your pointer to the appropriate tab group:

- Drag the tab to the desired tab group while still keeping it in place.
- For a minute, hold the tab above the tab group. You'll see that as the group grows, you can drop the tab here.

5. **Drop the Tab**

Release the tab at last to place it in the new tab group:

- When the tab is above the desired tab group, release it. You'll see the tab leave the previous group when it is added to the new one.

Rearrange Tab Groups

When it comes to maintaining an ordered and effective browsing process, Safari's tab groups may be a lifesaver. Apple added several new functions and enhancements to Safari with the release of the most recent MacBook Pro, including the ability to manage tab groups.

1. **Launch Safari**

Open Safari on your new MacBook Pro to get going. You can accomplish this by selecting the Safari icon in your Dock or by using Spotlight to look for **"Safari"**.

2. **Create Tab Groups (Optional)**

You must first establish some tab groups before you can reorganize them.

The steps:

- **Open Multiple Tabs:** Click on each tab individually while depressing the **Command key** on your keyboard to open the ones you want to group.

- Create a tab group by selecting "**New Tab Group from [X] Tabs**" from the context menu when you right-click on one of the chosen tabs. You can also choose "**New Tab Group from [X] Tabs**" from the "**Tabs**" option at the top.
- Give your tab group a name in the pop-up box that will display. Hit Enter after entering a pertinent name.

3. **Rearrange Tab Groups**

You can now rearrange the tab groupings you've made as you like:

1. Find the tab group icon in the upper right corner of your Safari window to access tab groups. It resembles a deck of cards. To see your tab groupings, click it.
2. **Drag and Drop**: To reposition a tab group inside the tab group bar, click and hold the tab group you want to move, and then drag it to the appropriate location. When you let go of the mouse button, a visual cue will indicate where the tab group will be positioned.
3. Once the tab group is where you want it to be, release the mouse button to rearrange it. Accordingly, Safari will automatically reorder the tab groups.

4. **Modify Tab Groups (Optional)**

You may decide to adjust the individual tabs inside each set of tabs while changing the tab groupings.

Here's how to go about it:

- **Expand Tab Group**: To view all of the tabs in the tab group you wish to change, expand the tab group by clicking on it.
- **Reorder Tabs:** To move a tab to a different place inside a group, just click and drag it there.
- **Adding Tabs**: You can add new tabs to an existing tab group by dragging them from the tab bar or by right-clicking a link and selecting **"Open in [Tab Group Name]."**

- **Remove Tabs**: You can either drag a tab out of a group and back into the main tab bar to remove it from the group, or you can right-click the tab and choose "**Remove from Tab Group.**"

5. **Save and Sync**

You should be aware that any modifications you make to your tab groups are immediately preserved. These modifications will also be synchronized throughout all of your devices connected to the same iCloud account if you are using Safari with iCloud. This implies that rearranging tab groups on your MacBook Pro will also change how they appear on your other Apple devices.

Access Tabs Group in a Grid

The steps:

1. **Update Safari to the Latest Version**

Make sure your Safari browser is updated before you start exploring the Tab Groups feature. Apple often provides upgrades that enhance efficiency and security in addition to adding new features.

Use these procedures to check for updates:

- In the upper-left corner of your screen, click the Apple logo.
- From the dropdown menu, choose **"System Settings".**
- Choose "**Software Update**."
- If a Safari update is available, choose "**Update Now**."

2. **Open Safari and Create Tab Groups**

Once Safari is updated, adhere to these instructions to create and arrange Tab Groups:

- From your dock, Applications folder, or Spotlight search, open **Safari**.
- Click on the links to the websites you want to include in a Tab Group to open them.
- Right-click (or Control-click) on one of the tabs you want to add to the group to create a new Tab Group.
- Hover your mouse over the "**Add to Tab Group**" option in the context menu.

- Choose "**New Tab Group**" from the submenu.
- There will be a pop-up box that lets you give the Tab Group a name and choose the color of its icon. Although this step is optional, it might aid in visually distinguishing between various groups.
- To create the new Tab Group, click "**Save**".

3. **Access Tab Groups in a Grid Layout**

You can now quickly access and manage Tab Groups in a grid layout after creating them:
- If it's not already open, launch **Safari**.
- On the far-right side of the tab bar, look for the Tab Groups icon, which resembles four squares grouped in a grid?
- To see the grid arrangement, click the **Tab Groups button**.

4. **Manage and Organize Tab Groups**

All of your currently open Tab Groups and the individual tabs inside them are shown in the grid arrangement.

Here are some tips for organizing and managing them:
- Simply click on a Tab Group's symbol in the grid to transition to that Tab Group. You may begin surfing inside that group once the linked tabs are shown.
- Drag the tab from the main tab bar and drop it into the relevant group in the grid layout to add a new tab to an existing Tab Group.
- Hover your mouse pointer over a group's icon in the grid and click the close (X) button that appears in the top-left corner to dismiss the whole tab group.
- Click on a Tab Group's icon in the grid and choose "**Edit Tab Group**" from the menu to change the name of the group. The group's name and color may then be changed.
- Drag and drop the icons of your Tab Groups around the grid to reorganize them. You may then order your most often-used groups in this manner.

Remove a Tab Group

Tab Groups provide you the ability to group relevant tabs, which improves the organization and clutter-free surfing experience.

Here are the steps to remove a tab group:

1. **Launch Safari**

Click on the icon for Safari in the Dock, which is normally found at the bottom of your MacBook Pro's display, to open it. You can also use Spotlight to look for Safari by hitting **Command + Space** and putting **"Safari"** into the search box.

2. **Access Tab Groups**

Look in the upper left corner of the screen once Safari has loaded. The "**Show Tab Overview**" button can be found here. It looks like two squares stacked on top of one another. To get the overview of the Tab Groups, click this icon.

3. **Identify the Tab Group**

You can see how each of your open tabs is organized into a different Tab Group in the Tab Groups overview. Each Tab Group will be identified by its title and a preview of the tabs it contains. Locate the Tab Group you want to delete with care. To see more possibilities, move your mouse over the Tab Group.

4. **Remove the Tab Group**

A collection of icons will start to display in the upper right corner of the preview as soon as you hover over the Tab Group. For the option to remove the Tab Group, look for the "**X**" symbol. By clicking on this button, Safari will request your approval before continuing.

5. **Confirm Removal**

A confirmation dialog box will show up when you click the "**X**" symbol, asking you whether you want to delete the Tab Group. This step is essential since closing a Tab Group will shut all of the tabs it contains. Before continuing, make sure you've saved any crucial information from these tabs. Simply click the "**Delete**" button to confirm removal.

6. **Verify Removal**

Safari will immediately shut all the tabs included in that group and delete the Tab Group after you confirm its removal. The Tab Group will no longer be shown in the Tab Groups overview when you return to the primary browsing interface.

7. **Organize Remaining Tabs**

You can simply manage tabs that you want to stay open after removing a Tab Group by making new Tab Groups or adding them to existing ones. Simply drag a tab from the Tab Groups overview and drop it into the main browsing area to create a new Tab Group. With that tab, Safari will automatically establish a new Tab Group. Drag the tab and drop it into the chosen Tab Group in the overview to add it to an existing Tab Group.

Frequently Asked Questions

1. How do you visit a website in Safari?
2. How do you bookmark a site in Safari?
3. How do you create and rename a Tab Group in Safari?
4. How do you use Tab Groups in Safari?
5. How to access and remove Tab Groups in Safari?

CHAPTER ELEVEN
AIRPLAY AND VOICE RECORDINGS

Overview

Are you looking to share content from your MacBook Pro with other Apple devices or make voice recordings? Well, this chapter shows you how best to use AirPlay on your new MacBook Pro. Also, you will learn how to create and customize voice recordings, how to create voice recordings with voice memos and so much more.

How to Set Up and Use AirPlay

Make sure that all the devices you want to connect are on the same Wi-Fi network before you start using AirPlay. This is essential for creating a trustworthy relationship.

Following confirmation, do the following actions to configure AirPlay on your MacBook Pro:

1. **Enable AirPlay on your MacBook Pro:**
- In the upper-left corner of your screen, click the **Apple logo**.
- From the drop-down menu, choose **"System Settings"**.
- Select **"Displays"** and then **"AirPlay Display"** from the dropdown menu.
- From the list, choose the device you want to connect to.
2. **Set Up AirPlay on Additional Devices**:
- Make sure your smart TV or Apple TV is plugged into the same Wi-Fi network as your MacBook Pro.
- Open **"Settings" > "AirPlay"** on your Apple TV and enable AirPlay.
- To enable AirPlay on other smart TVs, follow the manufacturer's instructions.
3. **Connect your MacBook Pro:**
- Your MacBook Pro ought to make a connection after choosing the device from the AirPlay Display dropdown menu. Now, you may expand your display or reflect it.

Using AirPlay for Screen Mirroring

For presentations, viewing movies, or sharing images with a bigger audience, you can duplicate the screen of your MacBook Pro using AirPlay's screen mirroring capability.

How to use screen mirroring

1. **Access the AirPlay Menu:**
- Select the AirPlay icon (which resembles a rectangle with an arrow pointing into it) from the menu bar in the top-right corner of your MacBook Pro's display.
2. **Select the Device:**
- From the available device list, choose the one you want to mirror to.

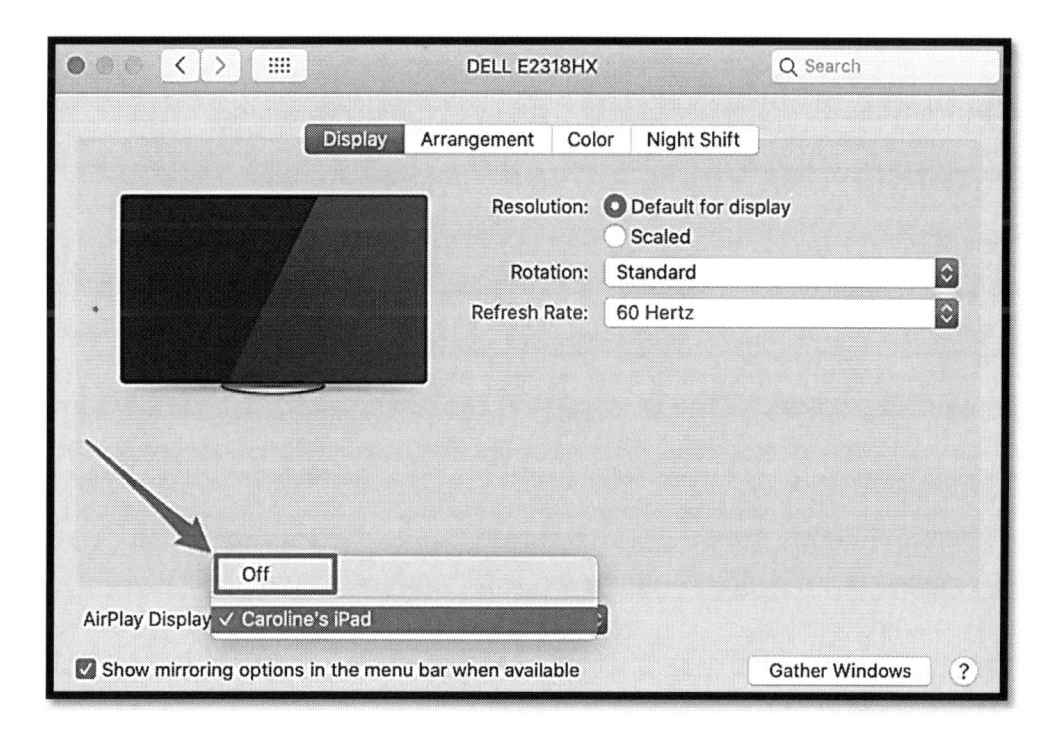

3. **Activate Mirroring:**

- Turn on "**Mirroring**" by flipping the switch. The screen of your MacBook Pro ought to now be mirrored on the chosen gadget.

Using AirPlay for Audio Streaming

You can broadcast audio from your MacBook Pro to speakers, Apple TV, or other devices that use AirPlay.

This is how you do it:

1. **Open the AirPlay Menu**:
   - While under the top-right corner of your screen, under the menu bar, choose the **Volume icon**.
2. **Choose the Output Device:**
   - To change the audio output device presently chosen, click the dropdown arrow next to it.
   - From the list, choose the device you want to stream audio to.
3. **Play Audio:**
   - Use your MacBook Pro to listen to any audio material. The chosen output device will now start receiving the sound through streaming.

Using AirPlay for Video Streaming

Streaming films from your MacBook Pro to a bigger screen is also supported using AirPlay. This is fantastic for using a bigger display for viewing videos, movies, or even playing games.

1. **Launch the Video:**
   - Using a video player that is compatible with your MacBook Pro, launch the video you wish to view.
2. **Open the AirPlay Menu:**
   - In the menu bar or the video player, click the **AirPlay symbol**.
3. **Choose the Device:**
   - From the list of supported devices, choose the device to which you wish to stream the video.
4. **Begin Streaming:**
   - The chosen device should now begin playing the video, delivering a more engaging watching experience.

Ending the AirPlay Connection

You should unplug your devices after you've finished utilizing AirPlay. This is how:

1. **Stop Screen Mirroring:**
   - In the menu bar, click the **AirPlay symbol**.
   - Click "**Turn Off AirPlay**" or "**Disconnect**."
2. **Stop Audio or Video Streaming:**
   - In the menu bar, click the **Volume icon**.
   - To stop audio streaming, choose your MacBook Pro's speakers or another audio output device.
   - To cease streaming video on your MacBook Pro, just shut off the video player.

Enable Mac to Receive AirPlay Content

The steps:

1. **Check System Compatibility**

Make sure your new MacBook Pro is running macOS High Sierra (10.13) or a newer version (such as the macOS Ventura) before starting the setup procedure. This is a necessary condition for the proper operation of AirPlay. Click on the Apple logo in the top-left corner of the screen, choose "**About This Mac**," and then look at the "**Overview**" page to see what version of macOS you are using.

2. **Connect to the Same Wi-Fi Network**

Your MacBook Pro must be connected to the same Wi-Fi network as the transmitting device (such as an iPhone or iPad) for AirPlay to operate properly. Ensure that the device you're streaming from is connected to the same network as your MacBook Pro.

3. **Activate AirPlay on your new MacBook Pro**

   - The Apple logo is located in the upper-left corner of your MacBook Pro's screen. Click on it.
   - From the dropdown menu, choose "**System Settings**".

- Click "**Displays**" in the System Settings box.
- Go to the "**Arrangement**" tab by navigating.
- To add the AirPlay icon to the menu bar for easy access, choose the checkbox next to "**Show mirroring options in the menu bar when available**."

4. **Receive AirPlay Content**

- Make sure the device you want to stream from is awake and unlocked, such as an iPhone or iPad.
- In the menu bar, click the AirPlay symbol (which resembles a rectangle with an arrow pointing inside it).
- There will be a drop-down menu with a list of accessible AirPlay devices. You should see your MacBook Pro listed below.
- To begin streaming or mirroring content, click on the name of your MacBook Pro.

5. **Adjust the AirPlay Settings**

You can change a few parameters related to receiving AirPlay content based on your preferences.

- Click the AirPlay icon in the menu bar and choose "**AirPlay Display**" choices to access further settings.
- Decide whether to enable AirPlay over a wired network connection (if necessary) in the AirPlay Display options box.
- For connections to AirPlay, you may also specify a password. Ensuring that only approved devices may connect to your MacBook Pro offers an added degree of protection.

6. **Mirror or Stream Content**

Choose to broadcast particular content or mirror your screen after successfully using AirPlay to connect your MacBook Pro to another device.

- Select "**Mirror Built-in Display**" from the menu bar's AirPlay icon to mirror the display on your MacBook Pro.

- The target device will now display a mirror of your MacBook Pro's screen. Your actions on your MacBook Pro will appear in mirror form on the other screen.

Also,

- On your MacBook Pro, launch the application or content you want to stream.
- In the menu bar, click the **AirPlay symbol**.
- From the list, choose the desired device.
- The device of your choice will immediately begin streaming the material you selected.

Enable Mac to Receive AirPlay Content

The steps:

1. **Verify Compatibility and Connectivity**

Make sure your iPhone and MacBook Pro are both AirPlay compatible before you start. Your MacBook Pro should have a macOS operating system that supports AirPlay, and your iPhone should be running a current version of iOS. It is advised to maintain both devices updated to the most recent software versions for best performance. Ensure that both devices are logged in to the same Wi-Fi network for a smooth connection. To stream material without interruption, you need a strong and quick Wi-Fi connection.

2. **Activate AirPlay on your MacBook Pro**

Navigate to the menu bar at the top of the screen on your MacBook Pro. A rectangle with a little triangle at the bottom serves as the AirPlay icon. The AirPlay menu may be accessed by clicking this button. You can choose from a list of available AirPlay devices in the dropdown menu. Your MacBook Pro may be chosen from this list. You also have the choice to activate "**Mirroring**," which mirrors the screen of your iPhone on the display of your MacBook Pro.

3. **Initiate AirPlay from your iPhone**

Grab your iPhone and launch the Control Center right away. Swipe down from the top-right corner of the screen on iPhones with Face ID. Swipe up from the bottom of the screen on Touch ID iPhones. The AirPlay icon, which looks like a rectangle with a solid triangle at the bottom, may be found in the Control Center. To see a list of compatible AirPlay devices, tap the **AirPlay symbol**. Your MacBook Pro should be listed among the choices. To make the connection, tap on it.

4. **Select Your Content**

Once the connection has been made, you can begin streaming. The content from your iPhone will now be seen on the screen of your MacBook Pro, including images, movies, music, and even games. Go to the app or piece of content you want to AirPlay. For instance, launch the **Photos app**, choose the album, and then hit the **AirPlay symbol** to display a photo slideshow from your iPhone on your MacBook Pro. Similarly, to start AirPlay for streaming music or video, launch the corresponding app. Control the playing during an AirPlay session from either your iPhone or MacBook Pro, depending on which is most convenient for you. You can easily change the volume, stop, play, and move around your media.

5. **Ending the AirPlay Session**

After you've finished viewing your content, it's crucial to correctly stop the AirPlay session. Alternatively, you can cancel the AirPlay session from the AirPlay menu on your MacBook Pro. To do this, open the Control Center on your iPhone, hit the AirPlay icon, and chooses **"Turn off AirPlay Mirroring."**

How to Create & Customize Voice Recordings

Voice recordings have become a crucial aspect of message delivery, information exchange, and emotional expression in the era of digital communication. The new MacBook Pro's cutting-edge technology makes it simpler than ever to create and customize voice recordings.

Here are the steps:

1. **Choosing the Right Software**: The flexible and user-friendly GarageBand program is preinstalled on your new MacBook Pro. Due to its user-friendly design and comprehensive feature set, this program is a great place to start for generating and modifying voice recordings.

2. **Setting up Your Recording:** Open GarageBand to get started. You'll see a variety of project templates. To optimize the settings for voice recording, choose the "**Voice**" template. Alternatively, you can choose an empty project and adjust the parameters to your liking.
3. **Using an External Microphone**: Attach your external microphone to your MacBook Pro for better recording quality. The built-in microphone on the MacBook Pro is also enough for simple recordings.
4. **Adjusting Input Levels**: Make sure your input levels are adequate before recording. To prevent distortion during recording, click on the track's name to open the "**Track Header**" and then adjust the input level slider.
5. **Recording your Voice**: By pressing the red record button, you may begin recording your voice. The "**Count In**" option in GarageBand provides a lead-in before recording starts. To get the greatest outcomes, speak clearly and consistently.
6. **Editing Your Recording**: After you've finished recording, edit your work. For trimming, cutting, and arranging your audio, GarageBand offers a variety of options. For a polished result, you can remove errors, insert pauses, or even rearrange phrases.
7. **Applying Effects**: To improve your voice recording, GarageBand provides a range of audio effects. You can use equalization to balance the frequencies, reverb to create a roomy sound, and compression to balance the volume levels. To get the desired result, experiment with various effects.
8. **Background Music**: You may think about using background music or sound effects to offer an additional degree of inventiveness. GarageBand allows you to input audio files and arrange them with voice recordings. This is particularly helpful for podcast openings, interviews, or narratives.
9. **Mixing and Mastering**: It's time to mix and master your track if you're happy with the arrangement and effects. To create a seamless mix, alter the loudness of the various songs. Make sure your voice is loud and clear, and pay attention to the overall sound quality.
10. **Exporting Your Recording**: Now that your voice recording is excellent, it's time to make it available to the public. In GarageBand, choose "**Share**" from the menu and then "**Format**" to specify how you wish to export your track. The most popular file types are MP3, WAV, or AIFF. For the best sound, be sure to use a high-quality setting.

11. **Using Shortcuts to Customize Voice Recordings**: The MacBook Pro is renowned for its practical shortcuts that improve user experience. To make the voice recording process more efficient, you may configure your shortcuts. For instance, you can program a certain key combination to start and stop recording, which can speed up and improve the procedure.
12. **Automating Tasks with Automator**: The Automator program on your MacBook Pro may be used to automate repetitive tasks by more experienced users. To save time and effort, you may design processes that specifically process and alter your voice recordings.
13. **Using Voice Commands:** Siri is compatible with the MacBook Pro and supports voice commands. Although it has nothing to do with making voice recordings, this function might nonetheless make it easier for you to organize your workload. Siri may be used to control playback while editing, make reminders for recording sessions, and look for audio effects in GarageBand.
14. **Save Your Recordings**: Your voice recordings are important, therefore be sure to frequently save your recordings. Use external hard drives or cloud storage to protect your work from possible data loss.

Create Voice Recordings with Voice Memos

The steps:

1. **Open the Voice Memos App**

Be sure your MacBook Pro is switched on and logged in before anything else. Use Spotlight search to find the Voice Memos program, which is normally located in the Applications folder. To open the app, click on its icon.

2. **Accessing the Recording Interface**

The Voice Memos app has a user-friendly layout when you first use it. Any voice recordings you may already have are shown in the main window. Simply click the **"+"** (plus) button in the window's lower left corner to start a new recording. Performing this will start a fresh recording session.

3. **Adjusting Recording Settings (Optional)**

You can change a few settings before you begin recording. To reach the settings menu, click on the gear symbol in the recording window's top left corner. You can pick the audio input source (built-in or external microphone), the recording quality (High, Medium, or Low), and even turn on automated noise reduction for better audio clarity.

4. **Start Recording**

You've made the necessary adjustments and are prepared to begin recording. In the middle of the recording window, press the red "Record" button. The waveform of your voice will be shown on the screen while you are recording to show that the app is recording audio.

5. **Pausing and Resuming Recording (Optional)**

The "**Pause**" button, which takes the place of the "**Record**" button during recording, may be used to temporarily halt the recording. If you need to collect your thoughts or if you are interrupted, this might be helpful. Click the "**Resume**" button that appears in place of the "**Pause**" button to continue recording.

6. **Completing the Recording**

To stop recording, click the "**Stop**" button in the center of the square. The list of recordings in the Voice Memos app will now include your freshly recorded recording. A date and time stamp will be automatically added to the recording when it is stored.

7. **Editing the Recording (Optional)**

You can make simple edits to your recordings using the Voice Memos app. Simply choose the recording you want to modify, then click the "**Edit**" button (pencil icon) that appears next to the recording's name to cut the beginning or finish of the recording. When the waveform editor opens, you can drag the handles to choose the section you want to preserve. To complete the adjustments, click "**Trim**".

8. **Adding Labels and Notes**

Labels and comments may be added to keep your recordings organized. To add a label to a recording, right-click (or control-click) on it and choose **"Add Label"** from the context menu. The label may subsequently be given a name and a color. By selecting the "i" (info) symbol next to the recording and inputting the necessary information, you may also add notes to your recordings.

9. **Sharing and Exporting Recordings**

The Voice Memos app offers simple sharing options if you wish to distribute your recordings to others or save them somewhere else. You can choose to share through AirDrop, Messages, Mail, or other compatible applications by selecting **"Share"** from the context menu when you right-click on the recording you want to share.

10. **Delete Recordings**

If you want to delete a recording from the Voice Memos app, just right-click on the recording in the list and choose **"Delete."** After you confirm your choice, the recording will be permanently deleted.

Customize Voice Recordings on Voice Memos

Your new MacBook Pro's Voice Memos software provides a practical method to conveniently record significant thoughts, moments, and notes orally. Even more intriguing is that you may organize and personalize these speech recordings by customizing and improving them. The Voice Memos app provides a variety of tools to allow you to customize your recordings to your tastes, whether you're a student, professional, or simply someone who likes to collect audio notes.

1. **Recording High-Quality Audio**: It's critical to make sure your recordings are of the greatest quality before exploring customizing options. To get the greatest results, look for a place with less ambient noise. To avoid distortion and keep crystal-clear audio, adjust the microphone input settings.
2. **Adding Custom Labels:** Voice Memos gives you the option to give your recordings labels, which makes it simpler to classify and find certain recordings afterward. Simply right-click on the recording in the list, chooses

"**Edit**," and provides a useful label. You can, for instance, title some of your notes **"Meeting Notes," "Ideas," "Lectures,"** or **"Personal Thoughts."**

3. **Trimming and Editing:** This is especially helpful if you wish to cut out extraneous starting or ending bits from a recording. To accomplish this, choose the recording, click the "Edit" button (which looks like a pencil), and then use the editing tools to remove the bits you don't want to hear.
4. **Organizing Recordings with Folders:** As your collection of recordings expands, you may want to use folders to maintain order. To accomplish this, choose "**New Folder**" from the "**File**" menu, then give the folder a name. Then, for convenient access, drag & drop the recordings into the relevant folders.
5. **Adding Notes to Recordings:** Add comments to a recording to give it context or other information. Then, put your comments in the space given after selecting the recording and clicking the "**Edit**" button. This is especially helpful if you need to recall a recording's goal or essential elements.
6. **Changing Recording Names**: If you're working with several recordings, the default recording names may not always be sufficiently clear. Right-click on the recording, chooses "**Edit**," and then modifies the title to something appropriate.
7. **Customizing Playback Speed**: Voice Memos allow you to alter the recording's replay speed. This might be helpful if you want to listen more quickly when studying a lecture or an interview. By clicking on the playback speed icon while the video is playing and choosing your chosen pace, you can change the playback speed.
8. **Sharing and Exporting**: App customization is just one aspect of personalization. Additionally, you can export and share your recordings in a variety of media types, such as audio files or iCloud links. Simply pick the recording you want to share, click the share button, and then choose the sharing strategy of your choice.
9. **Marking Important Sections with Bookmarks:** Add bookmarks to recordings if you want to quickly return to certain sections. Simply click the **bookmark button** while listening to a recording to jump to the appropriate spot. Later, by choosing them from the list, you may go directly to these bookmarks.
10. **Customizing Settings**: Exploring the app's options will allow you to further personalize your Voice Memos experience. You can change choices for things

like audio quality, where recordings are kept, and more. The settings can be accessed by clicking "**Voice Memos**" in the menu bar and choosing "**Preferences**."

Replace a Section of the Recording

Here are the steps:

1. **Open the Voice Memos app**

Make sure your MacBook Pro is turned on and ready to go before continuing. Use Spotlight Search or look for the Voice Memos app in the Applications folder to locate it. Clicking on the app will start it after you've found it.

2. **Create a New Voice Memo**

When you first launch the Voice Memos app, you'll see a red circle with a microphone symbol in the middle. To start recording a new voice memo, click this button. To make it simple to locate this voice memo when editing, be sure to clearly express your name or provide a little introduction.

3. **Recording the Replacement Section**

Navigate to the portion you want to replace if the recording you want to edit is open on your MacBook Pro. Play the recording while simultaneously speaking the desired content into a new voice memo. Make sure your voice memo is understandable and correctly synced with the previous recording.

4. **Stop Recording**

Click the square "**Stop**" button in the Voice Memos app to end the recording once you've recorded the replacement part. The voice memo is now kept in the library of the app.

5. **Trim the Voice Memo (If Needed)**

To make the recorded voice memo perfectly blend into the current audio, you may sometimes need to reduce the beginning or finish. To accomplish this, open the

Voice Memos app, choose the recorded voice memo, and then select the **"Edit"** button (shown as a pen icon). Now you may trim the memo appropriately by dragging the handles at the start and end of the waveform. When you're finished cutting, click "**Done**."

6. **Open the Recording for Editing**

Start editing the audio recording you desire. You can do this by using specialized audio editing software, like GarageBand or Audacity, or even your MacBook Pro's built-in QuickTime Player.

7. **Identify the Section to Replace**

Find the portion you want to change by playing the recording. Make a note of where this section begins and ends. When you are certain of the time, pause the recording.

8. **Cut the Section**

Select the part you chose in the previous step using the editing tools provided by the program you're using (for example, the selection and cut tools in GarageBand). Remove this part of the recording. As a result, there will be a pause in the audio where the replacement will be added.

9. **Insert the Voice Memo**

Locate the voice memo you previously produced by opening the Voice Memos app once again. Drag and drop this voice memo into the recording's void you just made. To keep the audio's natural flow, make sure the time is exact.

10. **Adjust Transitions (If needed)**

Make sure the transition between the original audio and the added voice memo is seamless by listening to the recording. If required, make a smooth transition by using the crossfade or fade-in/fade-out effects offered by your audio editing program.

11. **Save and Export**

Save your project in the audio editing program after you are happy with the edited recording. The final version should then be exported in the preferred audio format (such as MP3, or WAV) to guarantee compatibility across a range of hardware and software.

Trim a Section of the Recording

Here are the steps:

1. **Launch the Voice Memos app**

Locate and launch the Voice Memos app on your MacBook Pro to begin going. To easily discover and activate the software, look for it in the Applications folder or use Spotlight search.

2. **Access your Recordings**

You will see a list of your recorded voice memos when you first start the program. Find the recording you want to cut, and then click on it to choose it. The information and playback interface for the recording will then be shown.

3. **Play the Recording**

It's a good idea to listen to the tape and pinpoint the precise portion you want to cut out before editing the piece. To hear the recording, click the "Play" button on the playback interface.

4. **Set the Trim Points**

At the moment where you wish to begin cutting, pause the recording while it is still playing. Clicking the "**Pause**" button on the playback interface will do this. Once you've determined the beginning of the portion that has to be cut, record the time. Then, whilst the tape is still being played, pause it when you wish to finish the reduced segment. Note the time once again. Your trim bounds will be these two locations.

5. **Enter Edit Mode**

Click the "**Edit**" button, which is often represented by a pencil icon or another similar sign, once you've established the trim borders. The recording's editing interface will then be shown.

6. **Trim the Recording**

View a waveform representation of your recording in the editing interface. To traverse the waveform more accurately, utilize the playback controls. Click and drag the waveform's start or end point to the required trim points that you had previously specified to trim the portion. You will see that the waveform shortens as you move the points, showing the area that will be deleted.

7. **Preview and Adjust**

Use the playback controls to see the edited segment after changing the trim points. By doing so, you can make sure that the recording has been cut off at the appropriate point and that the transition sounds smooth. If you discover that you still need to make changes, you may go back to Step 6 and alter the trim points until you are happy with the outcome.

8. **Save the Trimmed Recording**

It's time to save your modifications after you're satisfied with the portion you've just cut. A "**Save**" or "**Done**" button should be included in the editing interface. To verify the changes you've made to the recording, click on it.

9. **Confirm the Changes**

The Voice Memos software will check your modifications once you save the revisions and refresh the recording as necessary. The portion of the recording you eliminated won't be visible in the waveform of the trimmed recording.

Create a Copy of a Recorded Audio

The steps:

1. **Find the Recorded Audio File**

Find the file in the Voice Memos app before you duplicate an audio recording. This is how you do it:

- Open the **Voice Memos App** by clicking on the "**Finder**" icon in your Dock or by searching for it in Spotlight.
- A list of your recorded audio files is available in the Voice Memos app. Choose the recording you want to copy from the list by scrolling through it.

2. **Export the Recorded Audio**

The next step is to export the recording from the Voice Memos app after you've found the one you want to replicate. You can then store or share the duplicate recording that is made as desired.

Take these actions:

- Right-click (or Ctrl-click) on the recording you want to copy to choose it. A context menu will appear as a result.
- **Select Share**: Click the "**Share**" option from the context menu. The submenu will show up.
- **Choose File**: Select "**File**" from the "**Share**" submenu. This will bring up a dialog window for saving files.
- Go to the spot on your MacBook Pro where you wish to store the copied audio file by choosing Destination. You can choose any place, including the desktop or a particular folder.
- **Name the File**: Give the audio file you copied a descriptive name. Enter a new name or leave the default one.
- **Choose Format**: To format your copied file as audio, click here. AAC and WAV are often available as choices. Select the format that best satisfies your requirements.

- After naming the file and selecting a format, click "**Save**" to finish. The recording will start exporting from the Voice Memos app to the chosen destination.

3. **Verify the Copied Audio**

It's crucial to check that the cloned audio file can be accessed and is playable when the export procedure is finished.

This is how you do it:

- Go to the spot on your MacBook Pro where you stored the copied audio file by using the navigational tools. The file ought to be on the desktop if you made that selection. Navigate to the folder you chose if a different location was chosen.
- Double-click on the copied audio file to play it using your MacBook Pro's built-in audio player. Verify that the audio plays flawlessly.

4. **Safely Store or Share the Copied Audio**

Once the cloned audio file has been verified to be functional, you can choose whether to keep it for your use or to share it with others.

Here are some recommendations:

- **Backup**: Store the cloned audio file on your MacBook Pro in a secure, well-organized spot. To make it simple to find relevant recordings later, think about creating a special folder for them.
- **Cloud Storage:** Consider transferring the duplicated audio file to a cloud storage service like iCloud, Google Drive, or Dropbox if you're worried about data loss. This offers an extra line of defense against hardware malfunctions or mishaps.
- **Sharing:** Attach the audio recording to emails, send it to friends through chat applications, or post it on websites like SoundCloud or YouTube.

Remove Background Noise from the Recorded Audio

The steps:

1. **Launch Voice Memos**

Launch the Voice Memos app on your MacBook Pro to get started. Using Spotlight search or the Applications folder, you may locate the software. You'll see a list of your recorded memos when the program is active.

2. **Choose the Recording**

Decide the audio recording you want to squelch background noise from. To choose a memo, click on it. The playing controls and an audio waveform representation will then appear.

3. **Access the Editing Tools**

You'll find an **"Edit"** button, denoted by a pencil icon, in the playback controls' upper-right corner. To access the editing tools for the chosen recording, click this button.

4. **Open the Noise Reduction Tool**

A menu with several editing choices will show after pressing the **"Edit"** button. To find the **"More"** option, look for the three dots. As soon as you click **"More,"** a dropdown menu will display. Go to this menu and choose **"Noise Reduction."**

5. **Adjust Noise Reduction Settings**

Choose the amount of noise reduction using a slider when the Noise Reduction tool first launches. The slider has a range of 0 to 100, where 0 means there is no noise reduction and 100 means there is the most noise reduction possible. Start by adjusting the slider to a modest level—roughly 50—and then listen to the audio preview to hear the results.

6. **Preview and Fine-Tune**

To hear a brief sample of the recording with the applied noise reduction settings, click the "**Preview**" button. You can get a sense of the final audio quality from here. You can also continue if you are OK with the preview. If not, move the slider until the audio quality is preserved while maintaining the desired level of noise reduction.

7. **Apply Noise Reduction**

Click the "**Apply**" button after fine-tuning the noise reduction settings. This will apply the chosen noise reduction level throughout the audio recording. Remember that applying noise reduction is permanent, so wait until you are happy with the outcome before continuing.

8. **Save the Edited Recording**

Return to the editing screen for the memo after applying the noise reduction. Replay the tape to make sure the background noise has been efficiently eliminated without degrading the audio quality. When you're satisfied with the outcome, press "**Done**" to save the altered recording.

9. **Export the Edited Recording**

The modified recording may be exported in the format of your choice after being saved. Choose the format you prefer, such as AAC or WAV, and select the destination folder for the exported file. Give the file a name and click "**Export**."

Frequently Asked Questions

1. How do you use AirPlay on your new MacBook Pro?
2. How do you AirPlay from iPhone to your MacBook Pro?
3. How do you create and customize voice recordings?
4. How do you trim and replace a section of your recording?
5. How do you remove background noise from your recorded video?

CHAPTER TWELVE
REMINDER APP

Overview

The Reminders app allows you to stay on track of certain tasks and events. You only need to set it up and wait for the app to alert you. Continue reading to learn a lot about the reminders app.

How to Use Reminder App

The steps:

1. **Getting Started:** The Reminder app is easily found in the Applications folder after turning on your new MacBook Pro and creating your user account. As an alternative, you can quickly find and launch the program by using Spotlight search (by pressing **Command + Spacebar**).
2. **Getting to know the design**: The Reminder app's design is simple and easy to use when you first open it. There are three primary components in the main window:
- **Lists:** The Lists panel is located on the left side of the window. Categorize your reminders into several categories, each devoted to a certain subject or undertaking. Simply click the **"+"** button in the panel's bottom left corner to start a new list.
- **Reminders:** The reminders from the chosen list are shown in the window's middle part. The title, due date (if specified), and any accompanying remarks are shown for each reminder. Click the **"+"** button in the top-right corner of this section to add a new reminder.
- **Details:** The right side of the window will display information when you click on a particular reminder. You can set the reminder's due date here as well as extra notes, priority levels, and other options.

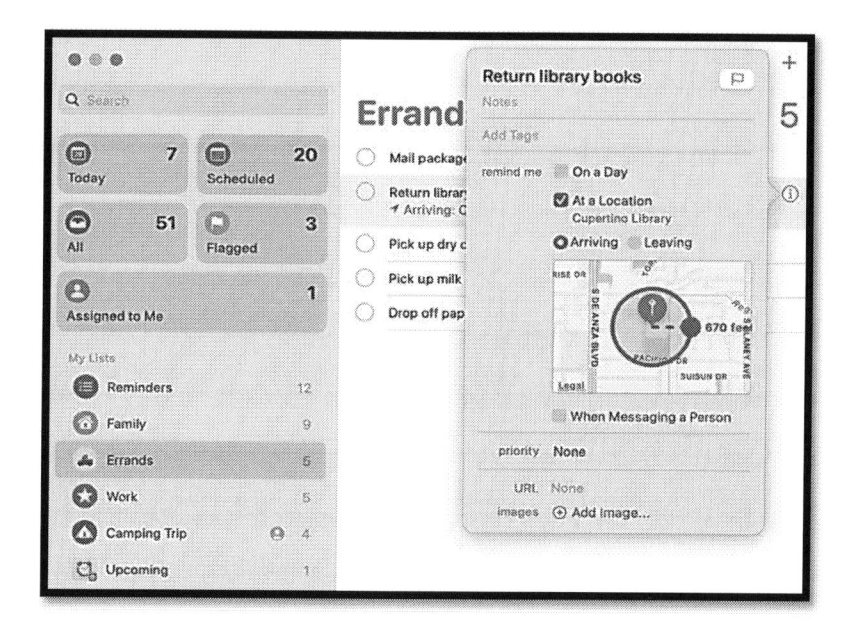

3. **Create and Manage Reminders**: To create a new reminder, go through the following steps:
- Click on the list (or make a new list) where you want to add the reminder.
- In the Reminders section, click the "+" button in the top-right corner.

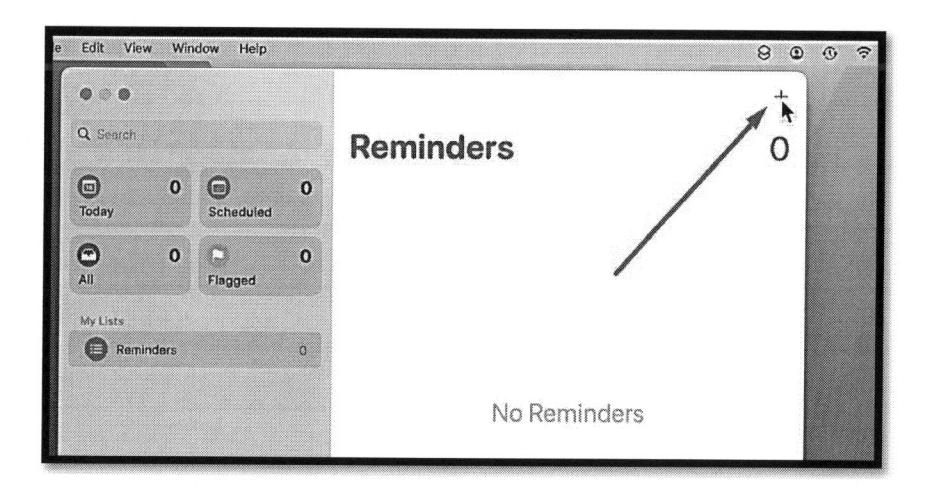

- Type the reminder's title here.
- By clicking the calendar icon and choosing a day and time, you can optionally establish a due date.
- Add any extra notes related to the reminder.

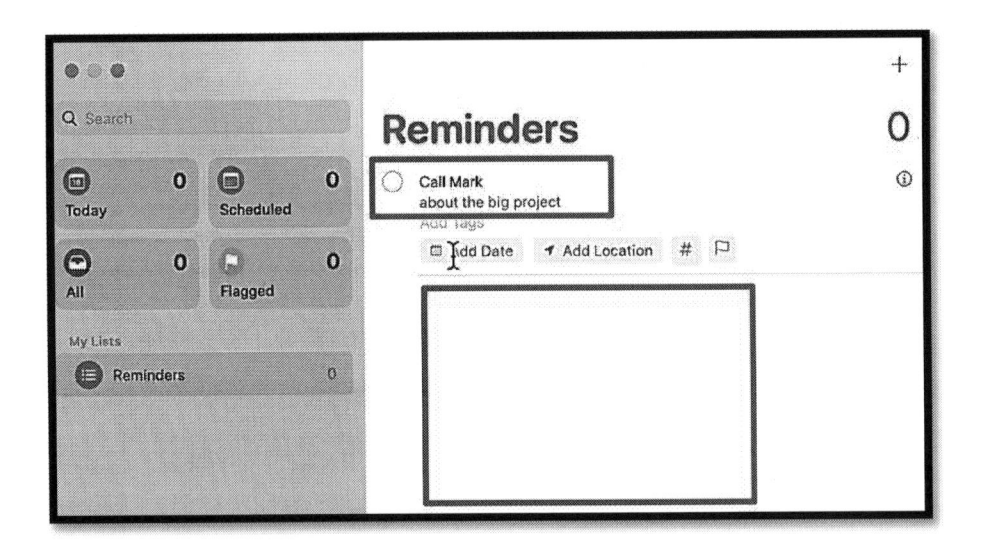

4. **Organizing Your Reminders:** Arrange your reminders in a variety of ways using the Reminder app.
- **Lists:** Make distinct lists for your job, personal chores, grocery lists, and other things. Click the "+" button in the Lists panel to add a new list, and then give it a name.

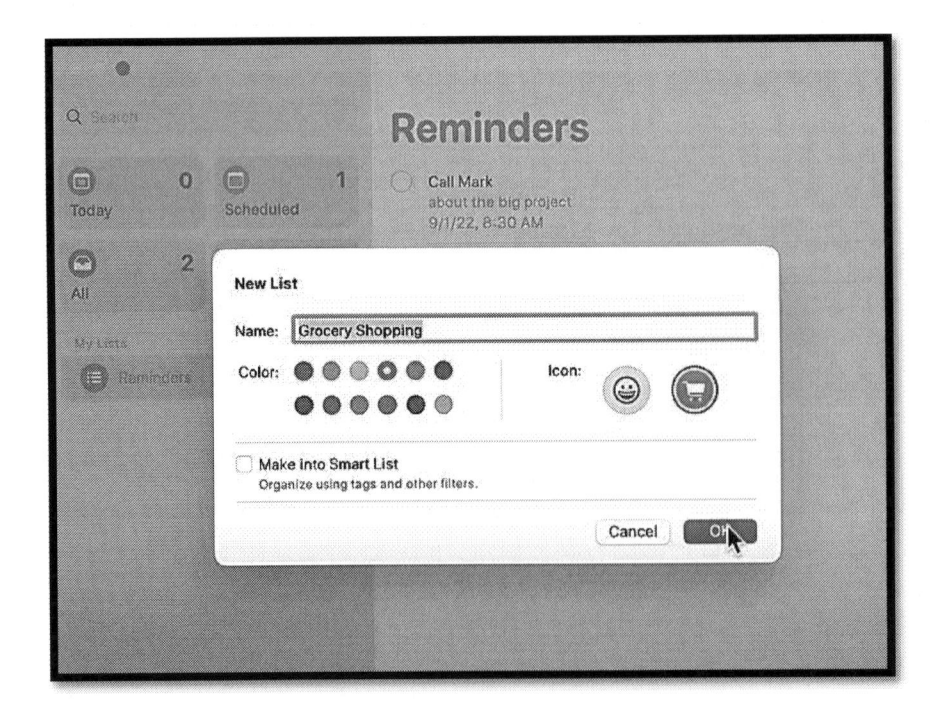

- **Priority Levels:** To make it simple to determine which chores are most essential, give your reminders a priority level. Click on a reminder, then choose the "i" symbol in the Details section and the preferred priority level to establish a priority level.
- **Subtasks:** For greater clarity, divide large jobs into more manageable subtasks. By selecting the "**Add**" button in the Details section of a reminder, subtasks may be created.
5. **Customizing Reminder Alerts**: The Reminder app lets you create alerts for specific tasks, ensuring you never forget a due date. Adjusting alerts:
- Make or choose a reminder.
- In the Details section, click the "**i**" symbol.

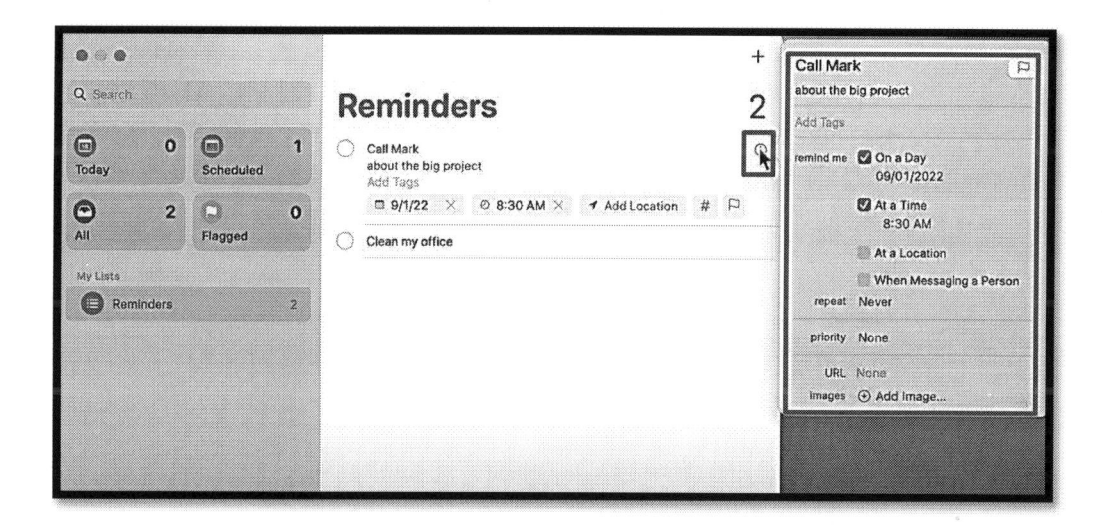

- Choose a time under "**Remind Me**" to get a reminder before the due date.
6. **Siri Integration:** The Reminder app on your MacBook Pro is smoothly connected with your virtual assistant, Siri. To create and manage reminders, use voice commands. Saying, "**Hey Siri, remind me to submit the report by Friday at 5 PM,**" for instance, will prompt Siri to set the reminder.
7. **Completing and Deleting Reminders:** A reminder can be deleted by selecting it and pressing the **"Delete" key** on your keyboard or by right-clicking and selecting "**Delete**."
8. **Syncing Between Devices**: The Reminder app's appeal goes beyond your MacBook Pro. Your reminders will be available on all of your Apple devices,

including your iPhone, iPad, and Apple Watch, thanks to its seamless iCloud account sync.

Set Up Recurring Reminders

The steps:

1. **Open the Reminders app**

Find the Reminders app on your MacBook Pro to get started. You can either find the app using the spotlight search (**Cmd + Space**) or by clicking on the "**Finder**" icon in your dock. Once you've located it, open the app by clicking the Reminders button.

2. **Creating a New List**

You will find the sidebar on the left when you first launch the Reminders app. Click on the "**Reminders**" area to see any lists or reminders that have already been created. Right-click on an empty spot, choose "**Add List**," and give your new list a suitable name, such as "**Recurring Tasks,**" to create a new list exclusively for your recurring reminders.

3. **Add a Recurring Reminder**

It's time to add your recurring reminder to your list now that it's ready. When you click on the newly formed list, a blank area with a flashing cursor will appear. To enter the task for which you wish to create a reminder, click there. Type your assignment and then hit "**Return**."

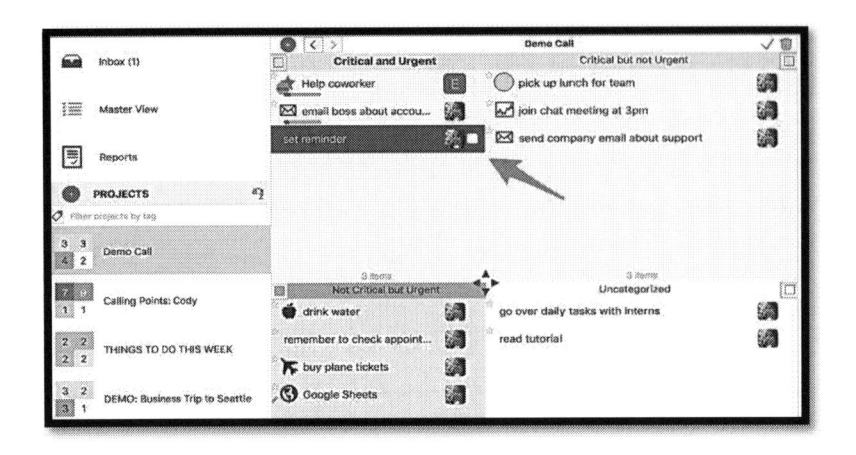

4. **Setting the Reminder Details**

It's time to set the reminder information once you've added the job. To get more information about the reminder, double-click the task you just entered. You can customize the reminder's details in this window.

- **Reminder Information**: Give your reminder a name that is descriptive and expresses the job clearly.
- **Date and Time**: Click on the calendar icon next to the "**Remind me on a day**" option to create a recurring reminder. Select the first day and hour when the reminder should occur. Use this as the basis for your regular schedule.
- **Frequency:** Select the number of times you want the reminder to recur from the dropdown menu under the "**Repeat**" section, which is located below the date and time selections. Daily, weekly, monthly, and annual options are available. Choose the one that best fits your needs.
- **End Repeat**: You can decide whether your repeating reminder should stop after a certain number of repetitions or on a specified date. This is especially helpful for jobs with a set completion date.

5. **Additional Options**

The Reminders app gives you some more customization options for your reminders.
- **Alerts**: You have the option of setting a custom time in advance or choosing to get an alert at the time of the reminder.
- **Priority**: Give your reminder a priority rating to help you concentrate on the most crucial activities first.
- **Notes**: Include any more remarks or information relevant to the assignment.

6. **Saving Your Recurring Reminder**

Click "**Add**" or "**Done**" to save your recurring reminder after you've finished configuring all the settings. The reminder will now appear in your list of "**Recurring Tasks**" and be generated automatically based on the schedule you've chosen.

7. **Managing and Completing Reminders**

By checking the box next to the reminder, you can mark your recurring tasks as finished as you do them. This will enable you to monitor your development and preserve your feeling of achievement.

8. **Changing or Deleting Recurring Reminders**

Life is dynamic, therefore you may sometimes need to change or get rid of a recurring reminder. Edit the reminder's information, and its frequency, or even erase it by simply right-clicking on the reminder and choosing **"Show Info."**

Share Reminders

The steps:

1. **Launch the Reminders app**

Find the Reminders app on your MacBook Pro to get started. It's accessible via Spotlight search or the Applications folder on your computer. Open the app after you've found it to view your lists and reminders.

2. **Create or Choose a Reminder List**

You need to have a list to share before you can post a reminder. If you don't currently have a list, you may make one by clicking the "+" icon in the bottom left corner of the app window and choosing "**New List**." Give your list a meaningful name, such as **"Team Project."** Ensure you select the list you want to share from the sidebar on the left if you already have one.

3. **Add Reminders to the List**

Start adding reminders to your list once it is ready. After opening the list by clicking its name, choose it and then select the "+" button at the bottom of the app window. Add the reminder's specifics, including the title, deadline, and any other remarks. To add all the reminders you want to share with others, repeat this procedure.

4. **Share the List**

The fun part now is letting people use your reminders. Take these actions:

- Click the sharing symbol, which resembles a person's silhouette with a plus sign (+) next to it, while the list is open. This icon is often seen in the program window's upper right corner.
- Once the sharing option appears, include more persons in the shared list. You may do this by entering their email addresses or, if they're using iCloud, by choosing them from your contacts.

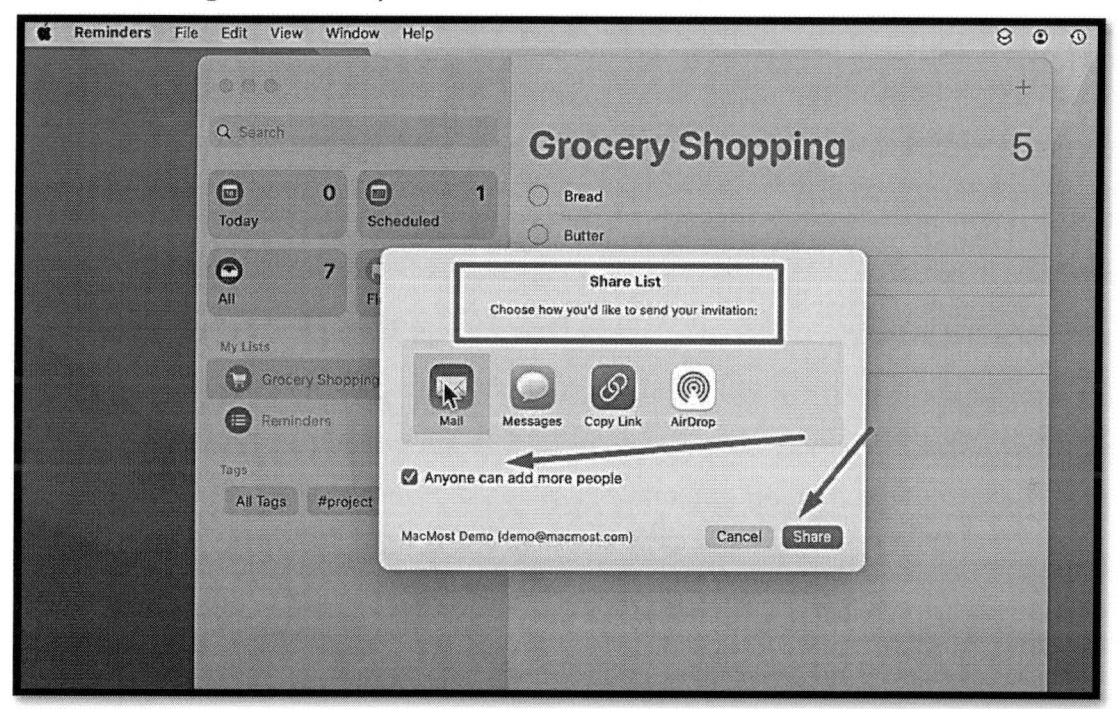

- Select the degree of access you want to give them after adding the persons you want to share the list with. The options are **"View & Edit"** or **"View only,"** with the former allowing collaborators to add, updates, and check off reminders and the latter allowing them to merely see the list and its contents.
- You can optionally attach a note with the invitation outlining the goal of the shared list.

- To send the invites, use the "**Share**" option.

    5. **Collaborate on Shared Reminders**

An email invitation to collaborate on the list will be sent to the recipients when you share it. The shared list will show up in their Reminders app as well if they accept the request.

Participants can now:

- View and modify the shared list's reminders.
- Add new remembrances to the list.
- Tick off accomplished reminders, which will sync across all devices used by collaborators.

When managing projects, scheduling family time, or organizing duties, this collaborative approach is very helpful.

    6. **Manage Sharing Settings**

A shared reminder list's sharing options can always be managed and changed. How to do it:

- Launch the Reminders app and access the shared list.
- Refresh your browser and click the sharing button (a person's outline).
- From this point, you can change the access permissions of your collaborators, add new ones, or delete old ones.
- By selecting the "**Stop Sharing**" option, you can also stop sharing the list completely.

Add People to a Shared List

On your MacBook Pro, adding individuals to a shared list is a simple procedure that allows you and your colleagues to work together effectively.

    1. **Launch the Reminders App**

Locate and launch the Reminders app on your MacBook Pro to begin going. You can look for it in the Applications folder or by putting "**Reminders**" into Spotlight search (**Cmd + Space**).

2. **Create a New List**

You must first make a list to share with others before adding individuals to it. You may skip this step if you already have a list that you wish to share. Click the "**+**" button in the bottom-left corner of the Reminders app to start a new list. The sidebar on the left will update with a fresh list.

3. **Give Your List a Name**

Give your list a name that accurately describes its function. Make it clear and descriptive since anyone you invite to the list will be able to see this name.

4. **Add Items to the List**

Start adding things to your list now that it has been created. These may be jobs, things on your to-do list, or anything else you wish to work on with other people. Enter your first item by clicking on the blank space inside the list. To add additional entries to the list, press "**Return**".

5. **Share the List**

It's time to share your list with others after it is complete and filled with goods. Right-click or control-click on the list's name in the sidebar. Go to the context menu that opens and choose "**Share List**."

6. **Select a Sharing Method**

There will be options for sharing the list in a popup that appears. You can decide to share via AirDrop, Messages, Mail, or another sharing-compatible app. Choose your favorite approach.

7. **Add Collaborators**

You may be asked to provide the email addresses or other contact information of the individuals you want to invite to the list, depending on the sharing option you choose. Multiple collaborators may be added at once. To guarantee that your colleagues get the invitation, double-check that you have the right email addresses or contacts.

8. **Set Permissions**

You have the option to decide what degree of access each collaborator will have before sending out the invites.

There are two permission levels:

- **View Only**: Users with this permission can see the list and its items, but they cannot edit them.
- **Add and Edit:** Users who have this privilege can browse the list as well as add new items and alter already-existing ones.

Depending on your preferences, decide the degree of authorization each collaborator should have.

9. **Send Invitations**

Send the invites when the collaborators have been added and the permissions have been specified. For the selected sharing method, click the **"Send"** button or a similar button. Each contributor will be notified and will also get an invitation.

10. **Collaborate in Real Time**

Your team members will be able to use their own devices to view the shared list after they accept the invitation. Real-time synchronization of any modifications made by you or your teammates enables smooth cooperation.

Set Up Task Sharing

Here are the steps:

1. Locate the Reminders app on your MacBook Pro and launch it to get started. It may be readily accessed by using Spotlight Search or by looking for it in the Applications folder. Make sure you are logged in with your Apple ID once you have launched the app.
2. **Create a New Reminder List:** You must first create a special reminder list before you can share tasks. All the tasks you want to share will be included in this list.

To create a new list, do the following actions:

- In the Reminders app's top menu bar, choose "**File**".
- From the drop-down menu, choose "**New List**".
- Name your list something that accurately describes what it is for, such as "Project Collaboration" or "Family Chores."

3. Now that you have a dedicated list, you can begin adding tasks to it. To add a new reminder, just click the "**+ New Reminder**" button at the bottom of the app window after clicking the list's name in the sidebar. To add a task, provide its information and, if required, its due date before pressing "**Enter**".
4. **Share the List with Others**: Collaborating with others is where task sharing shines. To share your reminder list with relatives, friends, or coworkers, follow these steps:

- In the sidebar, right-click (or control-click) the list you want to share.
- Choose "**Share List**" from the context menu.

5. After selecting "**Share List**," you will be given a variety of sharing choices to choose from. The list is sent through iCloud, Messages, Mail, or a third-party application like Slack. Let's go through the iCloud sharing procedure:

- Select "**Share with iCloud**" from the menu.
- People whose email addresses you want to share the list with should enter them. If you would like, you may also provide a customized message.
- Select the editing rights to control whether the recipients may just read the list or can also update it. Toggle the switch as necessary.
- To share the invites, click the "**Share**" button.

6. The individuals you invited will get an email inviting them to share the reminder list. To begin working together, they must accept the offer. What they can accomplish is as follows:
- Launch the invitation they got through email.
- In the email, choose the "**View List**" option. On their smartphone, this will launch the Reminders app.
- If they have an iCloud account, they may decide whether to "**Join**" the list. If not, users may view the list without having an iCloud account by selecting "**View in Browser**" from the menu.
7. After everyone has joined the shared list, start working together on projects. Any modifications made by one individual will be immediately visible on all devices. As necessary, you may add new tasks, edit task information, or mark tasks as completed.

You can access the shared tasks from your MacBook Pro, iPhone, iPad, or Apple Watch and stay up to date since the Reminders app syncs with all of your Apple devices.

Assign Task to Someone Else

Here are the steps:

1. **Create User Accounts**

Make sure you have user accounts set up for yourself and the others you'll be working with before you start giving assignments. It is possible to add new user accounts by going to "**System Settings**" from the Apple menu, choosing "**Users & Groups**," and then clicking the "**+**" button. Ensure you have the data you need to establish the person's account, including their name and email address.

2. **Create a Task List**

It's important to have a task list or project management solution in place to allocate work properly. Organize tasks by project, priority, or due date to guarantee smooth delegation. You can use the built-in "Reminders" app or use a third-party application like "**Todoist**" or "**Asana**."

3. **Assigning a Task**

When you're ready to give a job to someone else, do the following actions:

- Open the "**Reminders**" app or the task management app of your choice.
- By clicking on it, you can choose the assignment you want to assign.
- Look for a selection that indicates task cooperation or sharing. A "**Share**" button symbol might be used to illustrate this.
- Select the sharing button or symbol. You will be prompted to enter the email address or username of the person you want to assign the task to in a dialogue box that will display.
- You can have the opportunity to provide a due date, comments, or extra information about the assignment after entering the recipient's information.
- To assign the work to the selected individual, click "**Send**" or "**Share**".

4. **Managing Shared Tasks**

After a work has been allocated, it's crucial to monitor its development and guarantee effective communication. Here's how to successfully handle jobs that are shared:

- Check your task management application often for changes on the shared task. When the assignment is accepted and finished, or if there are any comments or questions, you can get alerts.
- Keep the lines of communication open with the individual you've given the work to. Respond quickly if they have any questions or want clarification.
- Make sure to mark the work as done in your task management application once it has been finished. By doing so, you can accurately track your development.
- Within the task management tool, you can make adjustments to the assignment as needed, such as changing the due date or adding more details.

5. **Getting Tasks Assigned**

It works the same way whether you're the one getting the job assignment.

Managing the duties you've been given is as follows:

- Look for alerts regarding the allocated assignment in your email inbox or your task management application. An app notice or an email might be sent to you.
- View the specifics of the given job by opening the notice or going to your task management application.
- If you can do the work, accept it. Use the tool's comments or communication tools to get in touch with the person who assigned the assignment if you need any clarification or have any issues.
- Mark the work as done in the task management tool after you have finished it. You might also provide remarks or notes regarding your development, if appropriate.

Reassign the Task to another Person

The steps:

1. **Launch the Task Management App**

Make sure you have a task management app installed on your MacBook Pro before you can reassign a task. Apple's built-in **"Reminders"** app, third-party applications like Todoist or Microsoft To Do, or more thorough project management solutions like Asana or Trello are also popular options. To begin, launch the app of your choosing.

2. **Access Your Task List**

Once the app is launched, a list of your tasks should appear. Find the assignment you wish to give to a different individual. It's possible that you came up with this assignment on your own or that someone else gave it to you.

3. **Edit the Task**

Click on the task you want to change the assignment to. The **"Edit"** or **"Details"** button is often there; click on it to see the task's choices and information.

4. **Reassign the Task**

You should find a change assignee or responsible person option in the task details. Clicking on this option will display a list of possible team members or contacts. This option can be titled "**Assign to**" or "**Responsible**."

5. **Choose a New Assignee**

Choose the person to whom you want to transfer the assignment from the list of available alternatives. This may be a coworker, a member of your team, or someone else you've added to your task management program. To confirm the reassignment, click on their name.

6. **Save Changes**

Save your modifications after choosing the new assignee. The "**Update**" or "**Save**" button may often be found inside the job description. Your task management software will now show that the work has been assigned to the selected individual.

7. **Inform the New Assignee**

Although the task management tool may automatically send alerts, it is a good idea to directly tell the new assignee of the job reassignment. This may clear up any misunderstandings and guarantee a seamless transfer of duties.

8. **Check Task Status**

After reassigning the work, monitor its development. You can monitor how the job is proceeding in the hands of the new assignee thanks to the real-time updates and collaboration tools that are included in many task management programs.

9. **Follow Up and Provide Support**

Once the work has been successfully transferred, it is crucial to continue supporting the new assignee. Check-in on the task's progress often, give support if required, and keep lines of communication open to deal with any difficulties that may develop.

10. **Examine and Consider**

Take the time to evaluate the procedure once the new assignee has finished the work. Analyze the reassignment's success and if it resulted in increased productivity. Consider what went well and what may be improved for the next task redistribution.

Set an Alarm via Reminders

Here's how to set an alarm via reminders:

1. **Open the Reminders App**

Locate the Reminders app on your MacBook Pro to get started. To quickly locate and launch the program, either click on the Reminders icon in the Dock or use Spotlight Search (type **Command + Space** and begin entering "**Reminders**").

2. **Create a New Reminder**

When you first use the Reminders app, you'll notice its neat and well-organized user interface. You must make a new reminder before you can set a new alarm. In the lower-left corner of the window, click the plus button. As an alternative, you can use the shortcut **Command + N**.

3. **Add Reminder Information**

Enter the specifics of your alarm in a new window that will pop up as a reminder. Write a short description of the work or event you want to set the alarm for in the title area. For instance, you might use "**3:00 PM Meeting**" as the headline if your meeting is at 3:00 PM.

4. **Set the Due Date and Time**

You must enter the reminder's due date and time to set an alarm. Next to the title box, choose the calendar icon. There will be a time and calendar selector. Use the calendar to find the event's date, and then use the time picker to choose the right time.

5. **Choose the List**

Categorize your chores into separate lists using reminders. For your alarm, you may choose from an existing list or make one from scratch. Your current lists will appear in a dropdown menu when you choose the "**Add to List**" option. Choose the list that most closely matches the reminder category. You can have a "**Work**" or "**Personal**" list, for example.

6. **Add Notes (Optional)**

You can put notes in your reminder if you wish to provide further context. Notes may be used to add details or instructions about the activity or event. To access the text area where you can also enter your notes, click the "**Add Note**" button.

7. **Set the Alarm**

Choose how you want to be reminded in the "**Remind Me**" portion of the reminder box. We're creating a time-based alarm, so click the dropdown menu to show choices like **"On a Day," "At a Location," and "Time."**

8. **Configure Alarm Settings**

After choosing "**Time**," you'll be given many options to set your alarm. You have the option of receiving a reminder "**At the time of day,**" "**Before,**" or "**After**" the occasion. Choose "At time of day" and the time that you want the alarm to go off. In our example, if you want a 15-minute heads-up before the 3:00 PM meeting, this would be at 2:45 PM.

9. **Save the Reminder**

It's time to save the reminder now that all the settings have been established. In the lower right corner of the reminder window, click the "**Add**" button. The chosen list will now include your reminder with the provided due date, time, and alarm settings.

10. **Receive and Manage the Alarm**

Depending on the settings you've chosen, your MacBook Pro will notify you when the time for your alarm draws near. If your smartphone is not muted, you will also hear a sound alarm in addition to the popup notice. To mark the reminder as finished or to snooze it for later, click the notice.

Frequently Asked Questions

1. How do you use the Reminder app?
2. How do you set up recurring reminders on your MacBook Pro?
3. How do you set an alarm via reminders?
4. How do you add people to a shared list?
5. How to assign and reassign a task to another person?
6. How do you share reminders?

CHAPTER THIRTEEN
LIVE TEXT

Overview

Chapter thirteen talks about LiveText and how you can effectively use it on your new MacBook Pro. You will learn how to share text in images, how to drag and drop selected text, how to translate text and so much more.

How to use Live Text on MacBook Pro

Interact with text included in photos as if it were a live, editable element using Live Text, which blurs the distinction between printed text and digital data. This groundbreaking function brings up a universe of possibilities, from information extraction to productivity improvement.

Enabling Live Text

Make sure you are using macOS Ventura before you explore the world of Live Text.

There is no need to install extra software since Live Text is a built-in function.

1. Make sure your MacBook Pro is running macOS Ventura by updating your macOS. To check for updates, click the Apple menu in the top-left corner of the screen, choose **"System Settings,"** and then choose **"Software Update."**
2. Whether you take a picture with your MacBook Pro's camera or import one from another source, Live Text works with text-containing photos.

Using Live Text

Once Live Text is enabled, you can make use of its features:

1. **Identifying Text**

Any suitable app, such as Preview or Photos, may be used to open a text-filled picture. Move your mouse pointer over the text you wish to edit. Your cursor will change into a text selection tool if the text is pickable.

2. **Choosing Text**

To pick the text within the picture, click and drag. A contextual menu will appear above the highlighted portion of text, which will also be highlighted.

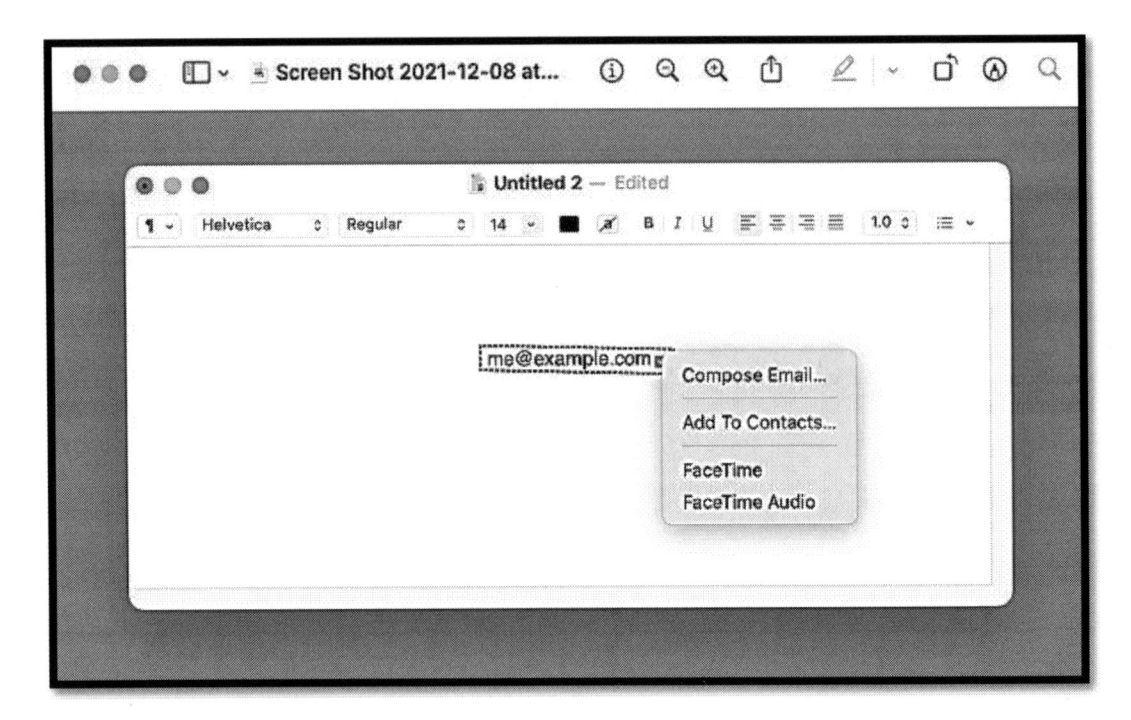

3. **Interacting with Text**

After you've chosen the text, the contextual menu will provide you with several options.

One can:

- **Copy and Paste:** To copy the text, choose "**Copy**" from the menu. Then, you can paste it into any text-input-capable app, including a document, note, email, and more.
- **Look Up**: Select "**Lookup**" to find out more about the text you've chosen. Definitions, pertinent data, and even online search results will be shown on your MacBook Pro to provide context.

- **Translate:** From the menu, pick "**Translate**" if the chosen text is in a different language. You can use the translation tools on your MacBook Pro to better comprehend the content.

4. **Editing and Correcting**

Live Text is more than simply data extraction. The text included inside the picture can also be changed and improved. Click on the text after choosing it to open the inline text editor. Just as you would in a standard text document, make your modifications.

5. **Looking Up Handwritten Text**

Live Text is not only for text that is printed. Additionally, it can find handwritten writing inside photos and identify it. You may choose the handwritten text in a scanned document or picture that includes handwritten notes and Live Text will try to turn it into editable text.

6. **Using Live Text in Third-Party Apps**

Live Text is now accessible to developers, thus several third-party applications should support it as well. Watch for upgrades to your favorite applications that could include Live Text.

Drag & Drop Selected Text

Follow the steps below:

1. **Upgrade your OS to macOS Ventura**

Ensure that the operating system on your MacBook Pro is up to date before exploring the fascinating world of Live Text. Apple provides software updates often to improve speed, address faults, and add new features. If an update is available, install it by following the on-screen instructions after selecting "**Software Update**" from the "**About This Mac**" menu by clicking on the Apple menu in the top-left corner of your screen.

2. **Enable Live Text**

A fundamental component of macOS Ventura versions is Live Text.

Follow these steps to activate Live Text on your MacBook Pro:

- Select the Apple Menu and **System Settings**.
- Choose "**Accessibility**."
- Go to the left sidebar and choose "**Display**."
- Select the checkbox next to "**Enable Live Text**."

3. **Using Live Text to Drag and Drop Selected Text**

Once Live Text is activated, you can use its drag-and-drop functionality to move chosen text around.

Follow these steps:

- Open the picture or screenshot from which you want to extract the text.
- Place the cursor on the text you want to choose. You'll see that the text is highlighted as you go.
- Select the highlighted text by clicking and holding it.
- You can now drag the chosen text to the location you want while continuing to depress the mouse or trackpad button.

4. **Dropping the Text**

Drop the chosen text by releasing the mouse or trackpad button after dragging it to the desired spot. This can be done in any text field where you want to insert the extracted information, including a document, email, note, or other text field.

Extracting Text

Let's look at the several things you can do now that you've enabled Live Text and chosen the text you want to work with:
- **Copy Text:** Right-click on the relevant text after choosing it, then pick "**Copy**" from the context menu. Alternatively, you can copy the text by pressing "**Command + C**" on your keyboard.

- **Look Up:** Live Text's capacity to rapidly look up text content is one of its most notable capabilities. You can get additional information about a word or phrase by right-clicking it after you've picked it and choosing "**Look Up**." This will launch the macOS dictionary.
- **Search:** To start a Google search for the highlighted text, right-click on it and choose **"Search with Google"**.
- **Share**: You can also send the chosen text from the image alone. Send the text via AirDrop, Messages, or other sharing options by right-clicking and choosing the "**Share**" option.
- **Translate**: If the text you've chosen is in another language, you can right-click and choose "**Translate**" to have it instantaneously translated into the language of your choice.

Editing Text

Basic text editing is also possible immediately inside photos with Live Text:

1. **Correction:** If the OCR fails to recognize the text correctly, you can manually fix it. To change the text, just click on it and begin entering the proper phrase.
2. **Formatting:** Although the text-editing features are simple, you can still use basic formatting features like bold, italics, and underlines.
3. **Copy as Plain Content**: From the context menu, choose "Copy as Plain Text" to copy the content in its original format.

Accessibility Benefits

Live Text is not simply a handy feature; it also has a lot to offer in terms of accessibility:

1. **Assistive Technology**: Using assistive technology, people with visual impairments may read text included inside pictures using Live Text, making it simpler for them to engage with a variety of information.
2. **Language Learning**: Words or phrases that are unknown to them may be easily translated and understood by language learners.
3. **Quick Information Retrieval:** For study and documentation, professionals and students may quickly and simply extract information from photographs.

Limitations and Considerations

Live Text is a strong tool, but it's crucial to understand its limitations:

1. **Font Recognition**: Live Text may have trouble reading certain typefaces or handwriting types, which might result in inaccurate text extraction.
2. **Image Quality:** Live Text's OCR performs better with clear, well-lit photographs; blurry or low-resolution images may provide less accurate text extraction.
3. **Language Support**: Live Text supports a wide range of languages, albeit the accuracy of recognition varies from language to language.

Search the Web for Highlighted Text

The steps:

1. **Update to the Latest macOS Version**

Make sure your MacBook Pro is running the most recent macOS version that supports this feature before you begin using Live Text to search the web for highlighted text. If an update is available, follow the instructions to download and install it by clicking the Apple menu in the top-left corner of your screen, choosing "**About This Mac**," and then clicking on "**Software Update**."

2. **Capture or Open an Image with Text**

You'll need a picture or screenshot of the text you want to interact with to use Live Text to search the web for highlighted text. Press **Shift + Command + 4** to choose the text-containing area of the screen and capture a screenshot of it. On your MacBook Pro, you can also use the screenshot tool located in the Control Center. Simply open an existing picture with text using the Preview app or your preferred image viewer.

3. **Enable Live Text**

It's time to turn on Live Text after you have the screenshot or picture with the text you wish to highlight. With photos that include legible and recognized text, this function works without a hitch.

Follow these procedures to turn on Live Text:

- Use the Preview app or any other appropriate Live Text-supporting app to see the screenshot or picture.
- Place the cursor on the text that you want to be highlighted. You'll see that when you do this, your cursor transforms into a text-selection tool.
- Click and drag the cursor over the text you want to highlight. A real-time selection of the highlighted text will be shown.

4. **Look up the Web for Highlighted Text**

You can now do a web search to get extra details or context about the relevant text after using Live Text to highlight it.

Here is how to go about it:

- Right-click the highlighted text to select it. Then a context menu will show up.
- Choose "**Search with Google**" (or "**Search with your preferred search engine**") from the context menu. The highlighted text will be used as the search query in the web search that results from this operation.
- The search results for the selected text will appear in a new browser window or tab that will open. You can research pertinent books, websites, and data on the text you choose.

5. **Interact with Search Results**

Interact with the search results once they are open, just as you would with any other online search. To read complete articles, websites, or other information, click on the search results. You may read, save, or share the information you uncover if it is what you were searching for.

6. **Refining your Search**

You can always hone your search phrase if the first search results don't provide the information you're searching for. Complete this by simply altering the selected text in your browser's search box. This enables you to alter the search query and carry out a more focused search for precise results.

Translate Text within Pictures

Here's how to translate text inside images after Live Text has been enabled:

1. **Open the Image**: Using your favorite image viewer, open the picture that includes the text you want to translate.
2. Hover your pointer over the picture to activate the live text. Live Text will highlight any text that it identifies in the picture. To enable Live Text, just click on the underlined text.
3. **Choose the Text:** Use your mouse to click and drag to choose the text you want to translate. The chosen text will be underlined.
4. The contextual menu will show after the text has been chosen, in other words. Select "**Translate**" from the menu's options.
5. Select a language and a translation box displaying the chosen text and its translation will appear. The dropdown options at the top of the translation box let you choose the source and destination languages.
6. **View Translation**: The translation of the text will be shown in the translation box after the languages have been chosen. The original context of the text and the translated text are both visible.
7. **Copy or Share**: By selecting the "**Copy Translation**" option, you can copy the translated content. Using the share option, you can share the translation with another person through messages, emails, or other messaging services.

Tips for Using Live Text Translation

- **Multiple Selections**: Repeat the procedure to pick and translate each text occurrence if a picture has many occurrences of it.
- **Language Accuracy:** Although Live Text's translation technology often provides correct translations, it's always a good idea to double-check the translation, particularly for important information.
- **Online and Offline**: Live Text's translation feature is adaptable for a range of situations since it works both online and offline.
- **Text Extraction**: In addition to translating, Live Text can be used to extract text from photos, such as names, addresses, and more.
- **Languages Supported**: Live Text offers translation for a sizable number of languages, making it a potent tool for multilingual communication.

Share the Text in Photos

Here are the steps:

1. **Ensure Your MacBook Pro is Updated**

Make sure your MacBook Pro's operating system is current before you begin utilizing the Live Text function. Updates to software often contain new functions and enhancements. If updates are available, install them by following the on-screen instructions after clicking the Apple menu in the top-left corner of your screen, selecting **"System Settings,"** and then clicking **"Software Update."**

2. **Open the Photo with the Text**

Once your MacBook Pro is up to date, launch the **"Photos"** app by searching for it in Spotlight or from your Applications folder. Locate the image on which the text you wish to extract is present. This might be a picture of a sign, a page from a book, a document, or anything else that has text in it.

3. **Enable Live Text**

Open the picture and place your cursor over it. The cursor will now be a "**Live Text**" symbol, which looks like a magnifying glass. Press and hold the "**Control**" key while clicking the picture, or clicking the icon.

4. **Choose the Text**

The image's text will become selectable and interactive once Live Text is turned on. When you want to share a particular section of text, you may highlight it by clicking and dragging your mouse over it. The highlighted text will become blue, and a contextual menu will show up with choices like "**Copy**," "**Look Up**," and "**Share**."

5. **Copy or Share the Text**

Depending on how you want to use the text, you may either copy it or share it right from the image. Simply choose "**Copy**" from the contextual menu if you want to copy the content and paste it somewhere else. The chosen text will be copied to your clipboard so that it may be pasted into a text field in a document, email, or anywhere else. Click on the **"Share"** option in the contextual menu to share the text straight from the image. This will open a share sheet with several sharing options, including the ability to transmit the text through mail, messages, or even social media. To finish the procedure, choose the preferred sharing method and follow the instructions.

6. **Use the Look-Up Feature**

Live Text offers more than simply copying and sharing text. To learn more about the chosen text, you may also use the "Lookup" option. To use this feature, simply select the text in the image, right-click or use the two-finger trackpad gesture, and then select **"Look Up**." This will use Apple's built-in dictionary and search tools to give you definitions, explanations, and pertinent information about the selected text.

7. **Edit and Correct Extracted Text**

When the picture quality is poor or the text is deformed, Live Text may sometimes struggle to accurately extract the text from the image. Fortunately, the retrieved text may be manually edited and improved. You may easily alter the text after choosing it in the Live Text box that displays on the image. Make the required modifications, then copy or distribute the updated text.

Speak the Highlighted Text

Live Text is a potent feature that uses optical character recognition (OCR) and machine learning to identify and extract text from photos. As a result, you can interact with text included inside pictures in the same way that you would with ordinary text found in books or online pages. The option to have the highlighted text read aloud to you is one of the valuable features of Live Text, which may be immensely helpful for those who prefer aural input or who have visual problems.

Enabling Live Text

Make sure Live Text is turned on in your MacBook Pro before you can use the voice highlighted text feature:

1. **Update to macOS Ventura**: A new feature in macOS Ventura is Live Text. Make sure this operating system or a newer version is installed on your MacBook Pro.
2. **Enable Live Text:** The checkbox next to "**Enable Live Text**" must be checked, however, so make sure it is by going to "**System Settings**" from the Apple menu, choosing "**Accessibility**," and then clicking on "**Live Text**" on the left sidebar.

Using Live Text to Speak Highlighted Text

Following these instructions will enable the functionality that will read highlighted text loudly once you have enabled Live Text:

1. **Open a Picture**: Click on the picture to see the text you want to change. This may be a screenshot, a picture, or another image containing words that can be seen.
2. To highlight a passage of text, just click and drag the mouse over it. You'll see a toolbar emerge above or around the highlighted text as you highlight it.
3. To make the "**Speak**" option active, choose it from the toolbar that displays. The symbol for it is often one of a speaker or sound waves.
4. **Listen to the Text**: By selecting the "**Speak**" option, your MacBook Pro will use its text-to-speech features to read aloud the selected text. Your computer will narrate the chosen text while you adjust the volume to your taste.

Customizing the Speech Settings

The voice settings on your MacBook Pro can change in many ways to suit your preferences:

1. **Speech Rate:** Increase the voice rate to read the text at a quicker rate; reduce it to read it at a slower rate.
2. **Voice:** macOS Ventura offers a variety of top-notch voices with various accents and tongues. From the Voice dropdown menu, you may choose a voice that meets your needs.

3. **Highlight Content**: The words being said will be highlighted in real-time when you choose the "**Highlight Content**" option in the Live Text toolbar, making it simpler for you to follow along visually as they are read aloud.

Translate Text on MacBook Pro

You are now prepared to begin translating text from photos with Live Text enabled:

1. **Open or Capture an Image**: Live Text works with photos from a variety of sources. You can use the camera on your MacBook Pro to capture a picture, scan a page, or just view an image file. To copy a picture to your clipboard, either choose "**Copy**" from the context menu when you right-click it or press "**Command + C**."
2. **Paste the Image**: Launch the app where you want to translate the text, such as Pages for a document or Notes for a note. To paste the picture, use "**Command + V**" or the "**Paste**" option from the context menu of the program.
3. **Enable Live Text:** After pasting the picture, moves your mouse over it to activate the live text feature. The cursor transforms into a magnifying glass icon, as you'll see. Live Text may be activated by clicking the picture.
4. **Choose the Text**: Drag the mouse pointer over the text you want to translate to select it. Live Text will highlight the text as you do this in real-time. Release the mouse button after selecting the text.
5. **Access the Translation:** After choosing the text, a little pop-up menu will appear next to the chosen text. You can choose from several alternatives by clicking the menu, among which is "**Translate**."
6. **Choose the Language:** A translation panel with the original text on the left and the translation on the right will show after selecting the language. The dropdown menu at the top of the panel lets you choose the translation's destination language.
7. **View the Translation**: After selecting a language, Live Text will instantly translate the text you've chosen. The translation may be used as required or copied to your clipboard.

Frequently Asked Questions

1. How do you use Live Text on your new MacBook Pro?
2. How do you drag and drop selected text?
3. How do you copy text from images on your MacBook Pro?
4. How to do translate and share text in Photos?
5. How do you search the web for highlighted text?

CHAPTER FOURTEEN
SPOTLIGHT, SPLIT SCREEN, AND SIRI

Overview

In chapter fourteen, you will learn all about these features, Spotlight, Split Screen, and Siri, and how to use them effectively on your MacBook Pro.

How to access and use Spotlight

On your MacBook Pro, Spotlight is a powerful search function that enables you to discover files, programs, documents, emails, and more with ease. Spotlight may substantially increase your productivity and make it easier for you to browse through the stuff on your computer thanks to its simple design and powerful features.

Enabling Spotlight

1. **Using the Keyboard Shortcut**: Using the keyboard shortcut is the simplest method to open Spotlight. The Spotlight search bar will appear in the middle of your screen when you simultaneously press "**Command**" and "**Spacebar**".
2. **Clicking the Magnifying Glass Icon**: The magnifying glass icon is located in the menu bar in the top-right corner of your screen. Additionally, clicking on it will bring up the Spotlight search box.

Using Spotlight

1. **Basic Search**: After opening the Spotlight search box, begin entering your search term. Real-time results from Spotlight, including apps, documents, emails, calendar events, and more, will start to appear as you type. The search can tolerate incomplete or misspelled queries and is not case-sensitive.

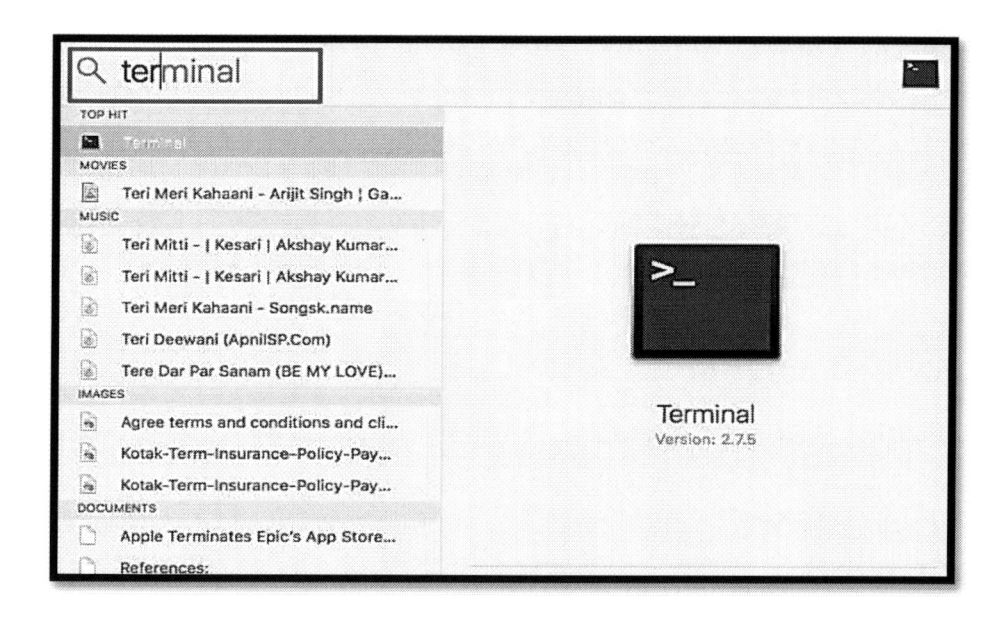

2. **Viewing Results**: Spotlight presents search results in a variety of categories, including Applications, Documents, Messages, Contacts, and more. To open a result right now, click on it. To browse the results, use the arrow keys.
3. **Previewing Results:** You can see the content of numerous file formats without launching the app. To obtain a brief preview, just highlight the outcome and hit the "**Spacebar**".
4. **Search Syntax:** Spotlight offers enhanced search syntax to help you focus your searches. For instance, "**kind**:" can be used to limit results by a particular file type (such as **"kind:pdf"),** and "**date**:" can be used to search within a specified time frame (such as **"date:last week").** You can efficiently limit your search results with this.
5. **Calculations and Unit Conversions:** The Spotlight search bar has an option for rapid calculations and unit conversions. Simply enter a mathematical formula or a unit conversion question (such as "25 USD to EUR"), and Spotlight will provide the answer.
6. **Launching Apps:** Spotlight can be used for more than simply locating files. By putting the names of programs in the search field, you can open them fast. By doing this, you won't need to search through your Applications folder.
7. **Searching the Web:** Spotlight can also be used to do quick online searches. Just use terms as the first part of your search query, and Spotlight will show you relevant online results from your preferred search engine.

8. **Searching Contacts and Emails**: Type the name of a contact to have Spotlight show you the appropriate contact information. Additionally, if you use Apple Mail, you may do a keyword or sender name search to find particular emails or chats.
9. **Accessing System Settings:** Typing relevant system preference-related keywords will also provide fruitful results. This is an excellent method for rapidly accessing and changing different MacBook Pro settings.

Customizing Spotlight

1. **Managing Search Categories**: You can choose the categories Spotlight searches through by managing the search categories. To achieve this, go to **"System Settings"** > **"Spotlight**," and from there, choose the categories you want to include or omit from your search results by checking or unchecking the appropriate boxes.
2. **Reordering Search Results**: Reorganize the search results if you decide that some results are more significant to you than others. To prioritize the order in which results are shown, just drag & drop the categories in the **"Spotlight"** section of System Settings.
3. **Keyboard Shortcuts**: Configure keyboard shortcuts for certain activities in the Spotlight options. You could create a shortcut to launch Spotlight, the calculator, or the dictionary, for example.

Edit Spotlight Search Results

The steps:

1. **Open Spotlight Settings**

You must access the Spotlight options to begin personalizing your search results. This is how:

- In the upper-left corner of your screen, choose the **Apple menu**.
- From the dropdown menu, choose "**System Settings**".

- Click "**Spotlight**" in the System Settings box.
2. **Selecting Search Result Categories**

When you search in Spotlight, you have the option of selecting which types of search results are shown. Depending on your preferences, you can activate or disable certain categories.

Here is how to go about it:

- Find the "**Search Results**" tab in the Spotlight settings box.
- A variety of categories, including ones for applications, documents, images, and more, will be visible.
- The checkbox next to a category must be ticked if you want it to appear in your search results. Simply deselect the checkbox next to a category to omit it.

3. **Reorder Search Result Categories**

It is also possible to change the order in which the categories of search results are displayed. If you often use certain file or program types and want them to show up at the top of your search results, this might be helpful.

The categories can be rearranged as follows:

- Click and drag the categories in the "**Search Results**" tab of the Spotlight settings to change their order.
- Your search results will show the categories at the top of the list first, then the categories below.

4. **Customize Search Result Sources**

Spotlight can get results from a variety of web sources, including Bing, Wikipedia, and more, in addition to searching your local files. Which sources appear in your search results is up to you.

Here's how:

- Find the "**Search Results**" tab in the Spotlight settings box.
- There is a list of online resources under the "**Other**" section, which can be found by scrolling down.
- Select the sources you want to see in your search results by checking or unchecking the boxes next to them.

5. **Exclude Folders from Spotlight Indexing**

You can prevent certain folders or places on your MacBook Pro from being indexed so they don't show up in Spotlight search results. This might assist you in maintaining clutter-free attention on pertinent outcomes.

How to exclude directories is as follows:

- Select the "**Privacy**" option in the Spotlight settings box.
- Navigate to the folder or place you want to exclude from indexing by clicking the "**+**" button.
- The folder won't show up in your Spotlight search results once you've added it.

6. **Reset Spotlight Preferences (Optional)**

You can quickly reset the preferences if you've made many changes to your Spotlight search results and want to go back to them.

This is how:

- Select the "**Search Results**" tab in the Spotlight settings box.
- The "**Restore Defaults**" option is located at the bottom of the window.
- To restore the default settings for your Spotlight search results, click this button.

Hide Items from Spotlight Search

The steps:

1. **Open System Settings**

Start by selecting "**System Settings**" from the drop-down menu when you click on the Apple logo in the top-left corner of your screen.

2. **Access Spotlight Preferences**

Find the "**Spotlight**" icon in the System Settings box and click it. The Spotlight preferences window will then be shown.

3. **Customize Search Results**

You'll notice a variety of categories, such as Applications, Documents, System Preferences, etc., while you're in the Spotlight preferences panel. All categories are by default checked, so your search results will include everything in them.

4. **Uncheck Items to Hide**

Simply uncheck the associated categories to make some objects invisible to Spotlight search. For instance, uncheck the "**Documents**" option if you wish to exclude Documents from the search results. By doing this, documents won't show up when you do a Spotlight search.

5. **Privacy Settings**

What if you just want to hide a few particular files or folders, not an entire category? The Privacy tab in the Spotlight options might be useful in this situation.

6. **Add Items to the Privacy List**

In the Spotlight settings window, choose the "**Privacy**" tab. The areas on your MacBook Pro that Spotlight is presently not allowed to search are listed below. Click the "**+**" button in the bottom left to add an item to this list.

7. **Select Items to Hide**

In the file window that displays, find the file or folder you wish to conceal. After choosing the item, press the "**Choose**" button. By doing this, Spotlight won't return that item in its search results.

8. **Remove the items from the Privacy List**

Return to the Privacy tab in the Spotlight options to make a hidden item searchable once again if you change your mind. Click the "**-**" button in the bottom left corner after choosing the item from the list that you wish to delete.

9. **Reindex Spotlight (Optional)**

You can see that the search results don't update right away after you hide anything from Spotlight. This is necessary so that macOS can re-index your machine. To do this, return to the "**Privacy**" tab and choose the location of your starting drive. To remove it from the privacy list, click the "**-**" button now. This will cause Spotlight to begin being re-indexed by macOS.

How to use Siri

In this aspect, Apple's virtual assistant Siri has changed the game. Your everyday duties will now be much more convenient and effective thanks to Siri's incorporation into the macOS environment, particularly on the new MacBook Pro.

Enabling Siri

On your MacBook Pro, you need to turn on Siri before exploring the features. Simply click the Siri symbol in the menu bar in the top right corner of your screen to accomplish this, or press the **Command** and **Space** keys simultaneously to use the keyboard shortcut. Alternatively, if your MacBook Pro is compatible with **"Hey Siri,"** you can also call Siri up by speaking those two secret phrases.

Siri's Basic Tasks

1. **Search and Information Retrieval:** Siri can be your go-to tool for online searches, information retrieval, and weather checks. You can obtain

immediate answers by asking Siri simple inquiries like, "What's the weather like today?" or "Tell me about the most recent Apple event.

2. **Setting Reminders and Alarms**: Do you need to set an alarm for a crucial meeting or a reminder to get groceries? That can be handled by Siri. Siri will set alarms and reminders for you when you say things like, "Set an alarm for 7 AM tomorrow" or "Remind me to buy milk when I leave the office."
3. **Sending Messages:** Siri can save you time by delivering messages for you without you having to write them out yourself. For example, you might say, **"Send a message to Sarah: I'll be there in 10 minutes,"** and Siri would write and send the message on your behalf.
4. **Making Calls:** Calling someone is as simple as asking Siri to do it. When you tell Siri to "Call Mom" or "Dial John's mobile number," she will do it.

Advanced Features

1. **File and App Navigation:** On your MacBook Pro, Siri can assist you in finding files and starting the app fast. If you ask Siri to "**Open Microsoft Word**" or "**Find my vacation photos,**" she'll take you right there.
2. **System Settings:** Change System Settings without navigating menus. Siri makes it simple to carry out commands like "**Turn on Do Not Disturb**" or "**Increase screen brightness**".
3. **Language Translation**: Siri can help you communicate with those who speak a different language. You can instantly translate common expressions like "**How are you?**" by asking Siri to translate them into the target language.
4. **Math and Conversions**: Siri also functions as a useful calculator and unit converter for math and conversions. Need to convert miles to kilometers or figure out a tip? Simply ask, and Siri will respond with the solution.
5. **Calendar Management:** By adding, rescheduling, or changing appointments on your calendar, Siri can keep you organized. Say something like, "Schedule a meeting for tomorrow at 2 PM" or "Move my dentist appointment to next week," and Siri will take care of the scheduling.

Integration with Apple Ecosystem

1. **HomeKit Control**: If your smart home appliances are compatible with Apple's HomeKit, you can use Siri on your MacBook Pro to manage them. Use voice commands to lock doors, change thermostat settings, or turn off lights.

2. **Apple Music Playback:** Use Siri to have a smooth music experience. You may ask Apple Music to play certain songs, albums, or playlists. The music will continue to play if orders like **"Play some upbeat music"** or **"Skip this song"** are given.
3. **Email Management:** Siri can assist you in effectively managing your emails. While you're focused on other chores, ask Siri to create a new message for a contact or read your most recent email.

What can Siri do for you?

They include the following:

Effortless Productivity

Several improvements in Siri on the new MacBook Pro are intended to increase productivity. Siri can help you in many ways, whether you're a student, a professional, or a creative person. Without moving a muscle, you can use voice commands to book appointments, set reminders, and make to-do lists. Need to locate a file or document quickly? You just need to ask Siri to look for it, and it will be at your disposal. Siri can handle emails and messages for mobile professionals, help them prepare replies, and even start video conversations. The proper interpretation of your orders is made possible by Siri's natural language understanding, which also speeds up your workflow and helps you save time.

Seamless Multitasking

The new MacBook Pro's Siri elevates multitasking, which is a fundamental component of contemporary work, to a whole new level. Without leaving your present job, you can easily navigate between programs, access files, and even manage music playing with Siri. You can successfully use your smartphone while maintaining your concentration on what you're doing by using the **"Hands-free"** mode. Think of a design project where you need to acquire data from numerous sources. Without interrupting your creative flow, you may ask Siri to read articles, summarize them, and present you with pertinent information.

Voice-Controlled Features

Siri is integrated into the new MacBook Pro in ways that go beyond basic chores. It makes a variety of system functions voice-controlled. It just takes a few voice commands to change settings like display brightness, volume, and keyboard lighting. This hands-free method provides a degree of practicality that may greatly improve your user experience. Additionally, Siri is capable of carrying out more difficult operations that require changes to the operating system, such as establishing Wi-Fi connections, turning Bluetooth on and off, or starting system upgrades. You can retain your focus on the wider picture if you delegate these jobs to Siri.

Knowledge at your Fingertips

The new MacBook Pro's incorporation of Siri changes how you access information. Asking Siri for weather updates, news headlines, or general information is as easy as using your voice. Students and professionals who require rapid access to data and numbers for their studies and presentations will find this feature to be extremely helpful. Beyond the gadget itself, Siri's voice-based search capabilities are available. Without typing a single letter, you may start online searches, look for local eateries, and receive directions. Since this is the case, Siri is a useful assistant for both personal and professional duties.

Personalized Experience

The new MacBook Pro's Siri is built to learn your preferences and routines. It gains knowledge from your interactions over time and makes recommendations depending on how you use it. It may, for instance, offer shortcuts that fit your workflow or remind you to take breaks if you often work long hours. Siri is an AI-powered personal assistant who also understands context. If you're working on a project and tell Siri, "Remind me about this," it will link the reminder to the task you're currently working on, keeping you focused and on task.

Inclusivity and Accessibility

With Siri's inclusion in the new MacBook Pro, its accessibility features are expanded, making the gadget more accommodating for users with a range of needs. Voice commands provide a different input method that can be especially useful for people who have mobility issues. They do this by eliminating the need for precise mouse movements or complex keyboard inputs.

How to use Split Screen

The steps:

1. **Activate Split Screen Mode**

Make sure you are using macOS Ventura before you start multitasking. To start using Split Screen mode, do the following:

- On your MacBook Pro, launch the apps you want to use.
- The top-left corner of the window for your active application has a green full-screen button, also known as a **"traffic light"** button. Click and hold this button.
- When you press and hold the button, screen-splitting options will appear.

2. **Selecting the Split Screen Setup**

There are several options for screen arrangement once Split Screen mode has been activated. **These consist of:**

- **Full Screen**: Selecting this option will fill the entire screen with the active application.
- **Tile Left**: A list of your open apps will appear on the right, and your active application will take up the left half of the screen.
- **Tile Right**: Similar to Tile Left, Tile Right places your active application in the right half of the screen.
- **Exit Split Screen**: This will bring your active application back to its standard windowed mode and end the full-screen mode.

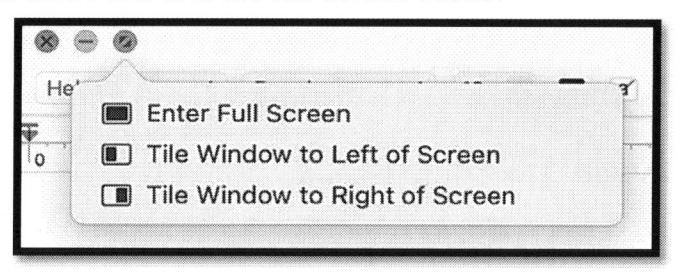

3. **Dragging and Resizing Applications**

Once you've decided on your preferred screen layout, you can drag and resize applications to effectively fit your workspace:

- Click and hold the secondary application's title bar, then drag it to the left or right side of the screen to reposition it.
- You can see a translucent blue outline as you drag the application, showing you where it will be placed when you release it.
- Hover your cursor over the space separating the apps until it transforms into a double-headed arrow to resize them. To change the width of each application, click and drag.

4. **Increasing Productivity with Split Screen**

Now that your applications are running simultaneously, it's time to make use of this configuration for increased productivity.

Here are some pointers for maximizing Split Screen mode:

- **Research and Writing:** When doing research or writing an essay, use one side of the screen for your word processor and the other for your source materials. As a result, there is no longer a need to go back and forth between windows.
- **Communication and Task Management:** Organize your communication applications, such as email or messaging, on one side, and your task management tools on the other. You may keep informed and organized at the same time by doing this.
- **Design and Preview**: Designers can use Split Screen mode to have their design program open on one side and a preview application open on the other while using their design software. Making modifications in real-time is made easier by this quick preview.
- **Code and Testing**: Programmers can create code one way and test it the other way in a development environment, which speeds up the debugging process.
- **Multilingual Work:** Working with papers in various languages? You can speed up the translation process by keeping translation tools open in addition to your writing program.

Use Split View on MacBook Pro

The steps:

1. **Select the Apps**

Choose the two applications that you want to use in Split View first. It's important to keep in mind that not all programs support this functionality, so you should first verify for compatibility. The majority of frequently used applications, including Safari, Mail, Pages, and Messages, function nicely with Split View.

2. **Switch to Full-Screen**

Open the app you want to use in Split View first. In the upper left corner of the program window, choose the green **"Full Screen"** button. The software will enter full-screen mode as a result.

3. **Enable Split View**

Place your cursor at the top of the screen once the first app has been opened in full-screen mode. The macOS Ventura menu bar should now display. Once more, press and hold the green **"Full Screen"** button. This time, a dropdown menu will show choices for the **"Tile Window to Left of Screen"** and **"Tile Window to Right of Screen."**

4. **Choose Your Layout**

Depending on where you want the second app to appear on the screen, choose either **"Tile Window to Left of Screen"** or **"Tile Window to Right of Screen."** The screen will automatically split in half when one of these options is selected, and the chosen app will be moved to one side.

5. **Choose the Second App**

On the empty side of the screen, a thumbnail view of all of your open apps will be visible. To use an app in Split View, click on it. The other half of the screen will then be taken up by the selected app.

6. **Adjust the Divider**

There is a partition between the two apps in Split View. Because this partition is movable, you can, if necessary, give one app more room. Move your cursor over the divider line until it transforms into a double-sided arrow to adjust the divider. To change the window width for each app, click and drag the divider left or right.

254

7. **Close Split View**

There are a few ways to leave Split View once you're done using it. To restore the app window to its default size, just click the green "**Full Screen**" button on either of the app windows. Alternatively, while using Split View, you can press the "**Esc**" key on your keyboard to end full-screen mode for both app windows.

Tips for Effective Split View Use

1. **Keyboard Shortcuts:** Use keyboard shortcuts to speed up the use of Split View. While clicking on the app icons in the Dock, hold down the "**Control**" key. Select **"Tile Window to Left of Screen" or "Tile Window to Right of Screen"** in the "**Options**" menu to enter Split View.
2. **Changing Apps**: Split View makes it simple to change the locations of the apps. Move one app's title bar to the other side of the screen by clicking and dragging it there. The two applications' positions will be switched as a result.
3. **Adding More Apps:** You have the option of adding a third app to your Split View configuration. Drag the window of the third application to the middle of the screen when in Split View. In turn, a three-way Split View will be produced.
4. **Exiting Split View for One App**: To end Split View for a single app, hold down the green "**Full Screen**" button on the app's window. The program will then revert to its normal window state.

Activate Split View via Mission Control

The steps:

1. **Find Mission Control**

Make sure the applications you want to use in Split View are already open before you start. Otherwise, start the apps you want to use. Press the "**Mission Control**" key on your keyboard (F3) or swipe up with three fingers on the trackpad to launch Mission Control.

2. **Enter Split View**

Once in Mission Control, all of your open windows will be shown at the screen's top as thumbnails. Click and hold on the title bar of one of the app windows you want to use to turn on Split View. Drag the window to the top of the screen, where a space has already been prepared for it, after briefly holding it there.

3. **Select a different app**

After installing the first app, you must choose the second app for Split View. You have two options in Mission Control: click on the window of the second program to make it the active one, or search for it using the **"Spaces"** bar at the top of the screen.

4. **Enable Split View**

Drag the window of the second app to the area you designated for it now that both programs are prepared. The screen will split into two halves as you move it, with each app occupying one side. To secure the window, let go of the window.

5. **Adjust the divider**

The two apps will be shown side by side on the screen by default. Hovering your mouse over the line between the two windows allows you to adjust how much space each program takes up. You may now click and drag the divider to the left or right with your double-sided arrow-shaped mouse.

6. **Exit Split View**

After finishing your work in Split View, you can switch out of the mode by moving your mouse up to the top of the screen until the menu bar appears. To dismiss Split View and return to a full-screen view of either app, click on the green circle symbol in either app's title bar.

View Other Apps in Split View

The steps:

1. **Launch Apps you want to use in Split View**

The applications you want to use on your MacBook Pro must be open before you can start using Split View. If the apps aren't open, you can access them by clicking on their icons in the Dock, searching for them in Spotlight, or going through the Applications folder.

2. **Enable Split View**

It's time to enable Split View after you have the desired applications open:

- In the top-left corner of the open window, click and hold the green "**full-screen**" button (the one with the plus sign).
- Tile the window to the left or right side of the screen using the options that will then display.
- The screen will be split in two when you drag the window to the left or right side of the display.
- To dock the app on that side, let go of the mouse button.

3. **Select the Second App**

The other half of the screen is now devoted to a grayed-out view, suggesting that it's accessible for another app now that you have one app in Split View.

How to choose the second app:

- Click the app icon you want to launch in the grayed-out portion of the screen.
- The app will immediately snap to the available spot if it is already open. You can start it using Spotlight or the Applications folder if it's not already open.

4. **Adjust the Divider**

The area between the two applications is divided by a separator by default, but you may move it to give one app more room if necessary

- Move the cursor over the division until a double-sided arrow appears.
- To change the size of each app's window, click and drag the divider to the left or right.

5. **Exit Split View**

To go back to a single app view after using Split View mode, do the following actions:

- To display the menu bar, move your pointer to the top of the screen.
- On the window of the current app, click the green **"+"**-shaped full-screen icon.
- The application switches back to its default windowed state.

Fix Split Screen Not Working

A MacBook Pro's Split Screen functionality makes it simple to multitask and increase productivity by enabling users to run two programs simultaneously. However, this functionality could sometimes fail to perform as intended.

Here are the steps to take:

1. **Verify System Requirements**: Verify that your MacBook Pro satisfies the system requirements for the Split Screen functionality before delving into complicated solutions. You should be using macOS El Capitan (10.11) or a later version like the macOS Ventura on your MacBook Pro. To find out what version of macOS you are running, click the Apple logo in the upper left corner of your screen and then choose "**About This Mac.**"
2. **Restart Your MacBook Pro**: This seemingly simple step may often fix minor software hiccups. After closing all open programs, click the Apple logo and choose "**Restart**." Try using Split Screen again once your MacBook Pro has restarted.
3. **Check Split Screen Options:** Access "**System Settings**" by using the Apple menu. Make sure the "**Displays have separate Spaces**" option is selected by clicking on "**Mission Control**" By giving each app its place; this option enables Split Screen to work effectively.

4. **Use Software That Supports Split Screen**: Not every software supports split screen. Make sure the programs you're using are compatible with the functionality. Split Screen must be activated by dragging a suitable application's window to the top of the screen. If not, carry through the further procedures.
5. **Reset NVRAM/PRAM:** Hardware-related problems are often resolved by resetting the non-volatile random-access memory (NVRAM) or parameter random-access memory (PRAM). Shut down your MacBook Pro to begin. Press and hold the Option, Command, P, and R keys simultaneously after turning it on. Hold the keys down for another 20 seconds or more, and your MacBook Pro should restart. Release the keys, and then see whether the Split Screen function is functional.
6. **Reset Mission Control:** Reset the Mission Control function if the Split Screen problem continues. Launch "**Terminal**" by selecting "**Applications > Utilities.**" enter after you type the following command: **defaults delete com.apple.dock; killall Dock**. The Mission Control and Dock settings will be reset as a result. Restart the Dock and then attempt to use Split Screen once again.
7. **Check that macOS is up to date**: Outdated software might cause compatibility difficulties, including Split Screen issues. Make sure macOS Ventura is up to date. Open the Apple menu, click "**System Settings**," and then choose "**Software Update**." Install updates if they are available, and then determine whether the problem has been fixed.
8. **Create a New User Account**: Split Screen issues may result from user-specific settings. Go to **System Settings > Users & Groups** to create a new user account. To make modifications, click the lock symbol; to add a new user, click the "**+**" button. Test out the Split Screen functionality by logging onto the new user account. If it solves the issue, your original user account may be at fault.
9. **Check for Third-Party Software Conflicts:** Some third-party programs and utilities may conflict with the functionality of macOS. Restart your MacBook Pro while pressing the Shift key until the Apple logo shows to start it in Safe Mode. Only necessary system files will load in Safe Mode. Try out the split-screen function. If it functions normally in Safe Mode, a third-party program could be the problem. Locate and remove any recent third-party installations.

10. **Reinstall macOS:** If none of the alternatives above work, you could think about doing so. Before continuing, make sure to back up any crucial data. Holding down Command and R when restarting your MacBook Pro will put it in Recovery Mode. You then have the option to reinstall macOS. The operating system will be installed completely throughout this procedure, perhaps correcting any underlying problems causing the Split Screen issue.

Frequently Asked Questions

1. How do you access and use Spotlight on your MacBook Pro?
2. How do you edit Spotlight search results?
3. How do you hide items from Spotlight search?
4. How do you set up and use Siri on your MacBook Pro?
5. How do you use Split View and Split Screen?
6. How do you fix Split Screen not working

CHAPTER FIFTEEN
MEMOJI AND APP STORE

Overview

This chapter brings you up to speed regarding how to use Memoji and the Mac app store to get apps and check for apps that need to be updated.

How to Use Memoji

Create your Memoji:

1. On your MacBook Pro, launch the Messages app to begin going. You will build and use your Memoji here.
2. Locate the **"Memoji"** button in the Messages app, which is often located on the bottom toolbar, and then click it. It resembles a tongue-protruding image of a monkey.
3. **Create a New Memoji:** When you click the Memoji button, a panel with several Memoji choices will display. Click the **"+"** button to add a new Memoji to the collection.

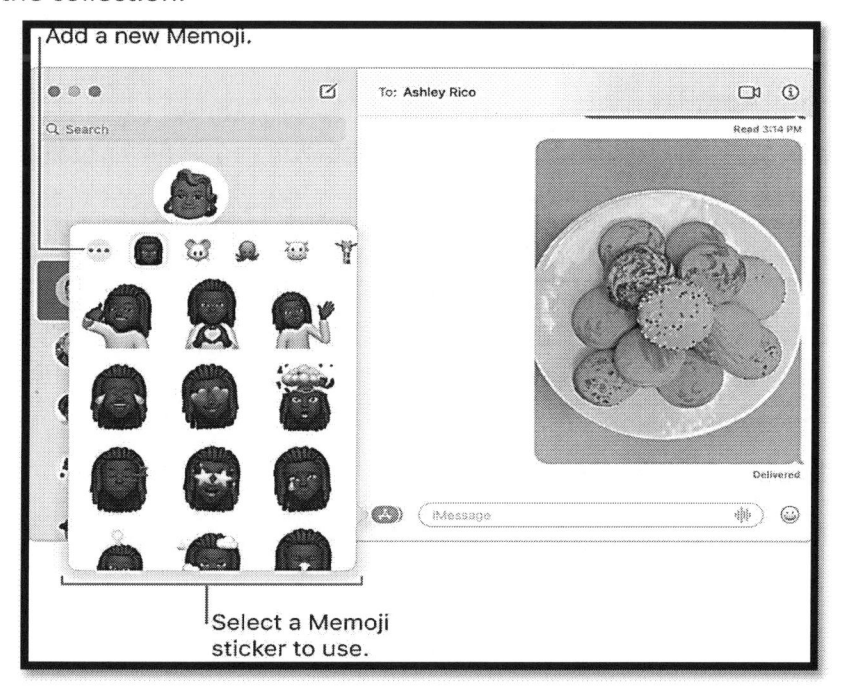

4. **Adding Features to Your Memoji:** A Memoji creation screen will display, enabling you to add features to your Memoji. The skin tone, haircut, hair color, eye color, accessories, and other features are all up to you. Make your Memoji one-of-a-kind by taking your time to perfect the details.
5. **Adding Information**: There are more customization options available than simply face characteristics. Additionally, you can add hats, eyeglasses, facial hair, and even piercings. Your Memoji is as accurate a representation of you as possible thanks to Apple.
6. When you are finished and are ready to save your Memoji, click the "**Done**" button. You can use your Memoji in your communications when it has been saved and added to the collection of Memoji stickers.

Using your Memoji

1. Open the Messages app and start a new discussion or respond to one that is already going on to use your Memoji in a message.
2. Select the "**App Store**" icon adjacent to the text input box to access Memoji Stickers. With that, a screen with several app selections will appear. Until you locate the Memoji stickers, scroll through.
3. **Choose Your Memoji:** Click or tap on the Memoji stickers to access your collection of Memojis. Pick the one that most accurately captures your attitude or the point you want to make.
4. **Drag and Drop:** Memoji stickers can be quickly added to your messages by just dragging them into the message box. They may be supplied with your wording or separately as stickers.
5. **Resizing Memoji:** You can resize a Memoji sticker by clicking on it and using the trackpad's pinch-to-zoom feature. This enables you to adjust the sticker's size as necessary.
6. **Sending Your Memoji:** After including your Memoji sticker in the message, click "**Send**" to send it to the recipient.

Using Memoji in FaceTime

1. On your MacBook Pro, launch the FaceTime app if you want to use your Memoji during a FaceTime chat.
2. **Start a Call:** Call the person you want to talk with on FaceTime.

3. To access the effects, choose the star-shaped "**Effects**" button during the call. By pressing this, a panel containing many effects, including Memoji, will open.
4. **Select Your Memoji:** Click the Memoji button in the effects panel. Your collection of Memoji stickers will be visible.
5. To use a Memoji, just click on it. It will then show up on your video stream while you are on the call. Your Memoji will replicate your facial emotions in real-time as you move and express yourself.
6. **Changing the Memoji**: You can change the Memoji you are using during the call by going to the effects panel and choosing a new one.

Create Memoji Stickers

Memoji stickers are an entertaining and original way to add personality to your chats and communications. Apple has made it even simpler to make and use Memoji stickers right from your laptop with the introduction of the new MacBook Pro.

1. **Update your MacBook Pro**

Make sure your MacBook Pro is running the most recent version of macOS before starting to create Memoji stickers. Check to see whether you are using the most recent version by choosing **"About This Mac" from** the Apple menu in the upper left corner of your screen. If not, go to **"System Settings" > "Software Update"** and apply any available updates.

2. **Open Messages**

On your MacBook Pro, use the Messages app to begin making Memoji stickers. You can look for it in your Dock or Spotlight by entering "**Messages**" and pressing **Command + Space**.

3. **Access Memoji Stickers**

Open an existing conversation or start a new one once you're in the Messages app. Click the **"App Store"** icon next to the message composition area to access Memoji stickers. It seems to be an "A" enclosed in a blue circle.

4. **Select the Icon for Memoji Stickers**

Find the Memoji stickers icon in the list of accessible app extensions. It resembles a happy face in yellow with many emotions. To access the interface for Memoji stickers, click on it.

5. **Create Your Memoji**

Your existing Memoji will be accessible on your MacBook Pro if you've previously made one on your iPhone or iPad. From the list, choose your Memoji. Click the "+" button to begin the creation process if you want to create a new one. You can change the skin tone, hairdo, eyes, lips, accessories, and more of your Memoji. It is simple to customize your Memoji to reflect your preferences and personality thanks to the tools and settings accessible on your MacBook Pro, which are identical to those on your iOS device.

6. **Select a Pose or Expression**

It's time to decide on a posture or emotion for your Memoji sticker once you've made or picked your Memoji. You may pick from a variety of pre-made positions and emotions provided by Apple. Choose an option that fits your mood, whether it's a wink, grin, thumbs-up, or funny face.

7. **Send Your Memoji Sticker**

After selecting the ideal position or emotion, click the Memoji sticker to include it in your message. To add the sticker to the chat, either click on it or drag it into the message composition space. You can add any extra text or remarks to go with your Memoji sticker.

8. **Resize and Adjust**

Like any other picture, Memoji stickers can be scaled and changed. Resize handles will appear around the sticker you've added to the message when you click on it. To enlarge or reduce the sticker, drag these knobs. The sticker can also be clicked and moved about the message by using your mouse.

9. **Add Multiple Stickers**

You can have more than one Memoji sticker. To make a creative and expressive collage, feel free to apply a variety of stickers to a single statement. To convey a range of emotions or responses, combine diverse positions and expressions.

10. **Send and Share**

It's time to send and share your Memoji stickers after you're happy with them. To send your message with the Memoji sticker to your recipient, click the blue send button, which is symbolized by an upward-pointing arrow. The sticker will be sent to your friends and family along with the message, and they may interact with it just like any other picture.

Edit, Duplicate, or Remove Memoji

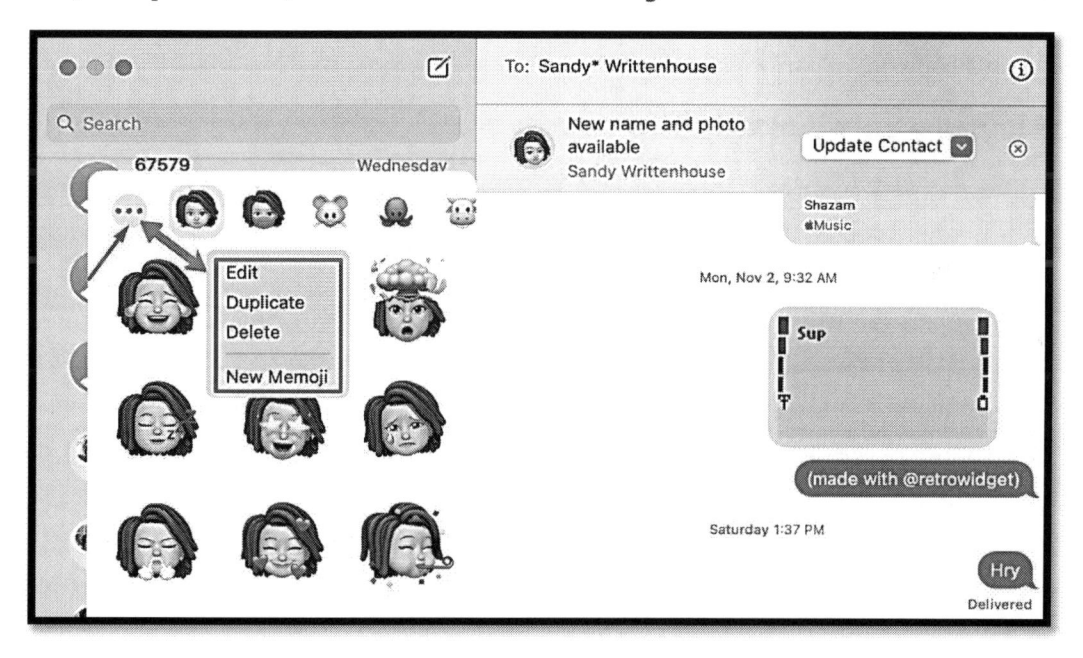

Editing your Memoji

1. Opening the Messages app on your MacBook Pro is the first step in editing your Memoji. Start a new message or rejoin an existing discussion with your Memoji next.

2. **Choose Memoji:** In the app drawer, choose **"Memoji"** by clicking on it. The Memoji interface will then appear, allowing you to see all of your accessible Memojis.
3. Locate the Memoji you want to change and click on it. Your Memoji will enlarge and appear on the screen. Click the **"Edit"** button at the bottom of the Memoji to make changes.
4. **Make Changes:** Your Memoji may be altered in several ways using the editing interface. Skin tone, haircut, eyes, mouth, accessories, and more are all modifiable. When you click on the element you wish to customize, a list of possibilities will show up.
5. **Preview Changes:** The Memoji on the screen will update in real-time as you make adjustments, enabling you to see how your changes affect its look. This makes sure you get the desired appearance.
6. **Save Changes:** When you are happy with your revisions, click **"Done"** to save them in your Memoji. You can now use your updated Memoji in messaging and other compatible applications.

Duplicating your Memoji

1. **Accessing Memoji:** Launch the Messages app as you did in the previous steps, and then select the **"Memoji"** icon in the app drawer to access the Memoji interface.
2. **Choose a Memoji:** Locate the Memoji you wish to reproduce and click on it to see a bigger version.
3. **Duplicate Memoji:** The **"Duplicate"** button is found at the bottom of the expanded Memoji. A duplicate of your Memoji will be made when you click on it.
4. **Rename (Optional):** The replicated Memoji will have the same name as the original, but you can rename it if you want to give it a more descriptive name. This might be especially useful if you have several Memoji designs.

Removing your Memoji

1. **Access Memoji**: The Memoji interface can be accessed by opening the Messages app as usual and selecting the **"Memoji"** button in the app drawer.

2. Select the Memoji you want to delete by finding it and clicking on it to view a bigger version.
3. **Remove Memoji:** The "**Delete**" button can be found at the bottom of the Memoji information screen in step three. When you click this button, a confirmation window will come up
4. **Confirm Deletion**: The confirmation popup will ask you whether you are certain that you want to remove the Memoji. The Memoji will be removed from your collection after you confirm the deletion.

Use Memoji as Group Picture in iMessage

The introduction of Memoji has completely changed how we communicate online. Users may design unique avatars that replicate their own emotions and facial expressions using Apple's Memoji function. Memoji isn't only for personal usage; it can also be an entertaining method for organizations to be represented in messaging services like iMessage.

The steps:

1. **Install the most recent version of macOS Ventura**

Make sure your new MacBook Pro is running the most recent version of macOS, which supports Memoji and its associated capabilities before you start. You can guarantee that you have access to the newest tools and advancements by routinely upgrading your system. If a new version is available, install it by following the on-screen instructions after clicking on the Apple logo in the upper left corner of your screen, selecting "**System Settings**," and then selecting "**Software Update.**"

2. **Create or Customize your Memoji**

You must first make or alter a Memoji that represents the whole group if you want to use it as a group image.

Follow these steps to do this:

- Launch the Messages app.
- Start a new group discussion or choose an existing one with the group for whom you want to personalize the Memoji.

- Click the group name or picture at the top of the discussion window.
- Select "**Details**."
- You can see the most recent group photograph in the group information section. Click on the collective picture to convert it to a Memoji.
- To edit or start a new Memoji, choose "**Edit**".

From here, you can change the skin tone, haircut, accessories, and other features of your Memoji to make it specifically reflect your group. When you are happy with the way your Memoji looks, click "**Done**."

3. **Set Your Memoji as the Group Picture**

It's time to make your personalized Memoji the group photo for your iMessage chat now that you have it.

Here are the steps:

- Click the Memoji you made while keeping the group information window open.
- Your Memoji will be shown in the preview along with the option to "**Choose**."
- To confirm your choice, click "**Choose**".
- The group photo for the iMessage chat has been changed to be your Memoji.

4. **Take Pleasure in Your Customized Group Photo**

Your selected Memoji will now show up anytime you send or receive messages in this group chat, adding some fun and personality to your online communications.

Use Memoji as Your iMessage Profile Image

Here are the steps:

1. **Create Your Memoji**

You must create a special Memoji before using it as your iMessage profile picture. How to do it:

- Launch the **Messages app** on your MacBook Pro to get started.

- In the top menu bar, pick "**Messages**" and then "**Preferences**." Click on the "**Messages**" tab.
- Go to the "**iMessage**" tab in the Preferences window to see the iMessage options.
- Select "**Edit**" next to your photo: In the "**Apple ID**" section, select "**Edit**" next to the picture that currently serves as your profile picture.

2. **Select "Add Photo"**

Choose the "**Add Photo**" option in the pop-up box that displays.

3. **Choose Your Memoji**

You can now choose a picture from your Mac or your Memoji. Click the "**Choose**" option beneath the Memoji area.

4. **Change your Memoji**

It will open a window with all of your Memojis. You can choose the Memoji image you want to use as your iMessage profile picture by browsing through your collection. Click on the "**+**" button to create a Memoji there if you haven't already.

5. **Confirm your Choice**

Click the "**Choose**" button after choosing or creating the Memoji you want. Your selected Memoji will become your iMessage profile picture as a result.

6. **Enjoy Your Customized Profile**

Your Memoji has been successfully configured as your iMessage profile picture. Your Memoji will now appear beside your name anytime you send someone a message through iMessage.

How to Choose a Memoji Profile Picture for iMessage – Tips

1. **Update Your Memoji**: You're not confined to using the same Memoji always. You can use the same procedures and a different Memoji to alter your profile picture.

2. Memoji is all about personal expression, so be yourself. Your Memoji's hairdo, facial characteristics, accessories, and other attributes may all be changed. Create it in your style.
3. **Use It Across Devices:** Your Memoji will sync across all of your Apple devices after you've configured it as your iMessage profile picture on your MacBook Pro. Therefore, your Memoji profile picture will remain the same whether you're using an iPhone, iPad, or another Apple device.
4. **Privacy Considerations:** Bear in mind that everyone you speak with over iMessage will be able to see your Memoji. Make sure your Memoji adequately reflects the online persona you want to project.

How to Use the App Store

Accessing the App Store

To begin, locate the "**App Store**" icon in your Dock and click it. You can also use Spotlight search (**Command + Space**) to discover and launch the App Store. When you first start it, you'll see a visually pleasing interface that displays highlighted applications, top charts, and other categories.

Browsing and Searching for Apps

1. **Featured Apps**: Apps that are highlighted as "**featured**" on the App Store's front page include recent releases, editor's picks, and themed collections. Discover well-known and important apps by exploring these areas.
2. **Top Charts:** To browse the most downloaded and highly rated applications across several categories, click the "**Top Charts**" item in the navigation bar. Finding popular and well-liked applications is a breeze with this method.
3. **Categories:** To see applications divided into different categories, such as productivity, entertainment, utilities, and more, choose the "**Categories**" option. Finding applications suited to your requirements and interests is now simpler as a result.
4. **Search**: To find certain applications, use the search box in the App Store's upper right corner. To find the applications you're searching for quickly, enter keywords or app names.

Installing Apps

When you locate an app you want to download, do it by following these instructions:

1. **Click on the App**: To see the app's detailed page, click on the app's name or icon. You can discover data about the software here, including a description, screenshots, user reviews, and contact information for the creator.
2. **Price or Get Button:** If the app is free, a **"Get"** button will be shown. Instead, you'll notice the app's pricing if it's a paid one. When you click the **"Get"** button, a **"Install"** button appears instead. If the app is purchased, clicking the price will ask you to use your Apple ID to finish the transaction.

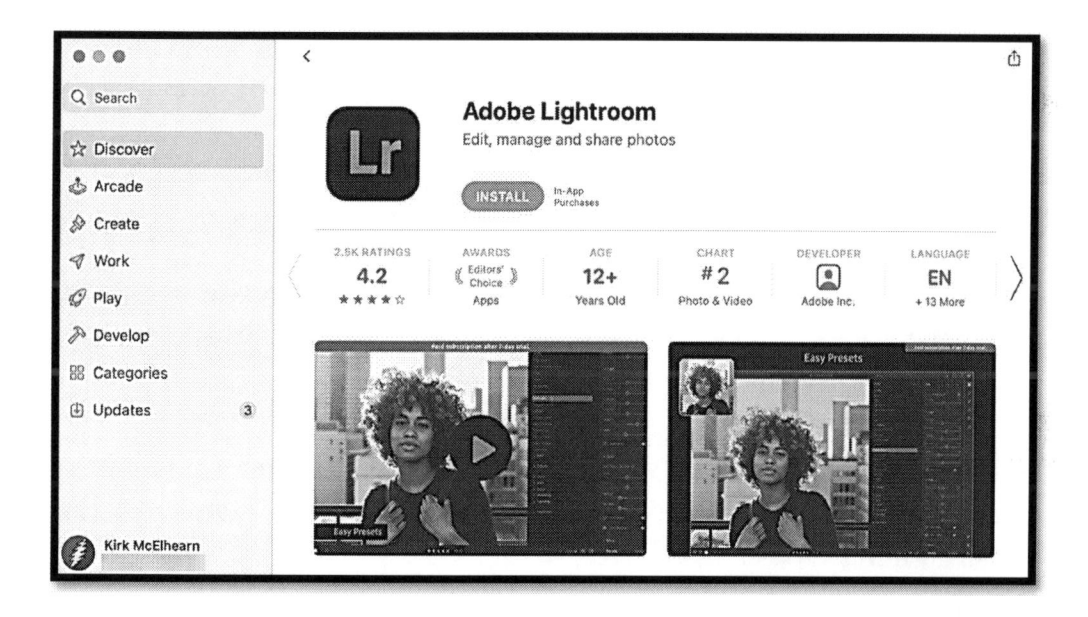

3. **Use your Apple ID:** When asked, enter your Apple ID and password or authenticate the download using Touch ID. This is a safety precaution to guarantee that only users with permission can download and install programs.
4. **Wait for Download**: The software will begin downloading after you have successfully authenticated. The **"Downloads"** area is located at the bottom of the App Store window, where you can keep track of the progress.

Managing Installed Apps

The ways:

1. **Launchpad:** Access installed applications using Launchpad, which you can launch by clicking its icon in the Dock or by using your trackpad's pinch-out motion. This is where you can arrange all of your applications, including any you've downloaded from the App Store.
2. **Updates:** The App Store often checks for new versions of the applications you have installed. If updates are available, a notice badge will appear on the "Updates" tab in the App Store. To see and install updates for your applications, click the tab.
3. **Purchased Applications**: You can re-download applications you've already purchased on other devices by tapping your profile image in the bottom-left corner of the App Store window and choosing "**Purchased**."

App Store Preferences

Use the following options to personalize your App Store experience:

1. **Automatic Downloads**: When you buy an app on one device and want it to be accessible on all your Apple devices, you can activate the automatic download feature by going to **"System Settings" > "App Store"** and checking the box next to "**Apps**."
2. **Family Sharing:** This feature allows you to share bought applications with your family. Follow the steps under **"System Settings" > "Family Sharing"** to configure this.

How to View Apps that Need Update

The steps:

1. **Launch the App Store**: Click the "**App Store**" icon in the Dock of your MacBook Pro, or go to the "**Applications**" folder in the Finder, to get started.
2. **Sign In:** You will be asked to sign in with your Apple ID if you aren't already logged in to the App Store. After providing your information, click "**Sign In**."

3. When logged in, the App Store window will have a row of tabs at the top where you may access the Updates tab. To continue, choose the "**Updates**" option.
4. **Check for Updates**: A list of all the programs that have updates available will be shown on the Updates page. Click the "**Update**" icon next to each app that needs to be updated to check for updates. To update every app at once, you can also click the **"Update All"** option in the top-right corner of the window.

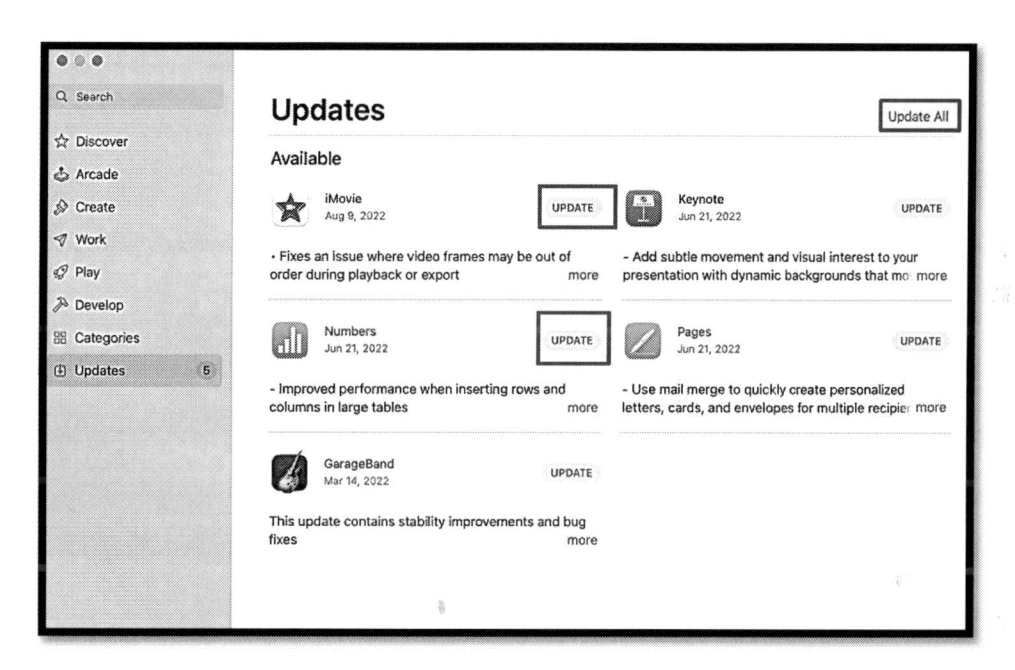

5. **View Update Details**: Click on an app's name to discover more information if you're wondering about the changes each update delivers. You can find information about the updates' enhancements, bug fixes, and new features in this window.
6. **Pause or Cancel Updates**: You have the option to delay or cancel updates while they are being applied, if necessary. This might be helpful if your internet connection is sluggish or if you want to update certain programs later. When updates are being applied, just click the "**Pause All**" or "**Cancel All**" buttons that appear.
7. **Automatic Updates (Optional):** Mac OS gives you the option to enable automatic program updates if you want to speed up the updating procedure. Check the boxes next to "**Automatically check for updates**" and "**Download**

newly available updates in the background" in "**System Settings**" and "**App Store**," then click the "Apple Menu" in the top-left corner of your screen to make this feature active.

8. **Manage App Alerts:** You'll automatically get alerts when new versions of an app are available. Return to the "**App Store**" section of "**System Settings**" to change these notification settings. Here, you can decide whether to get alerts for app updates or to restrict notifications to just crucial changes.

9. **Understanding App Update Icons:** You can see several icons for different applications on the Updates page. This is what they signify:

- **Update Available Icon:** A blue "**Update**" icon shows that the app has an update available.
- **Open Icon with Update:** If an app is open and needs to be updated, a gray icon with a downward-pointing arrow will appear. The app must be closed before clicking the "**Update**" button, as shown by this.
- **Update in Progress:** An update is presently downloading and being installed when a progress bar appears under the icon of an app.

10. **Restart Apps after Updates:** Restarting your apps after an update is a good idea to make sure the changes take effect. Restart the app after quitting it fully.

CHAPTER SIXTEEN
BASIC SETTINGS ON YOUR NEW MACBOOK PRO

Overview

Chapter sixteen talks about some of the basic settings found on your new MacBook Pro 2023.

How to Capture Screenshots and Record Your Screen

Capturing Screenshots

With its simple built-in features, the new MacBook Pro makes taking screenshots a snap.

Here are three typical approaches:

1. **Using Keyboard Shortcuts**: Using keyboard shortcuts is the easiest method to take screenshots. This is how:
- To capture the whole screen, use **Command + Shift + 3**. Your desktop will get a file containing the screenshot.
- Press **Shift + Command + 4** to capture the part you want to save. It will change from a cursor to a crosshair. To pick the area you want to capture, click and drag. To capture a screenshot, let go of the mouse button.
- Press **Shift + Command + 4**, and then press the **Spacebar** to capture the active window. The camera symbol will appear as your cursor. Select the window by clicking on it.
2. **Using the Screenshot Toolbar**: Apple introduced the Screenshot toolbar. To get to it:
- Hit **Shift + Command, and 5**. The Screenshot toolbar will then appear at the bottom of the screen.
- You can pick from many snapshot options, including taking a screenshot of the full screen, a specific area, or a specific window. This toolbar also enables you to record the screen.
3. **Using the Preview App**: The Preview app might be useful if you're seeking more sophisticated screenshot options.

- Click the **Preview app** in the Applications folder to launch it.
- Select **Take Screenshot** under File in the navigation bar. Select the selection for the desired screenshot.

Recording your Screen

Making lessons, presentations, or showing your artistic endeavors are all excellent uses for screen recording. Your MacBook Pro's built-in screen recording features have you covered.

Here are the steps:

1. **Using the Screenshot Toolbar**: The Screenshot toolbar is a strong tool that not only handles screenshots but also screen recording. It was previously stated.
   - To display the toolbar for taking screenshots, press **Shift + Command + 5**.
   - Depending on your desire, click the **Record Selected Portion** or **Record Entire Screen** buttons.
   - To begin recording, click the **Record icon** in the toolbar. To control the recording, a menu bar will appear at the top of the screen.
   - When finished, choose **Stop** from the menu bar. Your PC will get a file containing the recording.
2. **Using QuickTime Player**: QuickTime Player is a multi-functional multimedia player that also functions as a screen recorder.
   - Use Spotlight to do a search or launch **QuickTime Player** from the Applications folder.

- Select **New Movie Recording** under File in the navigation bar.

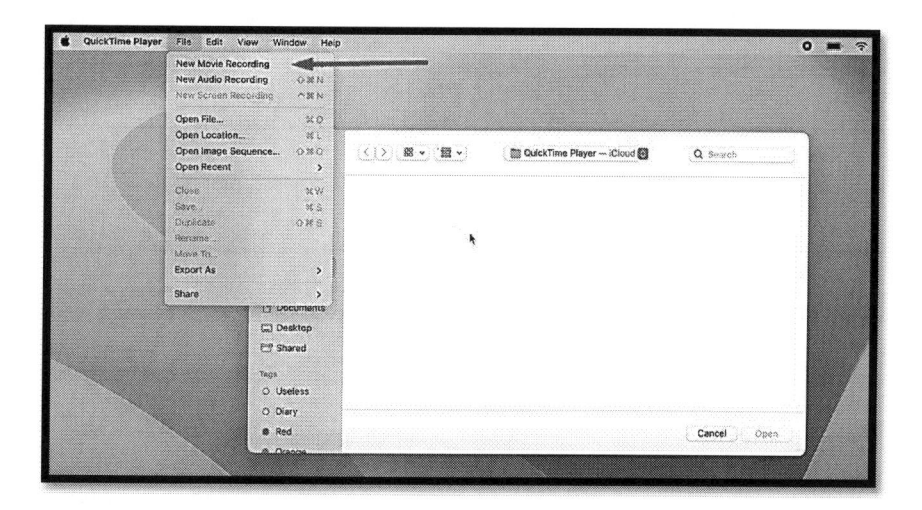

- Select your microphone input and camera input choices by clicking the arrow next to the record button.
- Select the record button to capture the screen. Click the stop button in the menu bar to halt recording.

Customizing Screenshot and Recording Settings

Change the screenshot and recording settings on your MacBook Pro to suit your requirements.

1. **Using Options in Screenshot Toolbar:** Using the Options button on the Screenshot toolbar will allow you to access options such as the place where recordings will be saved, how long the timer will delay, and if the pointer will be visible.
2. **Using Terminal Commands:** Advanced users can change default settings using Terminal commands. You can change the default screenshot format, location, and more, for instance.

How to Adjust the Brightness of the Display on your MacBook Pro

Your new MacBook Pro's display brightness is a key factor in improving your entire computing experience. Having the ideal brightness may significantly improve your comfort and clarity of vision whether you're working on a project, watching a movie, or just surfing the web. Having a basic understanding of how to change the display brightness on your MacBook Pro can substantially improve your use.

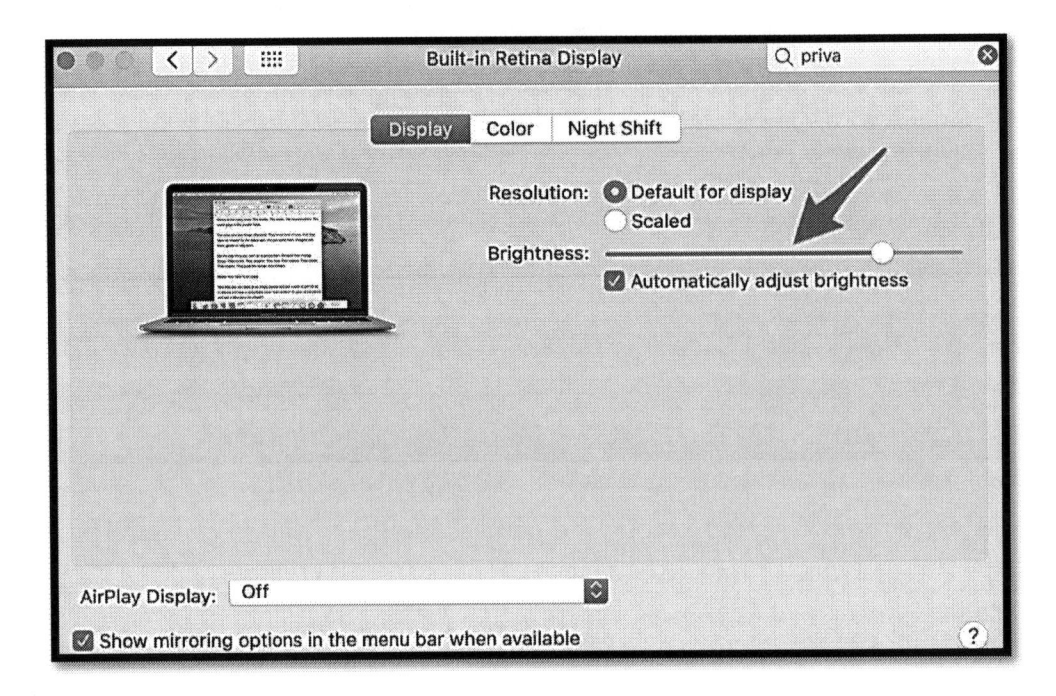

Method 1: Using Keyboard Shortcuts

Using keyboard shortcuts is one of the simplest and fastest methods to change the brightness of your MacBook Pro's display.

Here are the steps:

1. **Function Keys:** Take a look at the top row of the keyboard on your MacBook Pro. You'll see a row of keys with icon labels. The "**F1**" key often depicts a sun symbol with a downward arrow, whereas the "**F2**" key typically resembles a sun icon with an upward arrow. Among them, you will discover two keys specifically for brightness adjustment: "**F1**" and "**F2**."
2. **Brightness Decrease**: While holding down the "**Fn**" (function) key, hit the "**F1**" key (sun symbol with a downward arrow) to dim the lights. The brightness of the display should start to decrease.

3. **Brightness Increase:** To raise the brightness, hold down the "**Fn**" (function) key while pressing the "**F2**" key (a sun symbol with an upward arrow). The screen will become brighter.

Keep in mind that depending on the model of your MacBook Pro, the function keys' real appearances and their icons may differ somewhat.

Method 2: Using System Settings

Through the System Settings, you can also change the display brightness. This is how:

1. **Apple Menu**: In the top-left corner of your screen, click the Apple menu (logo).
2. **System Settings**: Click the dropdown menu and choose "**System Settings**."
3. **Displays:** Look for and choose the "**Displays**" icon in the System Settings window. The Display Preferences window will then be shown.
4. **Brightness Slider:** The "**Brightness**" slider can be found in the Display Preferences panel. This slider may be moved to the left or right to change the brightness. You can discover the ideal brightness level by using the slider, which causes the display brightness to vary in real time.

Method 3: Using Control Center

Apple included the Control Center, which offers easy access to many settings, including display brightness, with macOS upgrades.

This is how to apply it:

1. **Control Center Icon**: The Control Center symbol can be seen on the menu bar. There seem to be many vertical sliders.
2. **Brightness Slider**: To access the Control Center, choose the icon and click. Among the settings is a slider for the brightness. To change the display brightness to your liking, slide it left or right.

Method 4: Using Siri

If you like using voice commands, you can even use Siri to change the display brightness on your MacBook Pro:

1. To activate Siri, either click on the icon in the menu bar or use the **Command + Space** keyboard shortcut.
2. **Adjust Brightness:** Simply say something like "**Hey Siri, increase/decrease the display brightness**." Siri will take your instructions and change the display brightness as necessary.

Method 5: Automatic Brightness Adjustment

The display brightness of MacBook Pro models may often be automatically adjusted by an ambient light sensor depending on the ambient illumination. For those who want a hands-free experience, this is a fantastic choice.

To activate or modify this feature:

1. Open the "**System Settings**" option from the Apple menu.
2. Navigate to the "**Display**" options window by clicking the "**Displays**" icon.
3. Search for an option that says "**Automatically adjust brightness**" or a phrase that sounds similar. Turn on this setting to enable automatic brightness adjustment for your MacBook Pro.

How to Adjust the Volume

Here are the methods:

Method 1: Using the Volume Keys

Using the specific volume keys on the keyboard is the simplest method to change the volume on your MacBook Pro. Along with other function keys, these keys are normally found on the top row of the keyboard.

Here are the steps:

1. **Find the Volume Keys**: Locate the volume keys on the keyboard of your MacBook Pro. The **"+"** and **"-"** symbols are used to identify these keys, which resemble speaker icons. Typically, you can find them next to the F10, F11, and F12 buttons.
2. **Increase Volume**: Press the **"Volume Up"** key, which is often the F12 key with the **"+"** symbol, to turn up the volume. The volume indication on the screen will rise, and a chime will sound to indicate the level adjustment.
3. **Reduce Volume**: Press the **"Volume Down"** key, which is often the F11 key with the **"-"** symbol, to lower the volume. Once again, you'll hear a chime and see the volume indication on the screen fading.
4. **Mute:** Press the **"Mute"** key, which is often the F10 key and features a crossed-out speaker symbol, to swiftly muffle the sound. A mute sign will show up on the screen and the volume will be turned off.

Method 2: Using the Menu Bar

The menu bar at the top of the screen is another method to adjust the volume on your MacBook Pro. The volume level can be shown visually using this technique.

Here's how:

1. **Locate the Volume Icon**: Look to the right of the menu bar at the top of your screen for the volume icon. A speaker icon will appear. To access the volume controls, click on it.
2. **Adjust the Volume**: A slider will show once you click the volume icon to change the volume. To change the volume, just slide it to the right or the left. The volume level will adjust as you slide the slider, and the change will be signaled by a chime.
3. **Mute or Unmute**: In the menu bar, click the speaker icon to either mute or unmute the audio. The mute status will change as a result. A crossed-out speaker icon will show up next to the volume slider when the speaker is muted.

Method 3: Using System Settings

Using the System Settings on your MacBook Pro will give you access to more sophisticated volume control settings.

Using this technique, you can adjust your audio settings:

1. Access System Settings by clicking the Apple logo in the top-left corner of your screen.
2. **Select Sound:** Navigate to and select the "**Sound**" button in the System Settings pane. The Sound Preferences window will then be shown.
3. **Change Volume Settings:** The "**Output**" tab of the Sound Preferences panel allows you to choose your preferred audio output device, such as internal speakers or external headphones. Using the given slider, you can easily change the output volume.

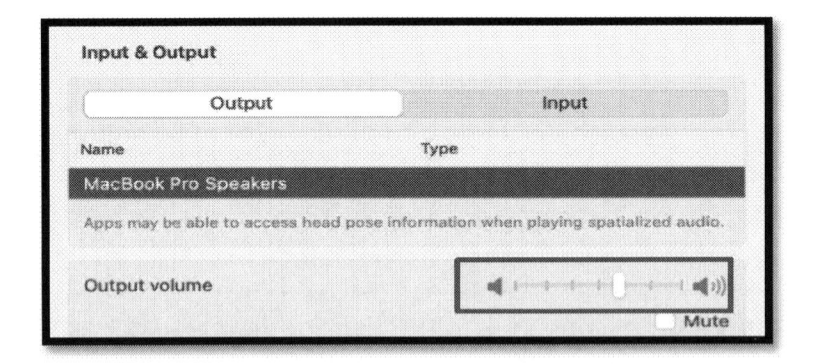

4. **Balance and Alert Sounds:** You can also change the balance between the left and right speakers in the Sound Preferences panel to get the best audio distribution. Additionally, you can customize your choices for alarm and feedback noises.

How to Perform Gestures Using the Trackpad and the Mouse

The Magic of the Trackpad Gestures

Your MacBook Pro's trackpad is a technical marvel that allows you to operate the computer with simple hand motions. You can move through your material, switch between apps, and manage Windows by becoming an expert at using the trackpad. **Here are some gestures you should be familiar with:**

1. **Scrolling**: Browse through documents, online pages, and lists with the simple two-finger scroll action. To scroll in the appropriate direction, use two fingers on the trackpad and swipe either upwards or downwards.
2. **Zoom**: Simply use the pinch-to-zoom motion to zoom in or out on content. Spreading out two fingers on the trackpad will zoom in while pinching them together will zoom out.
3. **Mission Control**: Mission Control, where you can view all of your open windows and desktop areas, can be accessed by three-finger swiping upwards. It's a great method to set up your workplace and move between programs fast.
4. **App Exposé:** It is activated by swiping down with three fingers and shows all the open windows for the currently open application. When you have numerous windows active in a single software, this is useful.
5. **Swipe Left or Right with Three Fingers to Move between Full-Screen Apps**: To move between full-screen apps, swipe left or right with three fingers. It resembles turning the pages of an electronic deck of cards.
6. **Desktop Management:** To get the desktop view, spread your thumb and three fingers apart. You can access files on your desktop with this motion without minimizing or shutting down any applications.
7. The **Notification Center**, which keeps you informed of your alerts and notifications, is accessible by swiping with two fingers from the right side of the trackpad.

Mastering Mouse Gestures

Although trackpad motions are effective, the magic continues. With your MacBook Pro, you can still make use of a variety of motions that increase productivity.

The most important mouse movements are listed below:

1. **Scrolling and Zooming:** Zooming and scrolling are both possible with a mouse, just as with a trackpad. You can travel vertically using a mouse with a scroll wheel. Additionally, by tilting the scroll wheel, certain mice provide horizontal scrolling.

2. **Mission Control and App Exposé:** Many mouse come with programmable buttons. You may designate a button to launch App Exposé or Mission Control, giving you easy access to these functions.
3. **Forward and Backward Navigation**: If your mouse includes side buttons, you can set them up in certain online browsers and software programs to act as forward and backward buttons. This makes browsing through documents and online sites easier.
4. **Desktop management:** Configure a gesture to display the desktop that works similarly to trackpad movements. You could do this with a mouse using a combination of button pushes or scrolling the wheel.
5. **Application Switching**: Some mouse includes buttons that may be set up to switch between different apps. This is very helpful when you need to switch activities quickly while juggling many chores.

Customizing and Fine-Tuning Gestures

The versatility of gestures on your MacBook Pro is what makes them beautiful. These gestures can be modified to fit your needs and method of operation. Depending on your device, go to "**System Settings**" and choose the "**Trackpad**" or "**Mouse**" options. From there, you may investigate the options for gesture modification and adjust them to suit your requirements.

How to Use the Stage Manager

Understanding the basic ideas behind the Stage Manager is crucial before delving into the details.

The Stage Manager's main function is to arrange your virtual workspace by letting you create and move between many desktops, each of which is designed for a certain activity or project. This allows you to have separate desktops for personal usage, work-related programs, and artistic activities, all without having your screen cluttered.

Creating and Managing Desktops

You must be able to create and manage desktops to fully use the Stage Manager. This is how:

1. **Open the Stage Manager:** Use the Mission Control interface by clicking the "**Mission Control**" icon on your dock or by swiping up with three or four fingers on your trackpad to access the Stage Manager.

2. **Create a Desktop:** To add a new desktop, click the "**+**" button in the Mission Control screen's upper right corner. You can give it a name that suits your tastes, **such as "Work," "Study," or "Entertainment."**

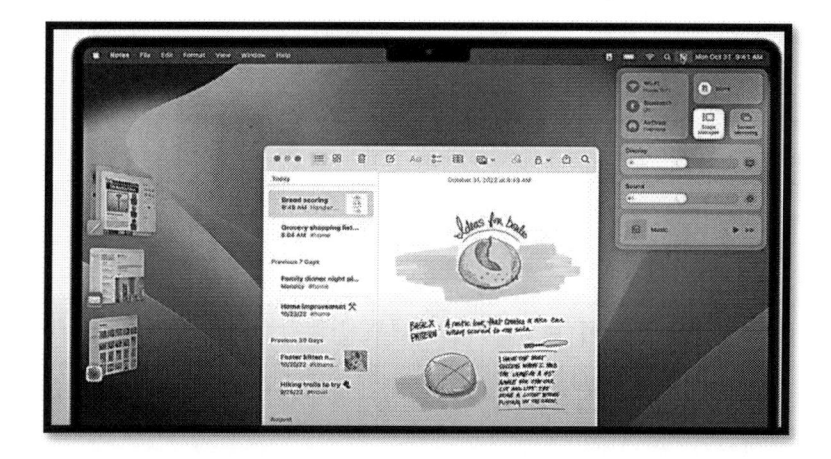

3. **Switch Between Desktops:** Use the four-finger swipe motion on your trackpad to switch between desktops, or hit the **"Control"** key and the right or left arrow keys simultaneously.
4. **Move Windows between Desktops:** The Mission Control interface allows you to move program windows across desktops. Simply choose the suitable desktop thumbnail at the top of the screen by clicking and dragging the window there.

Using Split View for Enhanced Multitasking

Divide your screen between two apps for effective multitasking with the Stage Manager's smooth integration with Split View.

1. **Enable Split View:** Click and hold the green maximize button in the top-left corner of an application window to activate Split View. The choice of whether to place the window on the left or right side of the screen will be made available to you.
2. **Choose the Second App**: From the other open windows in Mission Control, choose the second program you want to use in Split View.
3. **Adjust the Split:** The separator between the two apps can be moved by clicking and dragging it.

Using the App Exposé

The App Exposé feature in the Stage Manager makes it easier to handle many open windows inside an application on a single desktop.

1. **Open App Exposé:** When hovering over the program icon in the dock, swipe down with three or four fingers on the trackpad to activate App Exposé. As an alternative, you can simultaneously hit the downward arrow key and the **"Control"** key.
2. **Navigate Windows**: All open windows for the chosen program will be shown in the App Exposé view. To bring a window to the front, click on it.

Customizing the Stage Manager

The Stage Manager provides customization options so you may organize your workplace the way you choose.

1. Configure **Desktop Spaces** by going to **"System Settings"** > **"Mission Control,"** where you can change things like whether or not spaces are shown as spaces and whether or not they are automatically rearranged depending on recent usage.
2. Set hot corners so that you can reach Mission Control, the desktop, or App Exposé fast. Open **"System Settings"** and choose **"Mission Control"** > **"Hot Corners."**
3. **Keyboard Shortcuts:** Become familiar with the keyboard shortcuts for launching App Exposé, calling up Mission Control, and navigating between desktops.

Frequently Asked Questions

1. How do you capture screenshots and record your MacBook Pro screen?
2. How do you adjust the volume?
3. How do you adjust the brightness of the display on your MacBook Pro?
4. How do you use the stage manager feature?
5. How do you perform gestures using the trackpad and the mouse?

CHAPTER SEVENTEEN
TROUBLESHOOTING ISSUES

Overview

Students, business users, and creative professionals all like using the MacBook Pro. However, it could have problems, just like any other technology, and debugging can be difficult to fix. This chapter deals with the several MacBook Pro issues and potential solutions.

MacBook Pro Won't Turn On

Check the Battery

When your MacBook Pro won't power on, check the battery first. If the battery is dead, put it in the charger and give the gadget some time to charge before trying to turn it on.

Restart the SMC

Resetting the System Management Controller (SMC) may be helpful if the battery is not the problem. Hold down the **Power button, Shift, Control,** and **Option keys** all at once for 10 seconds. To start the MacBook Pro, release all the keys, and then hit the **Power button**.

Overheating

Close Resource-Intensive Applications

If your MacBook Pro is overheating, the cause can be resource-hungry programs that are open in the background. Close any unused apps to lessen the device's burden and the generation of heat.

Learn Debris and Dust

Your MacBook Pro's fans may get clogged with dust and dirt over time, overheating the device. To keep the gadget cool, blast the dust out of the vents and fans using compressed air.

Slow Performance

Clear Disk Space

You may not have enough disk space if your MacBook Pro is performing slowly. To increase efficiency and save up disk space, get rid of any superfluous programs or files.

Reset PRAM and NVRAM

Performance may be enhanced by clearing the Non-Volatile Random Access Memory (NVRAM) and Parameter Random Access Memory (PRAM). Hold down the Command, Option, P, and R keys at the same time as you turn on the MacBook Pro. After twice hearing the starter sound, let go of the keys.

Wi-Fi Connectivity Issues

The potential solutions include the following:

- Reset your modem and router.
- Disconnect from the Wi-Fi network and reconnect.
- Reset your MacBook's NVRAM and SMC.
- Verify if any other electrical gadgets are interfering.
- Under Network Preferences, try adding a new network location.

Trackpad and Keyboard Problems

- Use compressed air to gently blow trash from the keyboard and trackpad.
- Look for macOS upgrades that could address issues with the keyboard or trackpad.
- If a few keys aren't functioning, think about having Apple replace the keyboard.

Startup Problems

- When starting up, try holding Option-Command-P-R to reset the NVRAM (or PRAM).
- To troubleshoot software-related issues, boot into Safe Mode by holding down the Shift key at startup.
- Reinstall macOS from Recovery Mode if required.

Software Glitches or Crashes

- Upgrade macOS and any installed apps to the most recent releases.
- To verify and fix disk permissions, use Disk Utility.
- Make a new user account to check whether the problem still exists.
- Try deleting and reinstalling the offending software if you can.

External Devices Not Recognized

- Inspect the cable connections, and then test several ports.
- Restart your MacBook Pro while it is attached to the external device.
- Determine if the device requires special drivers and is compatible with macOS.

Screen Problems (black screen, flickering, etc.):

- Attempt to reset the SMC and NVRAM.
- Start your computer in Safe Mode to see whether the problem is software-related.
- If the issue continues, think about hiring an expert for hardware diagnostic and repair.

Data Corruption or Loss

- Using Time Machine or other backup programs, regularly backup your files.
- If data is lost, try to recover it using data recovery services or software.
- To avoid loss, save important data on external drives or cloud services.

It is advised to call Apple Support or visit an Apple Store for qualified assistance if the problem is more complicated or chronic. Before trying any troubleshooting activities that might result in data loss, always make sure your vital data is backed up.

Tips and Tricks for Navigating through MacBook Pro Functions

Here are some of the tips and tricks to help you navigate through the MacBook Pro functions:

1. **Quick Look**

One of the most often used Mac functions is Quick Look. Once you get in the habit of using it, you won't need to open any files since you can see their contents without opening them. Simply choose your file and press the spacebar once to initiate the fast glance Action. For instance, you may choose a PDF and rapidly scan its information without even opening it by selecting it and using the spacebar. Despite this, there are certain restrictions on this functionality. Depending on the file you are attempting to see, Quick Look may be able to provide a preview. If the file is a document or an image, you can use Quick Look to see the whole contents of the file, as shown in the images below. However, if it's a folder or an eBook, it will only provide rudimentary details like the file size and the date it was last edited. The glance tool will be quite beneficial once you understand when and when it is useful.

2. **Force Quit Apps**

While one of the advantages of owning a Mac is that you seldom ever have an unresponsive program, it does happen sometimes, and when it does, you'll need to know how to forcibly shut the app. On Windows, you must get into the habit of typing **Ctrl+Alt+Delete;** on Mac, the keyboard shortcut is a little different. You must use the **Cmd+Opt+Esc** keyboard shortcut (command, option, and escape key).

When you complete the combination, a floating window with the "**Force Quit Application**" box will appear. Simply choose the problematic app from the list and press the Force Quit button. You can use an alternative technique if you find it difficult to recall the keyboard combination. Force a quit by selecting the Force Quit option from the Apple Menu in the upper left corner.

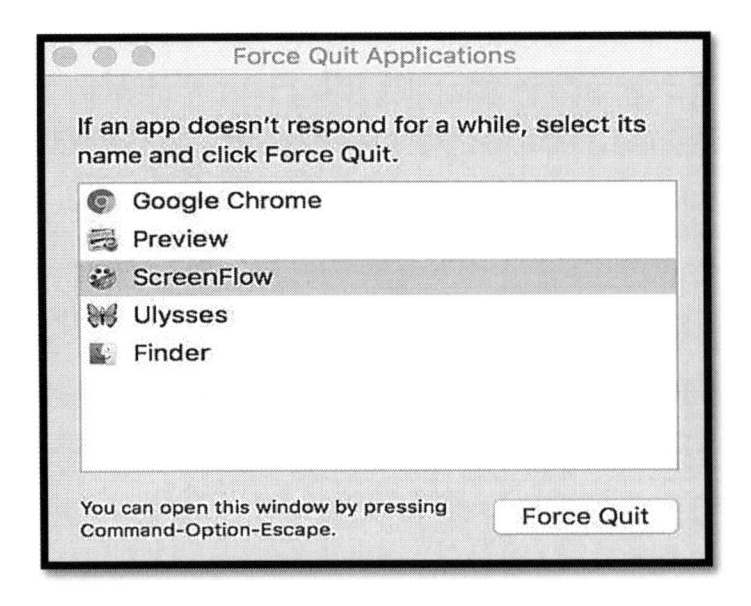

3. **Perform Spotlight's App Search more quickly**

This is a short and practical suggestion. When looking for an app in Spotlight, inputting the app's initials will provide results more quickly than typing the app's full name. For instance, you can only write the letters a and s to search for the App Store. Once you develop the habit, you will find apps more quickly and save a little bit of time at a time.

4. **Use Spotlight for calculations, definitions, and weather**

Spotlight has changed over time from being only a Mac search engine. You can now use it for a variety of tasks. For instance, Spotlight may be used to do unit and currency conversions. For instance, convert dimensions, money, and other things virtually every day using it. Spotlight may be used to do basic mathematical operations including addition, subtraction, multiplication, and more. Similar to this, Spotlight allows you to get weather data for any city in the globe. You can get the current weather by typing the term "**weather**" and the name of the city. Also available are word meanings. To get the term's definition, type the word and use the "**+L**" keyboard shortcut.

5. **Display Menu Bar even in Full-screen Mode**

The new MacBook Pro's smaller bezels provide you with more vertical space, which prevents the Menu Bar from taking up more real estate on your Mac's valuable display area. The Menu Bar is immediately removed by default when you use an app in full-screen mode, which is absurd since the applications can no longer use the Menu Bar space because of the notch. Fortunately, macOS lets you display the Menu Bar even while your programs are running in full-screen. You can do this by unchecking the box next to the option to "**Automatically hide and show the menu bar in full screen**" in System Settings Dock & Menu Bar.

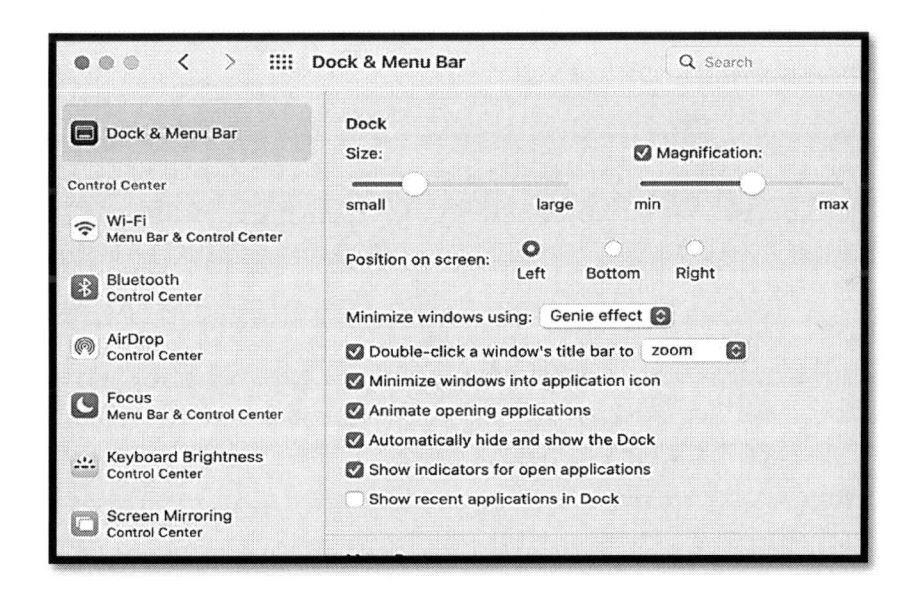

6. **Automatically Hide and Show Mac Dock**

You should enable the option to automatically hide and reveal the Mac Dock if you don't want it to take up extra space. To achieve this, go to System Settings Dock & Menu Bar and choose the checkbox next to the **'Automatically hide and reveal the Dock'** option. The pointer will relocate to the bottom of the screen and the Dock will be hidden until you need it. Check out the options for adjusting the Dock's size, magnification, and location while you're here.

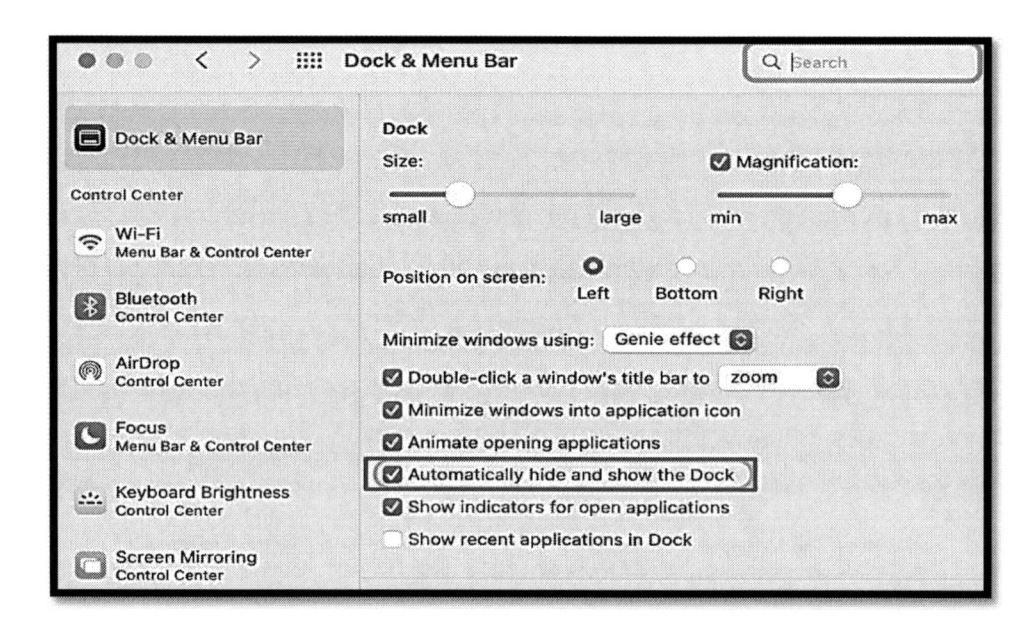

Keep the keyboard shortcut **CMD+Opt+D** in mind if you don't want the Dock to immediately disappear. When you want to, you can hide the Dock by using this keyboard shortcut. To re-activate the Dock, use the keyboard shortcut once more.

7. **Use Quick Note**

A new Quick Note feature debuted with macOS Monterey. With this feature, you can quickly take notes and brainstorm ideas while using other applications without interrupting your workflow. By default, you may open the Quick Note by placing your cursor in the display's lower-right corner on your Mac. Going to **Apple Menu > System Settings > Desktop & Screen Saver > Screen Saver Hot Corners** will allow you to change this behavior.

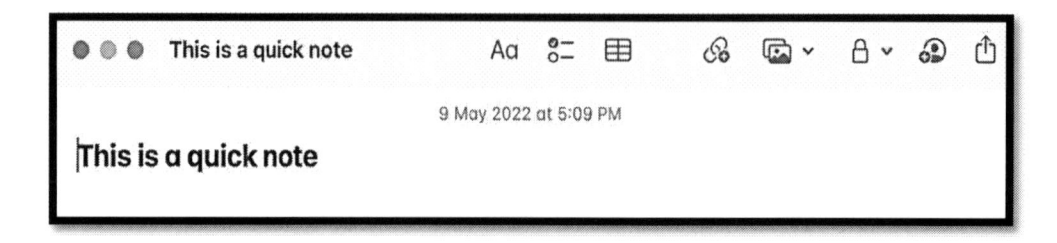

Holding down the Fn key or Globe key while pressing Q will activate the Quick Note function.

8. **Paste Copied Text Without Weird Formatting**

You'll notice that formatting information is included when you copy text from a website and paste it into a document. You will have to spend time reformatting the content if this behavior causes your document's formatting to be messed up. Use the **CMD+Shift+V** keyboard shortcut instead of the **CMD+V keyboard shortcut** to paste text into a page without any odd formatting. It will guarantee that the text you paste adheres to the formatting of your papers.

9. **Turn on "Tap to Click"**

No matter where you click on the trackpad of the MacBook Pro, the Taptic Engine underneath it provides you with exact feedback. If you don't like the feeling, you can switch on the trackpad's tap-to-click feature to eliminate the need to push down on it to click. Go to **Apple Menu > System Settings > Trackpad** and tick the box next to the **"Tap to Click"** option to activate this function.

The tracking speed and other trackpad capabilities, like two-finger scrolling, multi-touch gestures, and more, may all be controlled using this page's touchpad settings. You can see a video of each function on the settings page, so go through each one and adjust your trackpad options to configure it as you want.

10. **Using the Emoji Keyboard**

There is a simple method to access the Mac's emoji keyboard if you like using them. To accomplish that, press **Cmd+Ctrl+Space** on the keyboard and the emoji keyboard will appear. You can scroll down to locate the desired emoji here. To locate the person you're looking for, you may also search.

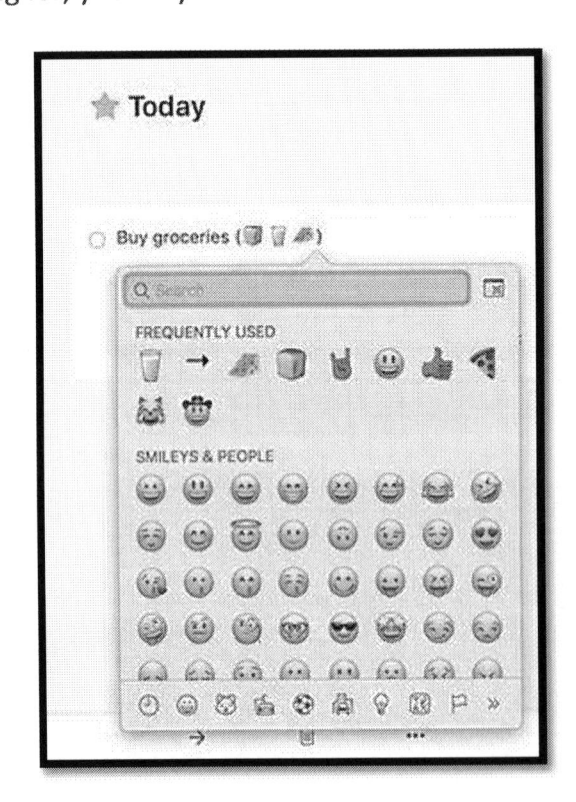

11. **Display File Path in the Finder**

The user interface on macOS is kept as minimal and uncluttered as possible. Even while it makes logic, it sometimes makes things less usable. For instance, the fact that macOS by default hides the file path irritates me. So you won't be able to determine how to go there if you search for a file in Spotlight and open its location.

The file path can be enabled using a helpful keyboard shortcut. The "**Cmd+Opt+P**" keyboard shortcut will show the file path if you want to see the location of a file. If you lose track of this keyboard shortcut, use the "**View**" option to locate it.

12. **Keep Your Search Limited to One Folder**

The fact that a search in a Finder window on a Mac starts a search for the whole Mac is one of the most annoying things about it. Although it makes no sense, this is how things have always been. Thankfully, the Finder Preferences allow you to alter this behavior. Therefore, open **Finder Preference > Advanced** and choose "**Search the current folder**" from the dropdown menu under the "**when performing a search**" option.

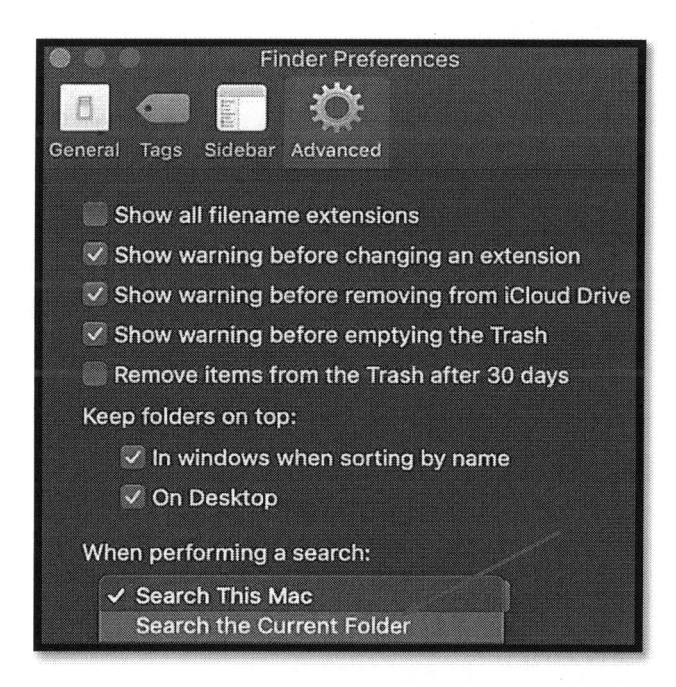

13. **Minutely Adjust the Volume and Brightness**

Although we can change the brightness and volume on your Mac devices using the keyboard keys (F1 & F2 for brightness and F11 & F12 for volume), there isn't enough flexibility. That's because the final few steps modify things excessively whereas the first few hardly change anything.

If you want to do that as well, press the volume or brightness buttons while simultaneously holding down the option and shift keys. If you don't use the option and shift keys, a single push will increase or reduce the bar by 1/4 instead of the complete bar as it would if you did.

14. **Move Files with Cut and Paste**

Being a Windows user, it truly infuriated me to not be able to utilize the keyboard's cut-and-paste function. The copying shortcut is **Cmd+C**, however, there is no Cmd+X for the cut action. If you use a Mac and are unfamiliar with the Cut Action, allow me to explain. While you can transfer files from one location to another using the **Cmd+C** or the transfer Action, the cut Action enables you to do the identical task with a significant distinction. On a Mac, to conduct the Cut Action, first copy the file using the **C (Cmd+C)** combination. The Copy Action preserves the original file or text in place and duplicates that file, but the Cut Action moves the original file without making a duplicate. Now enter the area where you want to paste the file, and instead of pressing **V (Cmd+V),** press **Cmd+Opt+V**.

15. **Trash Files in Seconds**

This little Mac technique might help you save time. When you need to remove anything on a Mac, you often drag it to the Trash icon on your dock or use the "**Move to Trash**" option when you right-click a file. The good news is that you can avoid the hassle of accomplishing these tasks by using a keyboard shortcut. Simply click on a file to select it, use the "**+Delete**" keyboard shortcut, and the file will be moved to the Trash. Use the "**++Delete**" keyboard shortcut to permanently delete a file instead of trashing it. A file will be permanently deleted and you won't be able to get it back.

16. **Put More Content on the Display of Your MacBook Pro**

Change the size of the text and objects on your screen using the resolution scaling capability built into the MacBook Pro's display. You can accommodate more material on your display if the text and objects are reduced in size. The display of the MacBook Pro comes with a resolution that is optimal for the display by default. However, you can use the Scaled option to acquire additional space on your Mac if you want to accommodate more stuff on the display. Go to the Apple menu, **System Settings**, and then click **Displays** to activate this scaled version. After that, click **Scaled** and choose "**More Space**."

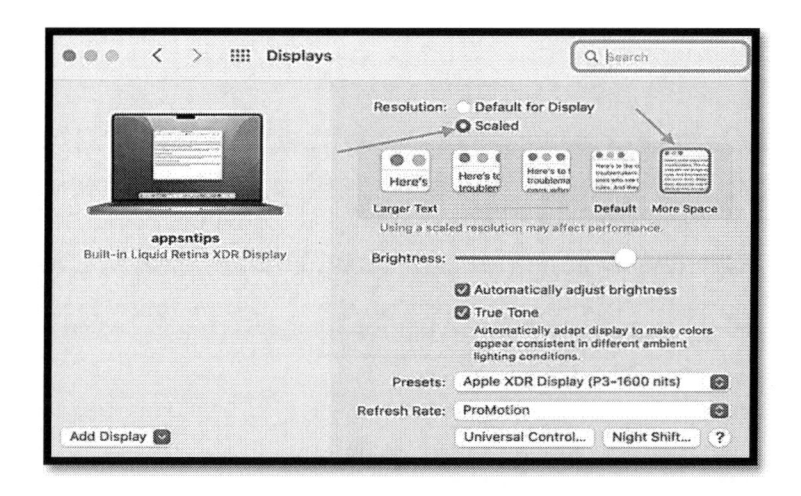

17. Master the Screenshot Tool

A built-in screenshot tool in macOS enables you to take screenshots of individual program windows, the full screen, or a specified portion of the screen. Use the keyboard shortcut **CMD+Shift+3** to capture a screenshot of the whole screen. Press the keyboard combination **CMD+Shift+4** and move the cursor over the area you want to screenshot while pressing the CMD key.

Use the **CMD+Shift+4 keyboard shortcut** to take a screenshot of an app's window. After that, press the spacebar once to watch the cursor transform into a camera symbol. Now click on the app window you want to screenshot, and the screenshot will be taken from that app window. Just remember the keyboard shortcut **CMD+Shift+5** if you find it tough to memorize so many keyboard shortcuts. The screenshot overlay tool will open, giving you access to all the tools we covered above as well as the option to screen record your Mac's display.

18. Sign PDFs using the Preview App

Did you know that the Mac's built-in Preview software allows you to sign PDF files? Open the PDF in the Preview app, and then choose the annotation tool to add your signature. Now, click the signature tool, and if you haven't already, you'll see the opportunity to add your signature. In the Preview app, adding a signature may be done in many ways.

You can use your MacBook Pro's trackpad to sign documents, the camera on your Mac to scan paper signatures, or even your iPhone or iPad's touch screen to import your signature. The Preview app preserves your signature after you add one, so you don't have to start from scratch each time you want to sign a new PDF.

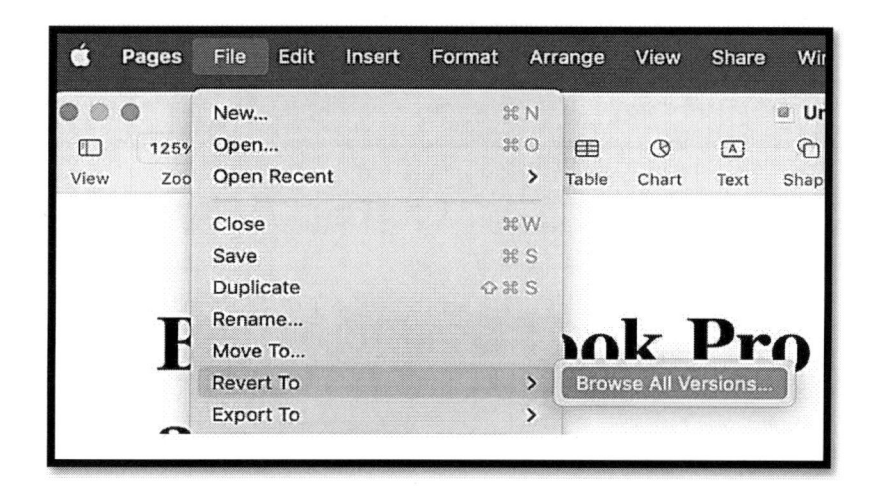

Pages will now launch in version history mode, with the most recent version on the right and the older ones on the left. Using the arrow button or timeline, you can view previous versions. Clicking the Restore button will return the document to that version after you've located the proper one. Choose the **CMD+C keyboard shortcut** to copy the necessary portions if you don't want to restore the complete text.

19. **Create Secret Notes using the Keychain Access App**

Use the Keychain Access App to make hidden notes if you want to secure important information on your MacBook Pro by keeping it behind a password-protected wall. Although the Apple Notes app now has a note-locking option as well, most people still prefer the secure notes feature since it is less likely that someone would be looking there because fewer people are aware of its existence. Launch the **Keychain Access** software using Spotlight (or choose Applications Utilities) to access this function. Now, choose File New Secure Note or press **CMD+Shift+N** on the keyboard. To save the note, write down anything you wish to keep private, then verify using your password.

20. **Know the Hot Spots**

One of the least recognized aspects of macOS is Hot Corners. Either they are unknown or people don't find them beneficial. A user can designate various actions for each of the display's corners using the Hot Corners functionality. You can do it by dragging the mouse cursor to that spot.

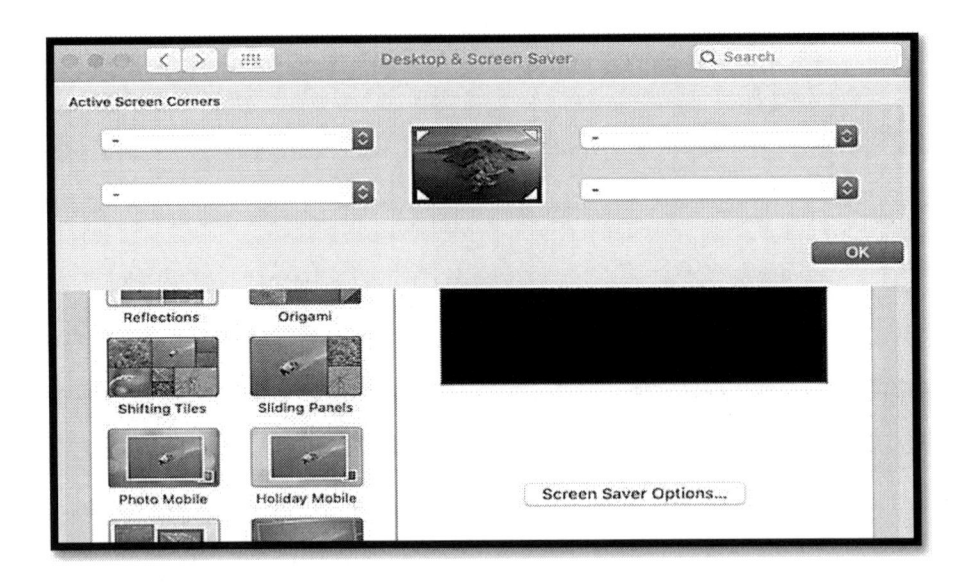

Therefore, if you need to grab a file to attach or do anything else that needs you to glance at the desktop when there are several windows open, move the pointer to the top-left corner. The four corners of your desktop are entirely up to you, but if you get in the habit of using them, you will notice a significant speedup in productivity.

21. **Quickly Access Folders using the Go Menu and Shortcuts**

The Go Menu, which is available on the Menu bar by default, is another underutilized item that may significantly speed up your productivity. Without initially launching the Finder window, you may quickly access folders by using the Go Menu. You can launch a window using the keyboard shortcuts without even using the Go Menu if you make an effort to memorize the keys that are listed there.

22. **Using the Delete Key both ways**

Users who recently made the move from Windows to Mac will undoubtedly value this functionality. The Backspace and Delete keys in Windows are used to delete text. The Delete button deletes text that is in front of the cursor, while the Backspace button deletes text that is behind the cursor. MacOS, meanwhile, just has the Delete key. The fact that the Delete key on macOS functions as the **Backspace key** on Windows just adds to the confusion. However, there is a technique to use the remove key in both directions, that is, to remove text both in front of and before the cursor. The **"fn"** key must be held down while pressing the delete key to remove the text that is now selected. If you just want to remove the text before the cursor, you don't need to hold down the function key.

23. **Intelligent Text Selection and Text Navigation**

Most people browse the text with the left, right, up, and down arrow keys. However, a surprising proportion of Mac users are unaware of the keyboard modifiers for easy text navigation. These navigation modifiers allow you to go not just by character but also by word, line, paragraph, and even to the beginning and finish of the text.

The navigation modifiers that you need to keep in mind are shown below.

- ⌥ + ←/→ = move cursor by word instead of by character
- ⌥ + ↑/↓ = move cursor by paragraph
- ⌘ + ←/→ = move cursor to beginning/end of line
- ⌘ + ↑/↓ = Move cursor to the beginning/end of all text

Similar to this, just add the Shift button to this combination when choosing text. For instance, if you use the shortcut **+Shift+,** the whole line in front of your cursor will be selected. These shortcuts make it simple to browse and choose text.

24. **Create Text Clipping**

It's an outdated yet helpful function that few people are aware of. To produce a straightforward text clipping using the .txt file format on your Mac, choose any text (works on most programs) and drag it to your Desktop or a Finder window. This tool is useful if you wish to summarize a piece of writing or preserve significant passages from a book.

Using the text clipping is likewise not that difficult. To copy from a file, double-click on it to open it, or simply drag & drop the file into any document to have the content pasted where the cursor is. Keep in mind that when you cut a text, the rich-text format is preserved. That implies that all text formatting and links are kept.

25. Rename Multiple Items at Once

Even while this one may not be helpful to everyone, it might save the life of someone who truly needs it. You may rename numerous files on your Mac in a single move, as the headline says. Select all of the files to be renamed before doing a right-click (control + click/secondary click). To rename numerous things, choose "**Rename multiple items**" from the right-click menu.

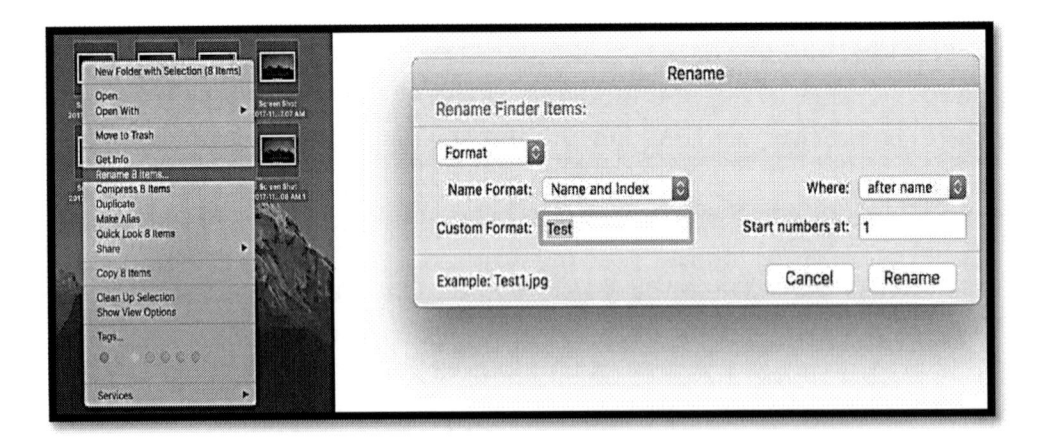

Then a menu will appear. Choose the corresponding option, and then type the desired name into the custom name area. Click the **Rename button** to continue. All of the files will now have their names changed to test, followed by a number. (Test 1, Test 2, Test 3, etc.). When you need to quickly rename files for organization, this option will save you a ton of time.

26. Organize your Files with Tags and Stacks

Tags may be thought of as colored dots that can be attached to any file or folder in their most basic forms. The left bar of your Finder window will display a Tags menu.

Once a file has been given a tag, clicking on that tag in the Finder window will immediately take you to it.

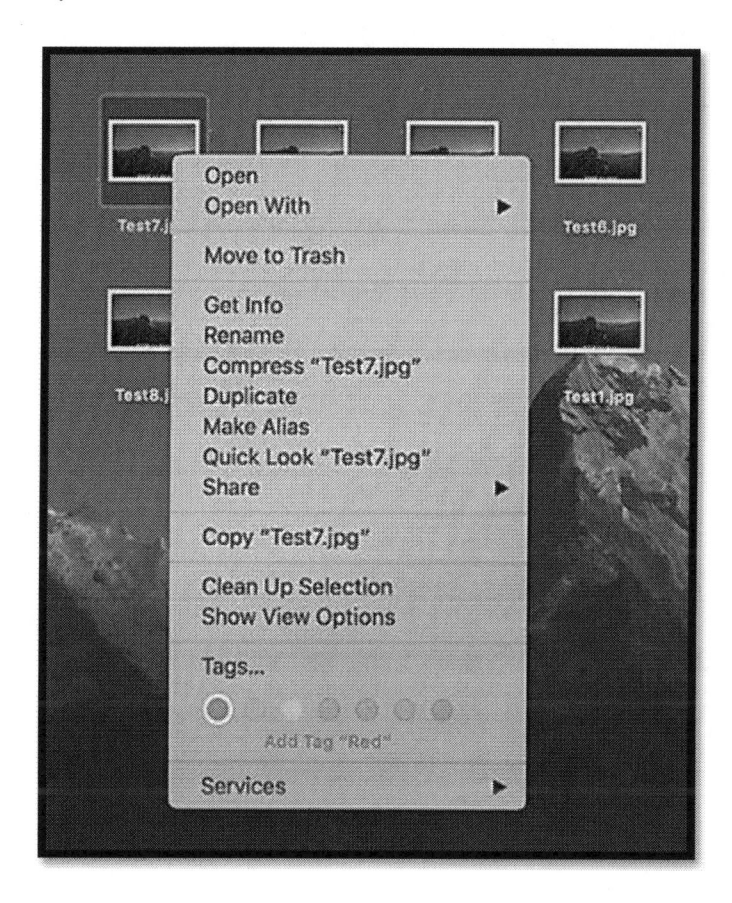

27. Take Screenshots in JPG Format

If you often capture screenshots on a MacBook Pro, you should be aware that these images are saved in PNG format. Although saving photographs in PNG format has several benefits (for example, it is lossless), it also has a significant drawback. Images in PNG format need more space on your Mac's hard disk because of their greater file sizes. Taken in JPG format, screenshots are thus usually a smart idea. JPG format saves space while maintaining almost the same screenshot quality. Additionally, since the files are lower in size, sharing them is made simpler. Teach your Mac to capture screenshots in JPG format extremely quickly. Simply launch the **Terminal app** on your Mac, input the aforementioned code, and then press the **Enter key**. Your Mac will now capture screenshots in a JPG format each time you do so. In reality, you can capture screenshots in PDF format by replacing jpg with pdf. Additionally, you can simply change the word "**jpg**" in the code above to "**png**" if you ever wish to resume capturing screenshots in PNG format.

28. **Mark the Hidden Apps**

We are all aware that the "**Command+H**" keyboard shortcut in macOS enables app hiding. An excellent approach to keep your desktop organized is to hide apps. You can use the "**Command+Tab**" keyboard shortcut to summon an app back if you want to hide it rather than minimize it, which is a significant advantage. Holding the option key while releasing the **tab key** and command-tabbing through the cycle will bring up a minimized app. It is not as simple to use as **CMD+Tab**. The difficulty with hiding applications, however, is one. Which applications are closed and which are hidden are not made clear. Since keyboard shortcuts don't bring up closed applications, it is more difficult to summon back apps. Simply open **Terminal**, copy and paste the aforementioned command, then press Enter. When you finish, you'll see that the hidden applications are a bit more grayed out than the other apps.

29. **Use Universal Control to use the keyboard and trackpad on your Mac to operate the iPad**

The Universal Control feature was unveiled by Apple with the release of macOS Monterey and iPadOS 15. With this function, you can use the keyboard and trackpad on your Mac to operate your iPad and vice versa. When using an external keyboard and mouse, the capability shines since it allows you to operate both devices with a single input.

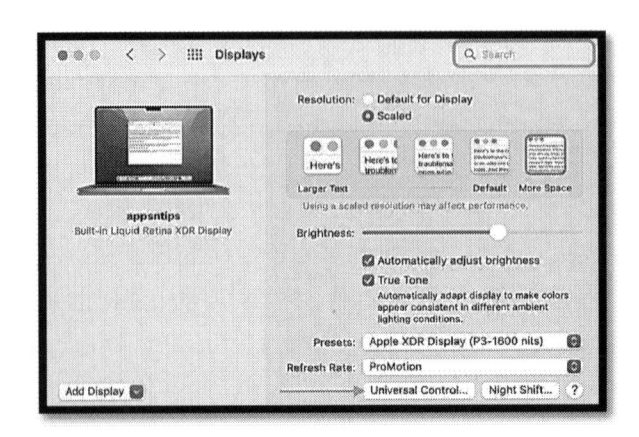

Go to the **Apple Menu > System Settings > Displays section** to activate Universal Control. Click on Universal Control in this area and confirm that the option is turned on. Keep your iPad close to your Mac and now drag your cursor to the screen's edge (on the side that the iPad is on). The other device shows the pointer starting to push through to its screen as you advance it beyond the edge of the screen. To connect to that device, fully advance the pointer.

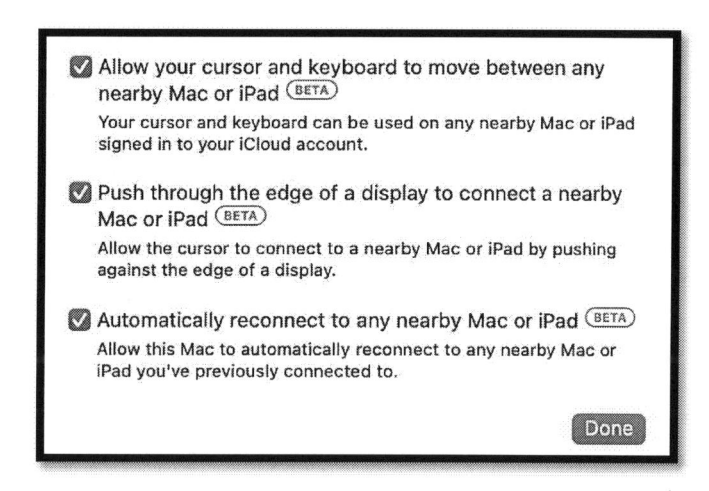

30. Change the Name of Your Computer

The name of your Mac is automatically assigned by macOS when you set it up. If you own more than one Mac, it gets complicated since macOS just adds digits to the end of the name while keeping the same name. Using System Settings, you can give each of your Macs a unique name to help you remember them.

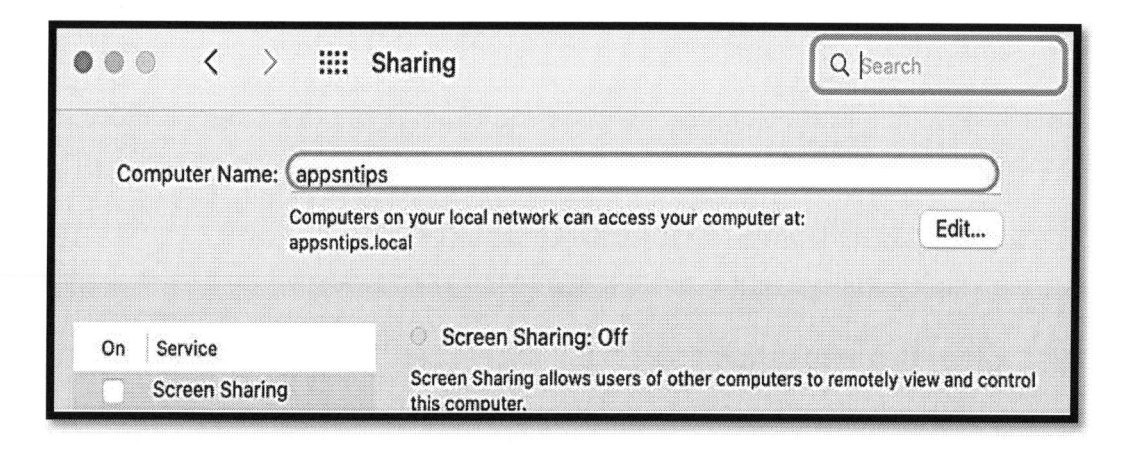

The machine name box may be selected by clicking on the **Apple Menu > System Settings > Sharing menu**. To save changes, modify the name as desired and then dismiss the System Settings window.

31. Launch certain apps automatically at login

This function is excellent if you often open up a certain app since you use it frequently. For instance, Mail, Slack, and Safari are some of the apps most people use the most often.

- To access **System Settings**, tap the Apple logo in the upper left corner and make sure your account is chosen in the drop-down box.
- Click **'General'** then **'Login Items'**.
- To add an application, click the "+" and look for the app or file you want to launch when you log in to Finder.
- Press **'Open'** after choosing the program or document from the list to add it to the list.

Tip: Right-click on the [[icon and choose "**Options**" from the pop-up menu, then choose **"Open at Login"** to quickly add an app to this list.

32. Use Mission Control to see all open windows

If you're anything like me, you probably have a lot of windows and programs open at once. You may not even be aware of how many distinct Safari tabs and all of your open applications are open in certain circumstances. Apple refers to the action that shows your open windows so you can quickly view whatever you're working on as Mission Control.

The following is one of the simplest methods to view all of your open windows out of all the options available:

- On the keyboard, press the **Mission Control (F3) key.**
- To switch, tap on any of the running apps or windows.

33. Digitally sign your documents

The rise of remote work has made signing papers from home a necessary duty.

Here's how to digitally sign your documents:

- Open Preview, then choose **Tools > Annotate > Signature > Manage Signatures** from the menu bar.
- From the pop-up window, choose **Create Signature**.
- After that, you can sign using your iPhone or trackpad, or you can use your Mac's camera to scan a paper signature.
- To sign a document, all you need to do is open it in Preview, choose **Tools > Annotate > Signature**, click the signature, and then drag it into position.

34. **Add a Guest user to your MacBook Pro**

If you have more than one person using your laptop at home, the ability to add extra users to your Mac is a terrific tool. The ability for each user to customize their experience with custom backgrounds, layouts, settings, and applications is awesome.

To include a new user:

- Click or tap the **Apple logo** in the upper-left corner.
- Select **Add Account** under Users & Groups by scrolling down.
- Select "**Allow guests to log in to this computer**" by clicking the "I" next to Guest User above Add Account.

Frequently Asked Questions

1. How do you fix MacBook Pro not turning on?
2. How do you fix your MacBook Pro overheating?
3. How do you solve your MacBook Pro having slow performance?
4. How do you fix keyboard and trackpad issues on your MacBook Pro?
5. How do you fix software glitches or crashes on your new MacBook Pro?
6. What are the tips and tricks that can help you navigate through the MacBook Pro functions?

CONCLUSION

Thanks to its M2 Pro CPU, the 2023 MacBook Pro 14-inch and 16-inch once again raises the bar for laptop performance. At least until we get the chance to test devices with 13th generation Intel Core CPUs, it outperforms the Windows competitors. Particularly when it comes to demanding operations like picture and video editing in Premiere Pro, the M2 Max is even quicker. Additionally, the M2 Max's graphical capabilities significantly outperform the M2 Pro. The 2023 MacBook Pro 14-inch and 16-inch model has an outstanding battery life of over 14 hours even with the performance upgrade. No other laptop provides this level of performance and longevity for the price. Additional changes include the quicker Wi-Fi 6E and an HDMI connector with more functionality.

Are you a good fit for the MacBook Pro 14-inch 2023 then? If you're ready to pay at least $1,999 and want a portable yet powerful device, then absolutely. It's undoubtedly a lot quicker than the 13-inch MacBook Pro with M2, but that model begins at $1,299 and has a battery life of almost 4 hours longer. The MacBook Pro 16-inch, which begins at $2,499, is another option; although it delivers the same specifications overall, it does have a larger screen and a design with a little more thermal headroom for sustained performance.

INDEX

1

100-watt-hour lithium-polymer battery, 9
1080p FaceTime HD, 1, 8
12-core CPU, 3, 5, 6
140W USB-C Power Adapter, 9
16-core GPU, 3

6

6x quicker, 1

A

A 10-core CPU, 3
A brand-new app, 10
About AirPrint, 36
accelerators, 9
Accept Terms, 35
Access All Notes, 94
Access Dock and Menu Bar, 164
access numerous sorts of data, 48
Access Payment, 50
access **System Settings**, 308
access the restricted note, 120
access your location, 68
Accessibility, 12, 13, 44, 45, 46, 90, 112, 230, 231, 237, 250
accessibility options, 13, 45
Accessing a Locked Note, 121
Accessing Applications, 40
Accessing Recent Notes, 94
Accessing Smart Links, 96
Account Information, 49
account name, 16
account name and password, 16
Activate & Use Screen Sharing, 157
Activate Focus, 82
Activate Focus from the Control Center, 82
Activate Focus from the Control Center and System, 82
activate specific features, 92
activate specific features or activities, 92
activate Touch ID., 28

Activity Monitor, 61, 62
Activity Stream, 11
ActivityWatch, 63
actual text in images., 10
Add a checkbox, 124
Add a Hint, 121
Add a Hint (Optional), 121
add a new fingerprint, 19
Add Additional Fingerprints, 20
Add Annotations, 98
Add Annotations (Optional), 98
Add another Participant, 153
Add Attachments to Notes, 132
Add Bookmark, 175, 177
Add Card, 35
Add Cards to Wallet, 29
Add Communication, 68
Add Communication Applications, 68
Add Contacts, 145, 150
Add Markups and Annotations, 131
Add Media, 129, 130
Add Media to Notes, 129
Add More Contacts, 150
Add More Contacts (Optional), 150
Add Participants, 153
Add Participants to the Call, 153
Add Smart Links, 95
Add Smart Links to Quick Note, 95
Add Text Content, 130
Add text or a photo, 98
Add the Printer, 37
Add to Quick Note, 98
Adding a Fingerprint, 19
Adding Apps, 40
Adding Attachments, 100, 114
Adding Images, 137
Adding/Removing Items, 41
Additional factors to consider, 67
Additional Options, 46, 169, 213
Additional Settings, 42
Additional Tips, 115, 149, 153
Adjust Print Settings, 39
Adjust Settings, 46
Adjust Size, 42
Adjust Table Dimensions, 136
Adjust the Scan, 172

311

Adjust/Turn off Universal Control, 164
Adjusting Battery Voltage, 23
adjusting charging patterns, 23
Adjusting Table Size, 137
admin password, 15
Administrator, 16
Adobe Photoshop, 6
Advanced Features, 95, 248
Advanced options, 52
advanced professional silicon, 1
Advanced Search, 115, 129
aesthetic options, 15
After initial setup, 12
Air Print services, 29
AirDrop, 132, 140, 198, 217, 231
AirPrint printer, 37, 38, 39
AirPrint-enabled printer, 37
Alert Style, 86
Allow alerts from Specific Persons, 86
Always Allow Apps, 66
Ambient light sensor, 9
animations, 5, 12
annotation tools, 98
Anti-Theft Measures, 70
App Limits, 60, 63, 65, 67
App Permissions, 69
App Store, 14, 18, 21, 67, 69, 72, 74, 75, 79, 80, 262, 263, 270, 271, 272, 273, 274, 292
App Store Apps, 69
App Store Purchases, 72
App time limits, 78
App Updates, 69
App Usage Limits, 63
Apple Books, 14, 21
Apple devices, 29, 36, 48, 72, 90, 99, 101, 103, 112, 117, 125, 132, 134, 136, 137, 138, 139, 148, 175, 184, 188, 211, 220, 270, 272
Apple icon, 41, 43
Apple ID, 14, 18, 19, 48, 49, 50, 51, 52, 54, 55, 69, 71, 73, 74, 75, 76, 77, 78, 79, 95, 103, 115, 134, 136, 138, 139, 143, 144, 147, 148, 150, 157, 162, 168, 171, 219, 269, 271, 272
Apple ID in the sidebar, 14
Apple M2 Pro chip, 9
Apple Music, 5, 72, 73, 74, 75, 78, 79, 80, 249
Apple Pay, 14, 15, 18, 20, 21, 22, 29, 30, 31, 32, 33, 34, 35, 39
APPLE PAY, 29

APPLE PAY AND AIRPRINT, 29
Apple Silicon, 5
Apple silicon's strength, 7
Apple TV, 5, 9, 14, 21, 73, 188, 190
Apple Watch or iPhone, 15
Apple Watches, 29
Apple's laptop's display, 3
Apple's Migration Assistant app, 18
Apple's strict energy efficiency, 7
Apple's web browser, 174
application asks for authorization, 67
apps, 18, 24, 26, 27, 41, 52, 62, 66, 67, 68, 70, 84, 85, 88, 240, 251, 252, 253, 254, 255, 256, 257, 261, 270, 274, 283, 284, 286, 288, 290, 292, 306, 308
App-Specific Permissions, 66
Arrange Folders, 109
Arrange Notes with Folders, 102
arrange windows, 4, 7
Ask to Share Screen, 157, 158
Asking for Screen Sharing, 158
asking Siri, 12, 248
Attach a File, 133
Attaching files, 134
Authorize Purchases, 73
Automatic device backups, 48
automatic message, 82
automatic message answers, 82
Automatic Preview Generation, 96
automation processes, 89
avoid accessing public Wi-Fi, 70
avoid accessing public Wi-Fi networks, 70

B

background music, 12, 195
Backing up Data, 24
Backlit Magic Keyboard, 9
Battery and Power, 8
Battery Health, 23, 24
Battery Health & Management, 23
battery life, 1, 5, 310
battery voltage, 23
Begin the Video Call, 160
benchmark, 3
benchmark performance, 3
better camera, 4
bigger directories, 106
billing and shipping addresses, 33

biometric authentication, 70
block distracting items, 10
Bluetooth and Wi-Fi, 140, 162, 164, 166, 171
brainstorming, 7, 10, 100, 112
brainstorming sessions, 100, 112
breakneck speed, 5
broad variety of graphics options, 3
Browse Attachments in Notes, 134
Browser History, 63
Browsing, 56, 270
built-in backup tool, 24
built-in utilities, 24
Built-in Utility, 61
bullet points, 98, 124, 131

C

Capturing your Thoughts, 99
card information, 30, 32, 33, 34, 35
categories, 11, 49, 51, 60, 63, 64, 68, 78, 84, 97, 100, 103, 126, 134, 138, 208, 241, 242, 243, 244, 246, 270
Change Settings, 20, 84
change the magnification level., 41
Change the Menu bar Size, 43
Change the settings, 44
Change the Shared Window, 159
changing the dock size, 40
changing the dock's orientation, 40
Changing the settings on a universal control, 164
Charging the battery, 22
Check Compatibility, 29, 36, 37
Check Connectivity, 165
Check Privacy, 56
Check System Requirements, 33
Check the Move, 116
Check the Recently Deleted Folder, 122
Check the Recently Deleted Folder (Optional), 122
Checklists, 94, 115, 138
chip and the 19-core GPU, 3
choice of formatting options, 111
Choose a Location, 104
Choose a Note-Taking App, 126
Choose a Source and Target, 26
Choose Dock Orientation, 42
choose new languages and voices, 12
Choose Printer, 36
Choose the Data to Transfer, 18

Choose the Document Type, 172
Choose the Focus Filter to Edit, 84
Choose the Note to Delete, 122
Choose the Note to Share, 139
Choose the Printer, 39
Choose your Device, 172
Choose your region or country, 13
Cinema 4D, 6
Clear Communication, 156
cognitive impairments, 13
Collaboration and Sharing, 132
Collaboration in Notes, 112
color grading, 1, 6
comfortable with the procedure., 156
Command-V, 22
common formatting faults, 12
communication limitations, 64, 67
Communication limits, 78
Communication Limits, 60, 65, 67
compatible devices, 36
compatible software, 168
Compiling in Xcode, 6
complete carbon, 7
complete carbon neutrality, 7
complete the transaction after authentication, 32
concept-illustration workshops, 100
Configure Account Settings, 16
Configure Apple, 33
configure custom, 84
configure custom notification, 84
configure custom notification sounds, 84
Configure Sharing Options, 73, 74
Configure Wi-Fi and Bluetooth, 171
configuring the sharing options, 73
configuring two-factor authentication, 69
Confirm Deletion, 111, 122, 267
Confirm Password, 121
Confirm the Addition, 154
confirmation popup, 36, 121, 267
Connecting a Previous Device, 26
Context Menu, 109
Continue your Call, 161
Continuity Camera, 4, 5, 7, 11, 166, 167, 168, 169, 171
CONTINUITY CAMERA, 162
Control Center, 14, 82, 89, 91, 93, 94, 95, 98, 99, 193, 194, 232, 279
Control or Right buttons, 125
controlling focus modes, 89

conversations with Voice Control, 12
create a computer account, 8, 15, 28
Create a New Focus Filter, 83
Create a New Folder, 102
Create a new note, 130, 132, 138
Create a New Note, 113, 123, 136
Create a new note or open an existing note, 132
Create a new note or open an existing one, 130, 138
Create Folders, 117, 126
Create or Select a Note, 119
create reminders, 12
Create Subfolders, 103, 109
Create Subfolders (Optional), 103
created user account, 16
Creating a Note, 93
Creating a Quick Note, 89
Creating and Formatting Notes, 111
creativity and productivity, 10
Creators, 1
credit card information, 33
credit or debit cards, 29, 33
crescent moon, 83
critical activity, 70
crucial information, 17, 99, 118, 119, 186
crucial information or settings, 17
customization options, 10, 213, 262, 286
customization options for a Focus, 10
Customize alerts, 86
Customize App Limits (Optional), 65
Customize Communication Limits, 65
Customize Communication Limits (Optional), 65
Customize Settings, 82
Customize the Call, 150
Customize the Call (Optional), 150
Customize the Folder's Look, 105
Customizing Appearance, 100
Customizing the Dock, 41
Customizing the Link, 96
Cut and Paste, 109, 298

D

DCI-P3 color range., 3
debut in the autumn of 2022, 4
Decide which Items to Transfer, 27
Delete a Note, 122
Delete Card, 35
delete cards, 33

demanding graphics workloads, 6
descriptive names, 128
design and operation of the dock, 42
designers, 97, 113
Developer Identification, 67
Device name, 8
Device Restarts, 166
dialog box, 67, 122, 123, 135, 179, 186
Disabling Universal Control, 165
Discover keyboard shortcuts, 22
Display, 2, 3, 44, 45, 88, 89, 188, 192, 230, 277, 279, 280, 293, 296, 299
display emoji and symbols, 22
Displays, 44, 165, 188, 192, 258, 279, 280, 299, 307
Dock & Menu Bar, 41, 42, 46, 293
DOCK AND MENU BAR, 40
Dock icons., 41
Dock visible, 43
dock's icons, 42
dock's size, 41, 42, 47
documents, 10, 14, 18, 27, 36, 37, 40, 48, 100, 108, 114, 130, 135, 170, 240, 243, 246, 283, 284, 300, 308, 309
documents and links, 10
Documents folder, 104
Downtime, 60, 64, 65, 78
Downtime and More, 64
Drag and Drop, 105, 116, 133, 183, 230, 262
Drag-and-Drop, 109
Drop the Note, 116
drop-down menu, 43, 46, 49, 52, 77, 79, 107, 131, 165, 188, 192, 219, 245

E

Edit an Existing Focus Filter, 84
Edit and Organize, 98
editable texts, 4
editable texts in iMessage, 4
effective conversation, 153
effective operation, 23
efficient operation, 166
efficient operation of Universal Control, 166
email addresses, 72, 86, 112, 125, 215, 218, 219
email addresses or Apple IDs, 72
emails, 10, 36, 69, 205, 234, 240, 242, 249
emoji choices, 22
enable dictation, 22

314

Enable Firewall, 69
Enable Hot Corners, 92
Enable Screen Sharing, 155
enable several fingers, 21
Enable Siri, 14
enables Force clicks, 9
Encrypt Your Data, 69
End Screen Sharing, 161
Ending Screen Sharing, 158
Energy Saver, 24
Enhanced Connectivity, 6
Enhanced Tracking Protection, 69
Ensure Compatibility, 168
Ensure Current Software, 157
Ethernet connection, 26
everyone's revisions, 11
Examine Favorites and Bookmarks, 175
Examine Favorites and Bookmarks (Optional), 175
external displays, 3
external monitor, 3
external storage device, 24
extraordinary 3D geometry, 6
extraordinary 3D geometry and textures, 6

F

FACETIME, 142
family members, 7, 58, 72, 73, 74, 75, 76, 77, 78, 79, 80
family member's library, 79
Family Sharing, 71, 72, 73, 74, 75, 76, 77, 78, 79, 80, 272
fastest Intel-based MacBook, 1
fastest Intel-based MacBook Pro, 1
favorite teams, 12
features and procedures, 89
Finder, 12, 50, 103, 104, 105, 106, 107, 108, 109, 110, 130, 133, 170, 173, 204, 212, 272, 296, 297, 302, 303, 304, 308
Finding the information, 129
Finish the Transfer, 27
Firewall, 69
fixing hardware-related, 166
fixing hardware-related problems, 166
Fixing Universal Control Problems, 165
flexible tool, 95, 97, 111
fluid 120Hz ProMotion, 3
Focus Filters, 84

FOCUS MODE, 81
FOCUS MODE AND QUICK NOTES, 81
focus modes, 81, 83, 89
focus modes or app alerts, 89
FOLDERS AND NOTES, 102
Force Touch trackpad, 9
force-canceling woofers, 3
format text, 117, 124
Format your Notes, 123
Formatting Options, 99, 114, 117
forthcoming events, 10
frames per second, 4
Freeform, 10
Frequently Asked Questions, 28, 39, 47, 57, 80, 101, 141, 161, 173, 187, 207, 226, 239, 260, 287, 309
From a Time Machine backup, 18
From a Windows PC, 18
From the Control Center, 82
full product life cycle, 7
full-height function keys, 9
functionality, 33, 36, 128, 134, 230, 237, 253, 258, 259, 291, 301, 303, 310

G

Gaming on Mac, 7
Gatekeeper Settings, 66
general privacy settings, 57
general productivity, 5
Gesture, 47
Get Information, 110
GETTING STARTED, 8
global clocks, 12
Globe key, 22, 295
Graphics and Gaming, 3
graphics performance, 5, 6
group assignments, 112

H

Handwritten Note, 93
Hang up FaceTime, 12
Hang up FaceTime conversations, 12
HDMI 2.1 standard, 3
HDMI connector, 2, 3
Headings, 94, 124
hearing, 13, 289

Hiding the Dock, 43
high-efficiency cores, 5, 6
Highlight Text, 95
highlighted content, 97, 98
high-performance, 5, 6
how Apple Pay works, 29
How do you add media to Notes?, 141
How do you add tables and checklists to Notes?, 141
How do you arrange Notes with Folders?, 141
How do you create and rename a folder?, 141
How do you move, pin, and lock a Note?, 141
How do you share your Notes?, 141
How do you show or hide the dock?, 47
How do you use the continuity camera?, 173
How do you work with Notes?, 141
How to Add a Credit Card, 34
How to Adjust the Menu bar Size, 45
How to back up and restore data, 24
How to change or remove payment cards with Apple, 34
How to Change the Dock's Orientation, 42
How to Change the Dock's Size, 41
How to charge the battery and adjust battery voltage, 22
How to Create a Folder, 103
How to Create a Note, 113
How to Create a Quick Note, 93
How to Enable Focus Mode, 81
How to Hide the Menu Bar, 46
How to Monitor App Usage, 61
How to Rearrange Folders, 108
How to Reduce Your Mac's Window, 46
How to Rename a Folder, 106
How to Set Downtime, 64
How to Set up & Edit iCloud, 48
How to set up Apple Pay, 29
how to set up family sharing, 70
How to Setup Family Sharing, 70
How to use AirPrint, 36
How to Use and Customize the Dock, 40
How to use Quick Notes, 89
How to Visit a Website, 174
Huawei Matebook, 2
Huawei Matebook X Pro, 2

I

ICLOUD, 48

iCloud account, 49, 51, 54, 90, 114, 115, 117, 162, 220
iCloud Drive files, 50
iCloud Private Relay, 54, 57
iCloud settings, 16, 48, 49, 51, 57, 76
iCloud Shared Photo, 11
iCloud Shared Photo Library, 11
Images and Attachments, 125, 137
Images and Links, 94
Import from iPhone or iPad, 169
Impose App Limits, 63
improved HDMI, 1
improved picture search, 4
in-built Touch ID sensor, 32
incoming calls, 10
Increased productivity, 97
Increased productivity and efficiency, 97
increasing number of applications, 5
informational content, 117
input the password, 13
Insert from iOS Device, 167, 168
Insert Smart Link, 96
Insert Table, 136, 137
Insert the Scan, 172
Inserting the Image, 169
install applications, 16
installation steps, 17
installing any drivers or software., 29
Instant Formatting, 115
integrated power management system, 23
integrating enormous panoramic panoramas, 6
Intel or Apple M1 processors, 4
Intel processor, 5, 6
Intel x86 software, 5
interactive forecast modules, 12
INTRODUCTION, 1
inverted-T arrangement, 9
Invite Family Members, 72, 78
Inviting Family Members, 74
iOS device, 14, 167, 168, 170, 264
iOS or macOS smartphone, 36
iOS smartphone, 168, 170, 171
iPad and iPhone, 12, 95
iStat Menus, 63

J

Join a Wi-Fi network, 13
Join the same wireless network, 37

K

Keep in Dock, 40
Keep your file structure logical, 106
key component, 40
keyboard and the Function, 22
Keyboard and Trackpad, 9
keyboard or input source, 22
keyboard shortcut, 46, 89, 91, 99, 102, 161, 176, 240, 247, 280, 291, 293, 294, 295, 297, 299, 300, 301, 306
Keyboard Shortcut, 28, 46, 93, 99, 111, 240
Keyboard Shortcuts, 109, 115, 242, 255, 275, 278, 287
Keynote presentation, 168

L

larger screen and a design, 310
later running macOS, 166
later version, 93, 166, 179, 258
Launch FileVault, 69
Launch Migration, 26
Launch System, 34, 57, 63, 70, 72
launch the corresponding app, 40, 194
Launch the Notes app, 102, 122, 132
Launching Screen Sharing, 157
Learning Resources, 89
Links, 94, 95, 96, 125
Lists and Bullets, 124
Locate and launch the Notes app, 123
Locate the Folder, 106
location of your finger, 20
Lock Screen, 70, 88

l

'Login Items', 308

L

Logout or Restart, 45
long-needed capabilities, 4
Look for Attachments, 134
Look for the Notes, 103

M

M2 Max, 1, 2, 3, 6, 8, 9, 10, 310
M2 Max model's, 1
M2 Pro and M2 Max, 1, 5
M2 Pro MacBook Pro, 4
M2 Pro's powerful media engine, 5
Mac devices, 95, 99, 297
Mac login password, 12
Mac models based on Intel, 5
MacBook controls, 23
MacBook controls battery, 23
MacBook controls battery voltage, 23
MacBook Pro 14-inch, 1, 3, 310
MacBook Pro 14-inch 2023, 310
MacBook Pro 14-inch display, 3
MacBook Pro document, 168
MacBook Pro models, 1, 29, 280
MacBook Pro's on-screen, 169
MacBook Pro's on-screen shutter button, 169
MacBooks, 29, 36
macOS interface, 40
macOS Ventura, 1, 4, 7, 9, 10, 12, 33, 41, 61, 64, 66, 68, 89, 108, 159, 162, 166, 168, 171, 191, 227, 229, 230, 237, 251, 253, 258, 259, 267
macOS version, 42, 45, 46, 88, 89, 92, 159, 232
macOS version., 42
macOS' built-in file, 106
macOS' built-in file manager by default, 106
Mac's language, 13
Magnification, 41
Mail message, 168
Making organization simple, 97
Manage Content, 68
manage content and privacy, 68
Manage Content and Privacy, 68
Manage Family, 72, 75
Manage the Call, 151
manage the family's planning, 71
manage your accessories, 11
Managing and Organizing, 94
Managing Cards, 33
Managing Participants, 154
Managing Permissions, 52
Manual Activation, 82
manufacturers, 36
Maps, 5
Markup and Sketching, 113

massive 38-core GPU, 1
Max's graphical capabilities, 310
measured HDR content, 3
memory usage, 62
Mentions, 12
menu bar, 12, 13, 14, 23, 36, 40, 42, 43, 44, 45, 46, 47, 63, 82, 89, 91, 100, 107, 114, 117, 119, 124, 125, 133, 144, 157, 165, 170, 175, 177, 178, 181, 189, 190, 191, 192, 193, 200, 219, 240, 247, 253, 256, 258, 269, 276, 277, 279, 280, 281, 293, 309
Menu Bar Options, 46
Merge Cells, 137
Message, 139, 152
Messages, 5, 7, 10, 11, 14, 67, 94, 139, 140, 148, 149, 198, 217, 219, 231, 241, 248, 253, 261, 262, 263, 265, 266, 267, 268, 269
messaging apps, 67
Migration Assistant, 14, 18, 24, 26, 27
mini-LED display, 3
Minimize Windows, 41
Minimize windows using, 41
minimizing distractions, 84
Mission Control, 47, 92, 255, 256, 258, 259, 283, 284, 285, 286, 287, 308
mix of system, 68
Modifications and Confirmations, 52
modify the operating system, 16
Monitor Activity, 78
Monitor Usage, 68
More Sharing Options, 140
Move the Notes to the Folder, 102
movie playback, 9
M-series CPUs, 5

N

native for M-series, 5
Navigate backward and Forth, 175
Navigate to the Folder, 108
nearby AirPrint, 36
nearby AirPrint printers, 36
necessary adjustments, 56, 68, 197
Neural Engine speed, 5
new 14- and 16-inch, 1
New Additions, 5
new development tools, 7
new features, 4, 8, 12, 28, 184, 229, 273
New features, 10

new languages, 12
new M2 Pro, 1
new MacBook Pro, 8, 174, 188
new tile style, 11
newer MacBooks, 28
next-generation GPU, 5
Notes App, 91, 99, 113, 116, 119, 123, 128, 129, 136
Notification Center, 62, 81, 88, 93, 152, 283
Notifications, 60, 68, 77, 83, 84, 85, 86, 87, 88, 92, 149, 151, 153
nuanced indication, 121
numbering, 98
numerous professional programs, 5
Nvidia GPU, 4
NVRAM, 166, 259, 289, 290

O

off Wi-Fi, 13
one-of-a-kind passwords, 69
Open at Login, 308
open Quick Note, 93
Open the Document or Image, 36
Open the Notes app, 94, 117, 118
Open the Notes app and search, 94
open windows, 47, 256, 283, 286, 308
operate the computer, 16, 282
Operating System, 9
optimized battery charging, 24
organizational system, 127
Organize within Folders, 109
Organize your Folders, 106
Organize Your Note, 131
Organize Your Notes, 134
Organizing and Editing, 90
Organizing with Tags, 100
Organizing Your Notes, 114
organizing your windows, 10
organizing your windows and programs, 10
Other Network Options, 13
Overview, 8, 29, 40, 48, 49, 51, 58, 60, 81, 102, 142, 162, 174, 186, 188, 191, 208, 227, 240, 261, 275, 288

P

packing list, 12

packing list for a vacation, 12
padlock symbol, 15, 61, 121
Pages, 5, 11, 36, 167, 168, 171, 238, 253, 301
painters, 113
paper quality, 38
particular program window, 155, 160
password hint, 16
password manager, 69
Password Manager, 69
Password Protection, 68
password-free, 7
password-free future with passkeys, 7
Paste Icon, 110
paste text, 97, 295
Payment & Shipping, 49, 50
payment information, 32
payment using NFC technology, 29
Performance, 3, 5, 289
personalized Clock shortcuts, 12
pertinent tags, 94, 128
phishing and data, 10
phishing and data breaches, 10
Phishing Awareness, 69
photographs, 36, 48, 89, 100, 117, 128, 135, 166, 231, 232, 305
Photos app, 50, 194
Pin a Note, 117
players in the News app, 12
playlists, 72, 79, 249
plug the, 23
Podcasts, 5
poof animation, 41
Populating the Table, 137
portable MacBook, 2
power outlet, 23
power-efficient performance, 1
preferred programs, 40
Prepare in Advance, 156
Prepare your Devices, 168
pressure-sensing, 9
pressure-sensing capabilities, 9
pressure-sensitive, 9
pressure-sensitive drawing, 9
previous version, 1, 5, 6
previously configured a Mac, 14
primary account for all transactions with Apple, 14
print dialog, 36, 39
Printers & Scanners, 37

Privacy and Security settings, 56
privacy-focused design. Passkeys, 10
Privacy-Focused Software, 69
pro laptop, 1
Proceed to Set Up Family Sharing, 70
process of customizing the dock, 40
process of gathering data, 97
producing scenes, 6
productive and expressive, 7
productivity programs, 5
productivity programs like Numbers, 5
professional users, 1
project checklist, 12
Project Update, 128
Public Wi-Fi, 70
purchasing a compatible app, 32

Q

Q3 Sales Projection Update, 128
QR Code Scanning, 168
quantity of copies, 37
Quick Actions, 10
Quick Actions using Spotlight,, 10
Quick Note Thumbnail, 96, 97, 101
Quick Note Thumbnails, 97
Quick Notes, 12, 89, 90, 91, 92, 94, 95, 97, 98, 99, 100, 101
quickest laptop, 1

R

random-access memory, 166, 259
rare earth elements, 7
realistic color, 4
Recent Applications, 41
recent version, 54, 70, 75, 76, 166, 168, 263, 267, 301
Recently Deleted, 122, 123
recommendations, 37, 153, 205, 250
Recovery of Deleted Items, 111
Redesigned System Settings, 4
reduce battery deterioration, 23
Reduce Distractions, 156
refresh rate, 3
Regular Maintenance, 127
Reminders, 12, 208, 209, 210, 211, 212, 213, 214, 216, 217, 219, 220, 221, 222, 224, 248

remove payment cards, 34, 39
Removing Payment Card, 35
Rename and Rearrange Folders, 103
Rename Files and Folders, 109
Requirements, 166, 258
Reset SMC and NVRAM, 166
Resetting the System Management, 166, 288
Resetting the System Management Controller, 166, 288
Resize and Format Media, 131
resolution, 3, 4, 44, 232, 299
Respect Privacy, 156
Restoring Data, 26
restrictions on communication during downtime, 65
Review and Insert, 169
Review and Modify, 52
Review the list of applications, 52
revised sidebar, 11
revolutionizes professional processes, 5
Right-click and choose "New Folder", 104
Rosetta 2, 5
running macOS High Sierra, 166, 168, 191

S

Safari, 5, 7, 10, 11, 31, 33, 34, 36, 39, 69, 94, 97, 98, 174, 175, 176, 177, 178, 179, 180, 181, 182, 183, 184, 185, 186, 187, 253, 308
SAFARI, 174
safeguard your connection, 70
Save and Secure your Notes, 132
Save and Share, 173
Save and Sync, 99, 134, 184
Save the Scan, 172
Save Your Changes, 137
Saving and Accessing Quick Notes, 90
Saving Your Note, 96
Scan Documents, 167, 168, 170, 172
Schedule, 82, 84, 248
scheduling send Redesigned System, 4
screen instructions, 20, 30, 72, 79, 229, 235, 267
screen sharing button, 155
Screen Time, 14, 58, 59, 60, 61, 63, 64, 65, 67, 68, 72, 77, 78, 80
SCREEN TIME AND FAMILY SHARING, 58
screen zoom, 44
SD card slot, 2
Search and Filter, 127

Search and Organization, 112
search in Spotlight, 4, 243
Search Notes, 127
Search within Folders, 129
Searching for Notes, 115
Secure Online Behavior, 69
Security, 33, 49, 56, 57, 66, 67, 68, 69, 70, 112
Select **"Time Machine."**, 25
Select a Sharing Method, 139, 217
Select Backup Disk, 25
Select Security, 16
Select Security Questions, 16
Select the "+" button, 150
Select the "Share" option, 139
Select the body of the note, 133
Select the Card to Remove, 35
Select the Icon for Screen Sharing, 157
Select the starting disk, 26
Select the Thrash Icon, 122
Select What to Share, 155
sending personal information, 69
Set a Password, 120
Set Communication, 67
Set Default Card, 30
Set Printer Options, 38
Set Printing Settings, 37
Set the Keyboard Settings, 22
Set Time Limits, 64, 68
Set up App Store Purchase Sharing, 75
Set up Apple Arcade, 79
Set up Apple Pay, 15
Set up Certain Apps, 18
Set up Family, 71, 76, 77
set up Screen Time, 12, 67, 68
Set up Time Machine, 24
set up Touch ID later, 14
settings screen, 71
Setup Assistant, 12, 13
Setup Assistant guides, 12
Several typical operators, 129
Share experiences and collaborate, 11
Share Sharing Screen, 159
Share Your Screen, 154, 160
Shared Notes, 95
shared purchasing restrictions, 75
Sharing Your Screen, 158
Shortcuts and Automation, 89
Show in Menu Bar, 14

Show Notification, 93
Showing the Dock, 43
sidebar icons, 15
sidebar icons and highlights, 15
Sign In and Grant Permissions, 150
Sign in to the New Account, 17
Sign in with your Apple ID, 14
six-speaker sound system, 1
size adjustment option, 44
Sketching and Drawing, 100
Smart Folders, 12
smart recommendations, 11
Smart Search, 117
Software Update, 70, 142, 184, 227, 229, 232, 235, 259, 263, 267
Sort Files, 109
Sort Search Results, 129
Sort your Notes, 126
specifications, 8, 28, 171, 310
Specifications, 8
specifications overall, 310
speed and security, 174
speeds up video playing and transcoding, 6
spoken notes, 12
Spotlight, 10, 62, 91, 102, 107, 111, 113, 116, 117, 119, 122, 123, 130, 132, 135, 136, 138, 139, 148, 149, 153, 157, 158, 160, 176, 182, 184, 186, 196, 200, 202, 204, 206, 208, 214, 217, 219, 224, 235, 240, 241, 242, 243, 244, 245, 246, 247, 257, 260, 263, 270, 276, 292, 296, 301
Spotlight's improved image, 10
spots a QR code, 168
sRGB color space, 3
Stage Manager, 4, 7, 10, 284, 285, 286
Standard, 16
Start a FaceTime call, 11
Start ScreenSaver, 93
Start the Call, 150
startup disk, 18
Stop Screen Sharing, 156
Storage, 9, 24, 49, 72, 76, 205
Store your files in iCloud, 14
straightforward procedures, 12
strong connection, 166
strong internet connection, 153
strong password, 120
studio-quality microphones, 1
Successful Screen, 156

Successfully Locked, 121
suit your requirements, 38, 98, 277, 284
suitable payment terminal, 29
Switching Between Apps, 40
symbol denotes, 121
Sync across Devices, 95, 138
Sync Across Devices, 137
Sync and Access Across Devices, 132
Sync and Save, 125
Syncing, 52, 90, 101, 112, 114, 136, 211
Syncing Across Devices, 101, 136
Syncing Procedure, 52
system administrator, 17
System Monitor Widgets, 62
system settings, 24, 29, 68

T

Tables, 125, 136
tabs reflecting, 52
Tagging, 94
Take a Document Photo, 172
Take a Picture, 169, 170
Take an Image, 168
Take Photo, 167, 168, 169, 170
Taking Notes Immediately, 97
Taking Position, 171
teams and leagues, 12
Test Ahead of Time, 156
Text Formatting, 123, 137
Text Recognition, 95
Text Recognition in Images, 95
text sizes, 111
The 13-inch MacBook Pro, 3
the 13-inch MacBook Pro with M2, 310
the Apple logo, 15, 17, 34, 42, 45, 46, 49, 50, 52, 57, 58, 61, 79, 87, 159, 165, 170, 184, 188, 191, 245, 258, 259, 267, 282, 308, 309
the Apple menu, 19, 22, 23, 24, 27, 28, 31, 33, 37, 46, 51, 66, 70, 76, 78, 83, 85, 142, 165, 220, 227, 229, 232, 235, 237, 242, 258, 259, 263, 279, 280, 299
the Apple Menu, 50, 74, 230, 291, 307, 308
The Apple Pay button, 34
The built-in Battery Health Management function, 23
The charging process, 23
the Clock app, 12
the Dell XPS 15 scored, 3
The dock, 40, 41, 42

The exact language, 46
The FaceTime session, 11
The focus mode, 82
the Focus Mode icon, 83
The Home app, 11
The HP Spectre, 2
The HP Spectre x360 14, 2
The keyboard keys, 175
the M1 Max, 6
the M1 Pro, 1, 5
the M2 Max, 3, 4, 310
The M2 Max, 1
the M2 Pro, 3, 4, 310
The Mac App Store, 62
the MacBook Pro, 1, 3, 5, 6, 7, 15, 32, 166, 195, 299
the MacBook Pro 14-inch, 3
The MacBook Pro 14-inch, 2, 3
The MacBook Pro 16, 310
The MacBook Pro 16-inch, 310
the mouse button., 42, 105, 109, 257, 275
The new freeform app, 7
The new MacBook Pro, 1, 68, 142, 194, 249, 250, 293
The new MacBook Pros, 4
The Notes app, 90, 101, 115, 117, 128, 129, 132, 137
the on-screen directions, 14, 34, 74, 76, 78
the ProRes acceleration, 6
the Quick Note symbol, 94
the relevant data, 168
the screen's bottom, 43
the size and color of sidebar, 15
the USB-C charging cable, 22
The USB-C power adapter, 22
the user's full name, 16
the Wi-Fi status indicator, 13
Third-Party Apps, 62, 229
third-party programs, 62, 259
three fingerprints per user account., 15
thumbnail picture, 96
thumbnails, 47, 256
Thunderbolt, 2, 6, 26
Thunderbolt 4 connections, 2
Thunderbolt/USB-C connectors, 2
Time Machine, 17, 18, 24, 25, 26, 27, 69, 290
Time Machine backup, 18, 26, 27
Time Machine Backups, 26
time zone, 13
timers, 12
Timing, 63

Tips for Successful Screen Sharing, 156
Today and Scheduled Lists, 12
Toggle Bluetooth, 166
Toggle Bluetooth and Wi-Fi, 166
Toggle the Switch, 57
Tokenization, 33
Touch Bar, 32
Touch ID, 2, 9, 14, 18, 19, 20, 21, 22, 28, 31, 32, 33, 34, 51, 70, 132, 194, 271
Touch ID & Password, 14, 22
toxic compounds, 7
Track Printing Progress, 39
trackpad, 22, 47, 93, 95, 99, 116, 117, 175, 230, 236, 255, 262, 272, 282, 283, 284, 285, 286, 287, 289, 295, 296, 300, 306, 309
Transfer Information, 14
transfer specific items, 27
transfer's target, 27
Trash symbol, 41
tremendous sound, 3
Troubleshooting, 56
troubleshooting techniques, 165
Turn hiding on, 43
tweeters, 3
Two-Factor Authentication, 69
Typed message, 93

U

unified memory, 1, 5, 6, 9
unified memory bandwidth, 5, 6
universal binaries, 5
UNIVERSAL CONTROL, 162
unmatched features, 1
Unmatched Power Efficiency, 5
unsend emails, 10
Up to 15 hours wireless web, 9
Update macOS, 54, 70
Update Software, 166
upload a profile photo, 16
USB-C, 2, 9, 18, 22, 23, 26
USB-C connection, 18
USB-C to MagSafe 3, 9
USB-C to MagSafe 3 Cable, 9
use Apple Pay, 15, 32
Use Descriptive Tiles and Tags, 128
Use Focus filters, 10
Use fresh approaches, 10

use Live Text, 10, 227, 232, 239
Use Mission Control to see all open windows, 308
Use Tabs to Multitask, 175
Use Tags, 117, 127
Use the Menu Bar, 107, 133
Use the Search Bar, 128
Use the USB-C charging cable, 22
useful accessories, 11
user accounts, 15, 18, 27, 220
Users & Groups, 15, 16, 220, 259, 309
using a reliable VPN, 69
using a small amount of power, 5
using a Thunderbolt, 18
using a USB cable, 24
using battery power, 5
using FaceTime., 11
using iCloud Shared Photo, 7
using iCloud Shared Photo Library, 7
Using the Dock, 40, 42
Using the Search Bar, 115
using Time Machine, 24
Using Universal Control, 164
using your new Mac, 12
Utilities, 18, 62, 259, 301

V

variety of fields, 5
variety of graphics, 3
various dock locations, 42
various fingerprint features., 20
various sources, 97
Ventura, 4, 54, 162, 237
Verification, 35, 36
Verify and Change Sharing Settings, 140
Verify Setup and Compatibility, 171
Verifying the Card, 30
version of macOS, 33, 44, 47, 54, 70, 75, 76, 166, 191, 258, 263, 267

version's 38-core GPU., 4
vibrant color scheme, 3
video playing, 5, 6
video processing quicker, 5
Virtual Private, 69
Virtual Private Network, 69
VoiceOver, 12
volume of data, 18, 52
VPN, 69, 70

W

Wait for the Transfer to Complete, 18
Wallet & Apple Pay, 15, 29, 31, 33, 35
Wallet app, 33
Weather, 12
web pages, 36, 174
webcam, 4, 5, 11
Webcam, 4
webcam captures excellent detail, 4
whole system, 16, 24
wide variety of credit and debit cards, 15
Wi-Fi 6E, 1, 6, 310
Wi-Fi 6E and an HDMI, 310
Wi-Fi 6E and an HDMI connector, 310
Wi-Fi in the sidebar of **System**, 13
Wi-Fi network, 19, 36, 37, 39, 151, 162, 165, 166, 167, 168, 170, 171, 188, 191, 193, 289
Windows PC, 18
Working with Notes, 111

Y

Your Username, 17

Z

Zoom In or Out, 175

323

Printed in Great Britain
by Amazon